EIGHT FEET IN THE ANDES

The men at Cajamarca were now ready to set out towards
Cuzco. They were attempting one of the most staggering
invasions in history. Without supplies, communications
or reinforcements, this tiny contingent was going to try to
force its way into the heart of an enormous hostile empire,
to seize its capital city. The road from Cajamarca to
Cuzco lies along the line of the central Andes. It crosses
and recrosses the watershed between the Amazon basin
and the Pacific, and traverses half a dozen subsidiary
ranges of mountains and wild torrents. The distance as
the crow flies between the two cities is some 750 miles, and
the journey was comparable to travelling from Lake
Geneva to the eastern Carpathians or from Pike's Peak to
the Canadian border, in each case following the line of the
mountains.

The Conquest of the Incas JOHN HEMMING

Full Tilt *Ireland to India with a Bicycle*
The Waiting Land *A Spell in Nepal*
In Ethiopia with a Mule
On a Shoestring to Coorg *An Experience of South India*
Where the Indus is Young *A Winter in Baltistan*
A Place Apart *Northern Ireland*
Wheels Within Wheels *Autobiography*
Race to the Finish? *The Nuclear Stakes*

Dervla Murphy

EIGHT FEET
IN THE ANDES

JOHN MURRAY

© Dervla Murphy 1983

First published 1983
by John Murray (Publishers) Ltd
50 Albemarle Street, London W1X 4BD

Reprinted 1983

Typeset by Inforum Ltd, Portsmouth
Printed in Great Britain
by The Pitman Press, Bath

British Library Cataloguing in Publication Data
Murphy, Dervla
Eight feet in the Andes.
1. South America—Description and travel—1951–
I. Title
918'.04'3   F2224
ISBN 0-7195-4083-6

Contents

Acknowledgements

We are grateful to: H. E. the then British Ambassador to Lima and Mrs Harding for advice and hospitality.

The staff of the British Embassy in Lima, who magnanimously solved a multitude of problems for two non-British travellers.

Amelia and George Calderbank, whose mule-buying help was invaluable and whose hospitality in Cajamarca remains unforgettable.

Carolyn and John Walton, who gave us a Happy Christmas at the end of our trek and whose understanding hospitality acted as a 'bridge' back to normal life.

Geraldine and Ken Brown, of the Potato Research Centre, Lima, who smoothed many paths for us and introduced us to a fascinating cross-section of Lima society.

Dr John Hemming, Secretary of the Royal Geographical Society, whose advice, encouragement and enthusiasm fortified us before our journey and whose book, *The Conquest of the Incas*, provided us with inspiration, instruction and entertainment between Cajamarca and Cuzco.

The staffs of the Library and Map Room of the R.G.S., whose co-operation was, as always, generous and whose fault it was not that we got lost so often.

Jaqueline Clark, who ruthlessly deleted a load of rubbish from the first draft.

Hallam Murray, who devoted much time and thought to helping us select suitable illustrations from among his superb collection of Andean photographs.

And last (but from the reader's point of view most important) – Diana Murray, who expended as much mental effort on this book as the author did, and to better effect. Without her editing, *Eight Feet in the Andes* would never have been fit for publication.

Illustrations

Glossary

aguarras	turpentine
aguardiente	home-distilled spirit
amigo	friend
antorcha	torch
aukis	mountain-spirits (Quechuan)
ayllu	Andean tribal community organised on co-op basis
baño	bathroom
barriadas	shanty town
bonito	beautiful
burro	donkey
Camino Real	royal road
campesino	Andean peasant
carretera	motor-road
carpa	tent
casa	house
cerdo	piglet
cerveza	beer
chicha	home-brewed maize beer
coca	plant from which cocaine is derived
comisariá	police station
conquistadores	Spanish conquerors of Latin America
curacas	Peruvian Indian tribal chief (Quechuan)
cuy	guinea-pig (Quechuan)
denuncia	accusation
desayuno	breakfast
encomendero	Spanish settler in Peru entitled to the *produce* of a given area of land though the Indians continued to *own* it
fideog	tin whistle (Gaelic)
flaco	lean or thin or meagre
gringo	white foreigner in Latin America
hacienda	country estate
hija	daughter

hombre	man
Inti	the Inca sun-god (Quechuan)
lomo saltado	dish of chopped meat, sauce and mixed vegetables
malo	lad
mercado	market
mestizo	mixed Indian and Spanish blood
mit'a	labour in the public service required under the Incas from each village as a form of tax (Quechuan)
mitayos	men who performed this labour (Quechuan)
montana	mountain
mula	female mule
mulato	mixed negro and white blood
niño	child
Ole!	hello
paja	straw
palo	stick
pan	bread
peligroso	dangerous
pisco	grape brandy (also used to describe various home-distilled spirits)
plata	money
posada	inn
pueblo	small town
puna	grassland above approximately 13,000 feet
redura	short cut
selva	jungle
sole	Peruvian unit of currency (at the time of our journey 100 soles equalled approximately 28 pence sterling)
tambo	Inca lodging and store house for travellers

This book has to be for the rest of the team —

Rachel and Juana

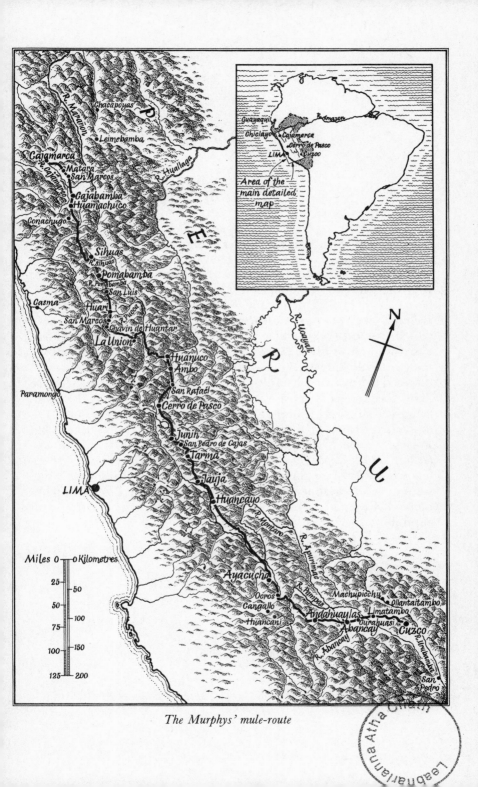

The Murphys' mule-route

Foreword

When we walked across the border bridge from Ecuador into Peru my daughter Rachel was aged nine years and eight months. For three years, since our return from trekking with a pony through Baltistan, she had been attending the primary school at our little home town of Lismore while I wrote a book about Northern Ireland. She was due soon to start her boarding-school career, which would preclude long journeys, and post-boarding-school she would naturally want to travel with her contemporaries, so I regarded this Andean frolic as our last major journey together. We planned to buy a riding-mule in Cajamarca, one of the main towns of northern Peru. Then I would walk while Rachel rode the 1300 miles (or so) from Cajamarca to Cuzco. We were not intent on following exactly the conquistadores' route as described by Prescott – the nineteenth-century American historian – in his *History of the Conquest of Peru*. But inevitably, because there are so few routes through the Andes, we would be covering much the same ground – at much the same season. Francisco Pizarro and his men left Cajamarca on 11 August 1533 and conquered the Inca capital on 15 November.

I

Cajamarca:
four plus four makes eight

Cajamarca. 3 September

This morning Rachel and I took a collectivo (communal taxi) from the coastal city of Chiclayo to Cajamarca: a five-hour journey. Nobody had bothered to heal our taxi's wounds after various misadventures (or was it just one major smash?) and it looked like something off a scrap-iron dump. If there are any rules of the road here, the brawny, dark-skinned mulatto driver hasn't yet heard of them. He chatted cheerfully to the couple in front, roaring with laughter at his own jokes and not noticing when the señora went white with terror. A restless five-year-old shared the back with us. His favourite game was pulling the driver's hair as we were about to overtake a truck on a blind corner, or knocking his cap over his eyes as we negotiated hairpin bends with yawning abysses on one side. I grew not to love him.

This must surely be the world's most dramatic approach to a great mountain range. For some thirty miles beyond Chiclayo we were crossing a flat, hot, grey desert, with lake mirages shimmering in the distance. Then came an area of scattered hillocks, their crests fuzzy with green scrub. And our excitement was ever increasing, as the faint mighty blur of the Andes, all along the horizon, became more solid, distinct, awesome. One approaches the Himalayas gradually, from 2,000 to 5,000 to 12,000 feet . . . But here one seems to leap from sea-level to 10,500, swirling and swivelling through sheer, rocky, barren gorges, glimpsing narrow valleys, sometimes sufficiently irrigated by glinting streams for ribbons of green to set off the dry colours of stone and sand — brown, red, grey. Minuscule dwellings perch on apparently inaccessible ledges. Tiny patches of maize flourish on almost sheer slopes. Diminutive, colourfully-attired campesinos, carrying loads or babies (or both) on their backs, sprint up near-vertical paths.

Burros abound, though our eagerly questing eyes spotted no mule. Often we looked back in disbelief at our road far below – a thin agile serpent, coiling itself around the flanks of the Andes. The many rattling plank bridges looked quite unable to bear a bus or truck and seemed not ideally suited to taxis. This road is quite new. Previously, luxuries like grand pianos and motor-cars were carried to Cajamarca by porters: as to Lhasa and Kathmandu.

At 3.30 p.m. we booked into Cajamarca's Gran Hotel Plaza, which the South American Handbook describes as 'dirty' (in brackets). To us it seems immaculate and we are paying only £1 a night for a spacious, high-ceilinged double room with two beds and handsome hand-carved red-wood furniture.

Our spirits were high as we set out to explore Cajamarca. Today being Sunday few people were about and those few were mostly Indians – on whom we'll be chiefly dependent for months to come, so we studied them closely. Their physical resemblance to the Tibetans dispels any doubts one might have had about migrations from Central Asia across the Bering Straits. Andean Indians are on average much smaller than Tibetans: otherwise the likeness is uncanny. Not only are their features Tibetan, but often their hair-styles (including some men's plaits), and the way they carry their babies, and sometimes even their gestures and expressions. Their gait, however, is different. Tibetans stride out – men and women alike – while the Indian women, many of whom go bare-footed, proceed most oddly with an irregular hopping/running/trotting movement not unlike a pheasant's. They also seem much less robust than the Tibetans and evidently they age quickly. We saw several apparent grandmothers suddenly swinging their infant burdens off their backs and sitting by the roadside to suckle them. Nor are they as out-going as Tibetans; rather the other extreme, with a tendency to keep their eyes averted or downcast on seeing gringoes. We are fascinated by the women's Panama hats and layers of skirts of varying hues. Often two or even three hats are worn simultaneously, as status symbols: the equivalent of the Hindu woman's gold bangles. Children wear them too: even toddlers, still travelling on Mamma's back.

In a small dark eating-house, where no food was available, silent Indian family groups were sipping Inca Colas (the name tells all) – presumably their Sunday treat. One wall was covered by a crude, sad, life-sized mural of Atahualpa, the last Inca ruler, hand-cuffed and gazing over a valley well stocked with anachronistic eucalyptus trees. The Indian proprietor asked, "You know Atahualpa?" When I nodded he went to the door, pointed towards the Plaza de Armas, where topiary freaks have a lovely time and the head of Atahualpa is unmistakable, and made a self-garrotting movement accompanied by a realistic death-rattle. "Muy triste", I murmured sympathetically. "Muy perfido!" retorted the proprietor grimly. How many local Indians retain in their racial memory some trace of the sickened horror that must have overwhelmed Cajamarca on Saturday 26 July 1533, when the Inca was garrotted at dusk after a repulsive exercise in Spanish hypocrisy which ended with his baptism into the Christian church? When we crossed the Plaza de Armas we were on that stage where the last act of the Pizarro-Atahualpa drama took place.

Scene One had taken place eight months earlier. On 15 November 1532 Francisco Pizarro and his 150 Spanish soldiers arrived on the pass above Cajamarca and found themselves overlooking the Inca's army: 40,000, at least, seasoned troops in full battle order. The illiterate Pizarro, who had started life as a child swine-herd in Estremadura, was then in his mid-fifties and a poor horseman – but a great leader. He at once realised that the Spaniards were trapped. If they retreated, showing their fear, they would probably be slaughtered by those Indians who had aided them on their march from the coast. The only course left was to attack. Throughout the night of 15/16 November the conquistadores remained on the alert while Pizarro devised a sixteenth-century 'psyop'. He reckoned that by capturing the Inca he might effectively demoralise his army and, as captor of Atahualpa's sacred person, be allowed to take command of the situation.

Next day 150 Spaniards defeated 40,000 Indians and captured Atahualpa. Within two hours each Spaniard killed at least fifteen of the Inca's immensely courageous bodyguard, all of whom died defending their ruler. No Spaniard was killed, or even seriously wounded. Atahualpa's offer of tons of gold and silver in exchange for his freedom was eagerly accepted by the Spaniards. Within months more than eleven tons of gold objects (the irreplaceable masterpieces of Inca goldsmiths) had been thrown into the Spanish furnaces. The silver objects produced 26,000 pounds of good silver. That ransom would now be worth almost three million sterling.

By July Atahualpa had realised that the Spaniards meant to keep him prisoner. When he tried to organise a rescue Pizarro decided, apparently on an impulse, to kill him. According to Prescott, Atahualpa was 'bold, high-minded and liberal. All agreed that he showed singular penetration and quickness of perception. His exploits as a warrior had placed his valour beyond dispute. The best homage to him is the reluctance shown by the Spaniards to restore him to freedom.'

Pizarro's crime was widely condemned in his own day by his compatriots. The Spanish court, like the rest of civilised Europe, was appalled. The Emperor himself wrote to Pizarro: 'We have been displeased by the death of Atahualpa, since he was a monarch, and particularly as it was done in the name of justice'. Many modern mestizos (of mixed Indian and Spanish blood) regard their Indian fellow-Peruvians with contempt. Yet the Emperor Charles V, then the most powerful ruler in the Western world, saw the Inca as a fellow-monarch who participated in the divine right of kings.

Towards sunset we walked to a carved rock, known as the Inca's Seat, which overlooks the valley from the top of a steep hill on the edge of the town. (Our ascent was slow: suddenly we were aware of being at 9,500 feet.) Here Atahualpa sat while inspecting his troops and since his day the view can have changed but little. Below stretched a town undefiled by modern architecture, its roofs all red-brown tiles, its church belfries curiously squat; these were left half-finished as a protest against a Spanish tax on completed churches. The valley floor is now drought-burned, a beautiful but tragic golden-brown expanse scattered with rare patches of irrigated green. Last season sixty per cent of Peru's rice crop was lost through drought and there is no foreign currency available for essential imported rice: many people are going hungry. And another calamitous season is on the way.

4 September

Outwardly Cajamarca is classic Spanish colonial: slow, tranquil, unspoiled. At noon the sun pours gold into narrow, quiet streets where the complacent carved façades of only slightly decaying mansions seem unaware that the Spanish Empire is no more. In the several market places rickety stalls sell a contrasting array of goods ancient and modern, including dried llama foetuses for use in magical rites. The air is pure, clear, invigorating: never too hot or too cold. Across the intense blue of the mountain sky high white clouds occasionally wander, their shadows seeming to alter the textures and colours of the nearby ranges. Long centuries before the Spaniards arrived – or indeed the Incas – this valley was settled and cultivated. And somehow one is aware of the tentacles of its experience stretching back through millenia of unwritten but not unimportant history. It has an old and secret soul; the colonial mansions seem quite modern.

We moved into one of those mansions this morning, as guests of Amelia and George Calderbank, a warm-hearted couple whose advice on mule-buying will be invaluable. Dr Calderbank is Director of the local Agricultural Institute, a British Government sponsored project to help raise the productivity of Peruvian farmers. Amelia has taken charge of our mule-hunt and today she expended a great deal of time and energy on letting it be known far and wide that a strong, quiet riding mule is urgently needed. It may take us several days to find one but I can think of no more enchanting town in which to be delayed.

5 September

Our mule-hunt continues and Rachel is in Paradise: riding de Paso horses, inspecting stud-farms, conversing at length with a variety of mules and generally being equine. She says riding a de Paso is like 'travelling in an armchair'. These extraordinary horses are now much in demand on the US market and fetch thousands of dollars at Lima sales. We looked this afternoon at one superb light chestnut mule whose dam was a de Paso. He is a family pet with a knowing look and at once we fell in love with him; but after a long suspenseful search for his owner our hopes were blitzed – £600 sterling and no haggling. Our limit is £150. A pony would be cheaper but an unwise choice given the terrain between here and Cuzco, plus drought conditions. Mules are incomparably more sure-footed and have more stamina and smaller appetites.

This afternoon we acquired our tack. A de Paso breeder sold me a saddle, blanket, bridle, leathers, stirrups (with shields made out of old motor tyres), a leather namdah, leather overpiece, leather head-collar, string girth, padded crupper and four yards of rope – all for £25. I requested a plain crupper instead of the long, elaborately fringed tailpiece worn here on formal occasions; this impressive relic from the caparison of a knight's steed would not be entirely suitable for the trails ahead. All this tack is well-worn but in perfect condition and the leather is of a far higher quality than anything now available in the local market.

6 September

This morning's mule-hunt took us to La Colpa, a Co-operative farm some seven miles away which was the British Agricultural Mission's first base. George's advice helped the new Co-op to use their government 'Improvement Grant' wisely and get off to an unusually good start. Previously La Colpa was an hacienda of 1200 hectares (400 irrigated) which had been in the same family for over 300 years. Then in 1972, under the military Junta's radical new Agrarian Reform law, it was given to the local campesinos whose ancestors had worked on it as semi-slaves since the 1660s. Luckily a good 'natural' leader came to the top – a rare type among campesinos – and he is able to take all the major decisions, telling the workers what to do and when, and generally standing in, psychologically, for the dispossessed landowner who now lives in Lima.

Peru's latest and most drastic Agrarian Reform programme was hurriedly implemented, as a political measure rather than a socio-economic reform, though the campesinos would have needed years of practical training and mental preparation to equip them for such an upheaval. Various sanguine 'experts' forecast that they would take naturally to Co-op farming because the Incas so brilliantly developed communal agriculture, which is the obvious way to deal with Andean terracing and irrigation problems. But the ancient *ayllu* and the modern Co-op make quite different demands on the community and the individual. Never before have the Indians had to plan ahead and few seem able to do so now; they put only enough work into Co-op land to provide for the immediate needs of their own family and as a result most Co-op farms are a wasteful shambles.

As La Colpa is comparatively successful, partly because of British advice, one rejoices to see the campesinos working the land for themselves rather than for some already too-rich landowner who lacks the Incas' sense of social responsibility. Yet there is an inevitable melancholy about the destruction of any traditional way of life. La Colpa, like all large haciendas, was a self-contained hamlet dominated by its church tower – white-washed, red-tiled, surmounted by a plain cross, handsome against a background of giant eucalyptus. The church is now disused and its attractively plain interior is disintegrating. All around it, separated by wide cobbled courtyards, are dozens of other white-washed, red-tiled buildings: cow byres, piggeries, granaries, dairies, a saddler's workroom, a smithy, a bakery, hay lofts, harness-rooms, hen houses and many neat workers' cottages. The family home, with a fine pillared portico and a long, deep verandah, has become the Co-op headquarters, its gracious rooms converted to a series of offices, stores, meeting-rooms and a scruffy cafeteria now closed because no one can afford to use it. Swarms of obese, half-tame rabbits are kept in the patio where an elegant stone fountain no longer plays. We walked through the pleasure garden between well-kept borders of exotic blooms shaded by towering eucalyptus. Little rockery 'islets', each with a miniature 'hacienda house' for geese, rose from a trout-filled ornamental lake fringed with weeping willows and crossed by wooden Chinese footbridges. In a far corner, swings and see-saws were discreetly concealed by crimson and gold flowering shrubs. Beyond a high cactus hedge several huge tiled barns, constructed of the local reddish mud, stood out against the sheer grey-blue rock-face of a nearby mountain. At a little distance from the barns were more workers' homes: two-storeyed, for the senior staff, including the primary teacher supplied by the hacienda for its own school. I wondered then if it is for the over-all benefit of Peruvian society that an hacienda like La Colpa – an oasis of order, dignity and simply beauty – should be, as it were, 'reduced to the ranks'. Does not mankind *need* such oases, when they can be maintained (as La Colpa was) without injustice to the masses?

7 September

Given time, the grape-vine always works. Today's mule-hunt started at 7.30 a.m. when Señor Federico Fernandez, a friend of the Calderbanks, collected us in his Landrover. He had heard of someone with several mules for sale: an unusual circumstance, probably connected with the drought. For miles we bumped over narrow tracks, the windows sealed against thick clouds of dust. Five campesinos gave us contradictory directions and it was 9 a.m. before we found our man, though he lives scarcely twelve miles from Cajamarca. "When you are trekking", advised Federico, "never ask these people for help. It's better to get lost your way than their's."

We had agreed that Federico should pretend to be the buyer so I made no comment when eight mules came cantering together across a steep, sun-browned mountainside. But at once my eye had fixed on an elegant, glossy young lady with an intelligent expression: about 12.1 h.h. and a dark bay, shading off on belly and legs to a most unusual creamy-russet. After much leisurely consideration of other animals we discovered that my secret instant-choice was aged three and a half, perfectly broken, good in traffic and the most expensive of the herd at 55,000 soles.* Federico seemed impatiently amused at the idea that anyone would ever pay even *half* 55,000 for such a miserable, weedy, highly-strung little animal who obviously had no stamina and couldn't carry anything more than a well-grown five-year-old. On that note he swept us all into the Landrover and quickly drove off. "Tomorrow", he said, "we return and offer forty and we get her for forty-five. She is a good choice – wiry and willing and docile. Also very beautiful. Maybe she is a little young, but better that than too old. In Cuzco you may sell her for 80,000 because there they have no good mules."

"Why didn't you haggle today?" I asked. Federico smiled. "It is better to leave our friend in anguish because he has lost a wonderful opportunity. Then tomorrow he is so glad to see me back it is easy to get for forty-five." "Or forty?" I suggested. Federico frowned and shook his head. "Maybe, but that would be unkind. She is worth forty-five on the local market now." I liked him all the more for that.

Federico now revealed two unexpected bureaucratic obstacles. "You must go to the Prefecture", he said briskly, "to get a document requesting everyone to help you in your troubles." I protested that we aren't expecting any troubles, my allergy to bureaucrats almost bringing me out in spots. But Federico was firm. "No one can walk from Cajamarca to Cuzco without having many troubles. This document you must obtain. Otherwise it is not safe to be in wild places." I remembered then that the Incas allowed no one to travel without a licence; had the population taken to wandering uncontrolled on their lovely new roads, the meticulous Inca organisation of society, from village level up, would have been jeopardised.

* About £155

"Also", continued Federico, "you must obtain from the police a stamped document, a certificate of mule-ownership, which you bring tomorrow to be signed when you have paid. Do you remember your animal's brand? No? You have not an eye for what is necessary in our country! But *I* remember! It is JL. So the police write all details, and exactly describe her, and when she is stolen other police help you. Without this document they believe *you* have stolen her – and you cannot sell her."

In the Prefecture – a labyrinthine and decaying colonial edifice – we had to deal with a horrible little man (round, yellowish, shiny) who took pompous stupidity to the furthest extreme. He was a minor official, a political appointee who under the Junta has no real power and so must seize every opportunity to inflate his self-importance. He spent twenty minutes going through our passports, scrutinising every document however irrelevant, and then he questioned my credentials as a writer. When I produced a letter of introduction from my publisher, mentioning all my books, he shrugged and flicked it aside. "Where are these books?" he asked insolently. "If I see no books, how can I believe you write books?"

Grinding my teeth, I was about to point out that people don't normally walk through the Andes carrying seven large volumes which they have no wish to read. But luckily Amelia – faithfully by my side as interpreter – got there first with a sweet-toned, casual reference to a telephone call she had had from the British Ambassador in Lima asking the Calderbanks to assist us. Ten minutes later we had our embossed, stamped, signed and sealed letter requesting every citizen throughout the length and breadth of Peru to render us every possible assistance. Let's hope we have no occasion to use this document.

At the Police Headquarters I was most courteously received by a kindly, unassuming man with a delightful sense of humour who turned out to be the Second-in-Command for Cajamarca Province and so of considerable importance. Without even glancing at our passports he organised the mule chit and, while it was being typed out, offered us coffee and much good advice about our route. When I explained that our main concern will be to avoid motor roads, wherever possible, he chuckled and pointed out that over part of our proposed route there aren't even footpaths marked on any of the available maps. He warned us to avoid fiestas in the smaller and more remote pueblos where pisco-maddened men occasionally kill strangers for no apparent reason. I didn't take this too seriously, though I'll remember it; it's the sort of warning one receives from townsfolk in every country with an unpoliced hinterland.

This is the beginning of the fiesta season and after an early supper we went to the near-by village of Los Baños del Inca to enjoy the beginning of a two-day celebration of the Virgin Mary's birthday. Christ's mother is still firmly identified in the Indian mind with the Inca Pacha-mama – Mother Earth, source of fertility. Vatican statisticians may count Peru's Indians as 'Christians' but their adaptation of Christianity bears little resemblance to the original. On the evening of Atahualpa's murder, future developments were foreshadowed when the conquistadores' Indian interpreter, translating for Pizarro's chaplain, told the doomed Inca, 'The Christians believe in three gods and one god and that makes four'. This was but the first of many crushing defeats for orthodoxy. It proved far easier to annex the Andes than to transmit any recognisable form of Christianity to a people already happy with their own simple rituals, all in some way related to the practicalities of everyday survival. Threats of Hell or promises of Heaven never really got through.

Few mestizo townspeople were present at Los Baños but Indians were swarming on the Plaza in front of the church. There a wicker cage, some thirty feet high, held an illuminated statue of the Virgin. Tomorrow morning, after a special Mass, this will be carried around the village in procession. Another, smaller wicker cage held a man wearing a black poncho and drinking chicha from a two-litre plastic jug. During the night he will be severely whipped as a scapegoat but he won't notice because by then his jug will have been often refilled from one of the many barrels of chicha that line the roadways. This mild, maize-based beer is succinctly described as 'murky drink' in the index to John Hemming's *The Conquest of the Incas*. It is refreshing and palatable, though some over-fastidious foreigners avoid it because the fermentation process is begun with the aid of human saliva.

8 September

This morning we went to a hairdresser and Rachel emerged red with rage looking as though some Amazonian headhunter had tried to scalp her. I pointed out consolingly that on the Andean highlands one's coiffure is of little moment. Officially all Peru's banks are now on strike but the indefatigable Amelia found one which admitted us, as desperate cases, and exchanged our 500 soles notes for a mini-sackful of small-denomination notes suitable for rural areas. Even in Cajamarca, it's hard to change anything above a 200 soles note. We were slightly disconcerted when a worried woman behind the counter of a chemist's shop, who had been informed of our plans by Amelia, presented me with half-a-dozen suppositories lest Rachel might develop an infection on a mountain-top. Apparently Peruvian medical opinion swears by these ghastly devices as a general panacea.

The exotic can come to seem normal within a week. Now I feel at home among the throng of campesinos who arrive in Cajamarca before dawn – the men and boys in swinging red/brown/orange ponchos, the tiny women comically squat in multitudinous skirts, the babies sleeping soundly on the pavements while Mamma sits cross-legged beside a little pile of eggs or potatoes, or a meagre spread of trinkets, or bunches of flowers, or herbs, or alfalfa for the cuys that are kept by most Andean households. I've even got used to the Indians' odd, faraway look, as though they live in a world so remote from ours that they cannot share things with us – and don't want to.

After lunch Federico drove us back to Martin the Mule-Merchant. As we got out of the Landrover all the herd approached, ever inquisitive, and from a distance we could recognise our choice, her long furry russet ears pricked forward as she trotted towards us, legs dainty as a Jersey cow's. I hope not *too* dainty for the task ahead . . . By 4.30 the deal was done and Rachel and I had solemnly named our travelling-companion 'Joanna' – Juana (pronounced Whanna) in Spanish. We had personal reasons for choosing Joanna but did not contradict Federico and Martin when they assumed that she was being pessimistically named in honour of Queen Juana la Loca – after all, her brand *is* JL!

Then we debated – to shoe or not to shoe? If shod, Juana might go over the edge on one of the many narrow, rocky paths between here and Huánuco. If unshod, she might go lame on such a long journey. Federico was for shoeing, Martin against. We looked at her feet which have never been shod and are in perfect condition. Eventually I decided against, arguing that there is a certain finality about going over a precipice, whereas going lame is a disagreeable but usually temporary misfortune. If her feet do prove too tender she can be shod somewhere along the way, preferably beyond Huánuco.

Juana has never worn a bit but responds well to a complicated rope noseband-cum-bridle which Martin presented to us. We had brought our own tack and I practised coping with the girth which has no buckles but is secured by a diabolically involved system of leather thongs and iron rings. When Rachel had mastered the art of riding without a bit, Juana was taken five miles across country to Federico's hacienda, from where we'll start our journey in the morning.

2

Left Foot Forward

Camp outside Matara. 9 September

Arriving at Federico's hacienda this morning, we were touched
to find a group from the British Agricultural Mission waiting to see
us off: a gesture that made both of us feel quite homesick on leaving
the Cajamarca valley. We won't quickly forget the kindness of the
entire Mission staff during this past week.

Juana emerged from her stable looking slightly puzzled yet
interested in the changing scene; this is, after all, her first day away
from an obviously loving owner. I groomed her briskly, murmuring sweet nothings – not because grooming was necessary (she
shines like a new coin) but to accustom her to my touch, voice and
smell before I began the less pleasurable process of saddling and
loading. Then Rachel held her, Federico's groom hovering watchfully nearby, while I struggled to come to terms with those esoteric
thongs and rings. (I've never been good with knots.) She stood
motionless, only her ears twitching – forward! – as she happily
received Rachel's fulsome compliments. Having at last secured
the girth and got the crupper on I relaxed; given this degree of
good behaviour, the day might even come when the crupper could
be left attached to the saddle.

Loading was easy. All our gear for the next four months is
tightly packed into two small attached saddle-bags (made in
England) and our two Diana-bags – one small, the other smaller.
Hard, heavy objects – books, emergency food rations – go in the
panniers, cushioned with clothes for Juana's sake. My Himalayan
flea-bag (one and a quarter pounds) and our high-altitude tent
(two and a half pounds including poles and pegs) go in my
Diana-bag with the two space-blankets. Rachel's flea-bag (two
pounds) provides the padding for one pannier and her Diana-bag
holds our high-altitude clothing which is very compact. The
panniers fit snugly behind the saddle and my Diana-bag is tied to
the crupper iron with a length of nylon clothes-line. Rachel's

Diana-bag, and the heavy iron picket and tethering rope, balance the five-litre water container across the pommel; as the water-level goes down, the picket can be adjusted to keep the balance right. A mug and saucepan hang from each pannier. On my back I carry the day's food and discarded garments in a light knapsack. My bush-shirt pockets hold notebooks, pens, maps (such as they are), compass, knife, whistle, passports and vital documents. Rachel has her own compass and whistle and we are both carrying prodigious quantities of cash in money-belts. When everything was in place, it seemed there would be no room for Rachel; yet she was able to mount unaided, despite the impedimenta fore and aft, and pronounced herself very comfortable. Then quickly we said our thank-yous and good-byes and to a fusillade of camera-clickings we were away.

Rachel was blushing under her riding-hat. "Just as well the media don't know what we're up to!" she muttered. And we shuddered in unison.

I was experiencing that familiar sense of unreality which always marks the first few miles of a trek into the unknown. One can hardly credit that the longed-for moment has arrived; and by the time one has come to believe in it, it has passed . . .

Already, at 9.15, the sun was hot in a cloudless sky. But soon we were climbing steadily, the land rising between what might here be described as 'rolling hills' – i.e., pretty impressive mountains, though not in the 'savage peak' category. Rachel marvelled at their colouring: great glowing patches of red and yellow, riven by wide streaks of orange and pink – as a painting this scene would have seemed vulgar, as Andes it was superb. But the drought-damage marred our joy. Beside the narrow stoney road, many hectares of withered young wheat lay on the cracked and desperate earth. Other fields were ploughed for planting; but if no rain comes, why waste seed? These fields had cactus hedges and when Juana noticed gaps on the right she made half-hearted attempts to turn towards home. Federico had advised me to lead her all day, foreseeing that she might take Rachel back to Martin.

When we reached our first plateau, at some 10,500 feet, a cool breeze came frisking over the red-brown dustiness from a massive mountain-range far ahead – a sheer wall (it seemed) of purple-gold-brown rock, rearing towards the deep blue sky. A few clouds were poised along its rough crest and we willed them to bring rain.

From the plateau we were overlooking a jumble of deep valleys, some blessed with vivid strips of green, marking the survival of streams. On steep slopes, far above the valley floors, hamlets of adobe hovels merged into their red-brown background. A few were thatched with sword cactus, most had red tiles bought at the nearest market and carried home on burros. We overtook one such caravan, driven by two barefooted campesino women who giggled nervously in response to our greeting.

Passing through a larger-than-usual pueblo in the early afternoon we saw a sheaf of dessicated maize stalks for sale. While Juana munched we drank beer and Inca-Cola, bought in quite a big shop from a polite but distant mestizo. His long shelves were ominously bare: salt, sugar, rice, macaroni, lavatory paper (unexpectedly!) but not much of anything. I mopped up the last of the beer. (Even in Cajamarca, the 'grandest' shops are now poorly stocked.) Juana was tethered outside and as we lent on the counter, gulping thirstily, an unkempt campesino couple appeared in the doorway dragging half a sheep's carcass, still dripping blood. This was duly weighed, and the shop-keeper said, "Eighteen kilos". Whereupon the campesinos erupted furiously, claiming that it was *at least* twenty kilos. The shop-keeper pointed to the scales needle, the campesinos shook their fists, stamped their feet and shouted. ("I thought they were meant to be a *docile* race!" said Rachel.) Then the shopkeeper shrugged, heaved their rather macabre property off the scales and made to return it to them. They looked at each other, then sulkily at the ground. The shop-keeper gave them a roll of notes and they trotted meekly away without counting them.

We continued down the long, deserted street between a straggle of detached, two-storey adobe houses given dignity by carved wooden balconies. Poverty was in the air, palpable as the dust that rose in the wake of a passing truck. All day we met only three motor vehicles, two buses and a truck; each left us shrouded and coughing. Juana completely ignored these horrors; she is an interesting animal, calm yet very alert.

Soon after, the road ran beneath shattered purple cliffs looking like stacked slates magnified 10,000 times. Here we paused to eat Amelia's *Cordon Bleu* sandwiches, which seemed incongruously epicurean in our grubby paws. Then I inspected my left foot and discovered that my Mexican-bought boots are not as good as they look. I had thought I was developing a standard blister, as would be normal – so I ignored the pain. But on removing my boot a torn and blood-soaked sock was revealed, plus a deep hole in my foot; and the errant cobbler's nail was virtually inaccessible. "What are you going to do?" asked Rachel, sympathetically. I surveyed my choices: I could either lie down and die or proceed according to plan. "Don't ask stupid questions!" I snapped ungratefully, lacing up the guilty boot. It is at such times that one pays the penalty for travelling light*est*; yet the advantages of that policy are greater than the occasional disadvantages.

Within a mile we had spotted our first redura (short-cut), a barely perceptible path across a level sandy plain where a few tall eucalyptus swayed in a gusty wind. Nearby, on our left, rose a sheer semi-circular wall of grey rock; on our right, the mountains were round and brown. Soon we entered a eucalyptus plantation where the young trees grew in rows some ten yards apart. Sheep, goats and a few skeletal cows grazed on sparse clumps of rough grass and scrub. Their herds – two tiny ragged children sitting in the shade of a eucalyptus – stared at us with alarmed eyes from beneath wide-brimmed hats. Next came a mile or so of curiously splintered land, its mini-abysses scattered with strange shrivelled shrubs. Then abruptly we were overlooking a deep, circular, irrigated hollow, containing the new dwellings of a Co-op farm. Turning left and keeping to the high ground, we crossed acres of stubble – the earth feather-light with drought – before negotiating a precipitous, shadowy ravine where Juana warned us of an inexplicable boggy patch. Mules are famed for their quick response to every sort of natural hazard. Remembering Juana's inadequate lunch, Rachel dismounted for the tough climb back to the road. Then she requested her sweater; it was 4.45 and suddenly cold.

Gradually the road dropped to a sad trickle of a river in a wide bed of pale, sun-bleached stones. *Green* grass grew on the level bank but we reluctantly decided against camping here; this grazing must at present be precious to someone. Another redura took us up a long, rough brown slope where dead leaves rattled as we pushed through the bushes. (Rachel was walking again.) Back on the road we met a young mestizo couple and asked anxiously where we could buy fodder. The husband leaped over a low stone wall and pulled an armload of wild oats and coarse grass which made it unnecessary to lead Juana; hugging this priceless burden I hastened on and she eagerly followed. A final steep climb, to Matara, slowed us. Here eucalyptus smoke drifting from adobe hovels instantly recalled the Ethiopian highlands – as only a smell can recall a place.

Matara has acquired much graffiti on gable-walls, proclaiming the rights of campesinos and extolling revolution. It was now 6 p.m. and heavy clouds were gathering but we had no faith in them, having observed the same false promise every evening in Caja-marca. In the handsome, oblong plaza we left Juana guzzling, and collecting a crowd of excited, bewildered children, while we entered another large, dark, ill-stocked shop. Mercifully the beer supply is better here. Four young mestizos were drinking chicha and one offered me a taste from his glass. This brew is so much more to my liking than commercial beer that I offered him my bottle in exchange; but he insisted that I must be his guest. The shop-keeper apologised for the expanding tumult of children out-side the door – "They are curious because tourists don't come here." Lucky Matara! While tethering Juana, Rachel had some-how dropped her shining silver-looking compass on the pavement outside the shop; and when we emerged one little boy shyly stepped forward and handed it to her. If Matara were on the tourist-map, would he have done so?

Juana's supper was a big worry; nobody in the shop had been able to help. When we consulted three policemen, sitting on a bench outside their station, they immediately sent two youngsters off in different directions. One officer had a round chubby face which he was evidently trying to render more intimidating by the cultivation of a fierce moustache. He laboriously wrote our names in a register, then opened his desk drawer and presented me with two eggs that had been wrapped in a handkerchief for safety. "Food to give the señorita," he explained, looking anxiously at Rachel – who was sitting outside the window attending to her print-deficiency by reading *Watership Down* in the fading twilight. Eleven hours is a long time to go bookless . . .

Darkness comes quickly here; at this altitude one tends to forget how close we are to the equator. Soon the stars were out above the irregular roofs of the substantial yet neglected houses surrounding the plaza. Then the youngsters returned – fodderless. But mean-while Chubby-face had been thinking and he ordered them to guide us to a large field of failed barley on the edge of the town where Juana is now filling her belly, though not getting the nourishment she requires. As the boys led us through narrow, rough, unlit streets, where only feeble lamp-light glimmered in living-room windows, a brilliant half-moon sailed into view. So my first battle with my own weird knots was by moonlight. We have tethered Juana to a huge fallen cactus trunk: the earth is too loose and dry for the picket to be trustworthy. On today's showing she is going to make an excellent Third Musketeer, though obviously we must expect minor differences of opinion during the first week or so.

This splendid camp-site is a trifle too bumpy to be described as 'ideal,' but one doesn't expect interior-sprung ground in the Andes. On three sides tall eucalyptus surround us, on the fourth a high, dense cactus hedge hides us from the road. In view of the anti-tent-peg state of the ground we are sleeping under the stars, wrapped in our space-blankets. After a supper of bread and Cajamarca cheese, Rachel was asleep before I had finished my first paragraph.

Camp outside San Marcos. 10 September

I awoke, puzzled, just before midnight. Was I dreaming? But no – for the first time in fourteen months, *rain* was falling on the Matara region. Quite heavy rain, too, and it continued for three and a half hours. I hastily pulled books, torches and clothes under our space-blankets, drew Rachel's space-blanket over her head and curled myself up in a ball. But Rachel is a lively sleeper and it proved impossible to keep her covered. When we rose at 5.45 her flea-bag and husky-suit were sodden. Yet one couldn't begrudge the thirsty earth its relief.

It was a cloudy, warm morning, the dawn light silver and soft. Less romantic were the town's powerful shit-smells, drawn out by the rain. Our field, I suspect, is a popular local latrine. As we loaded up, two trucks beyond the hedge were also loading up, with men going to the locally-famous animal-fair held every Sunday at San Marcos; many carried bound sheep and goats, slung over their shoulders.

By 7 we were climbing to a plateau bounded by arid red-brown slopes on which a maze of criss-crossing thread-like paths made a crazy pattern. Several groups of horsemen and a few horsewomen overtook us on their way to San Marcos and greeted us gravely. Juana brayed sociably to the ponies. Rachel was walking, so that her flea-bag and husky suit could be laid across the load and saddle to dry. In a small pueblo, where groups with churns were

awaiting the Cajamarca milk-lorry, a young man kindly pointed
out a redura down a steep slope of red earth between high red
embankments. Then came a grey-brown plain where emaciated
sheep grazed on nothing. At its edge we found ourselves staring
into an apparently fathomless ravine, long, narrow and veget-
ation-filled; this Andean landscape is wondrously unpredictable.
Suddenly an elderly limping campesino in a frayed poncho
appeared like a genie and indicated another redura, half overgrown by green thorny bushes, which hairpinned around the side
of the ravine. It then levelled out while taking us onto a bare,
boulder-strewn mountain-side where it plunged precipitously to
join the road near San Marcos.

Here Juana disgraced herself for the first time and had to be
disciplined. This evening Rachel noted in her diary, 'In one of
these patches of dust Juana committed one of the worst sins a
horse or mule can commit. When I was on her back she went down
on her knees and tried to roll. Luckily I got off in time and Mummy
pulled her up before she had time to roll on the rest of the things.
Mummy gave her a good walloping and Juana looked most put
out'.

Already scores of campesinos were returning from the market,
driving burros laden with hand-painted pottery, firewood, roof-
tiles and sacks of God-knows-what. Some were leading pigs on
strings, their squeals re-echoing from cliff to cliff in the narrow
gorge. Others were driving cows or sheep or ponies. A few of the
men had striking 'Inca' faces: aquiline noses, long bright eyes,
delicately-drawn mouths, haughty expressions. Most women
were carrying on their backs a bulky load of merchandise, packed
around the statutory infant. Each group plodded silently on, eyes
downcast, jaws rhythmically masticating coca-wads to blur
hunger and fatigue.

On the edge of San Marcos – by Andean standards a biggish
town – my questing eye spotted a small, square red flag above a
doorway: the sign that a householder sells chicha. A bottle cost ten
soles, as compared to seventy for a litre of beer. Sitting on the low
parapet of a humpy bridge over a dried-up stream, I emptied the
bottle before removing my left boot. "Sore?" suggested Rachel.
"Bloody!" I replied literally, displaying a sanguinary sock.
"You'd better find a cobbler", said Rachel, "otherwise you'll soon
need a blood transfusion." So we looked for a cobbler, but unsuccessfully because it was Sunday.

The animal market is held on a wide expanse of beaten earth below road level but as it was now 3.30 most of the fun was over. Yet the surrounding streets remained crowded and Juana was much admired by connoisseurs. "We'd better be careful tonight", said Rachel darkly. In the town centre we had to force our way through the traffic. Instead of motor vehicles, hundreds of horses and cattle were being ridden or led in every direction without benefit of traffic laws. In the main plaza a very small boy was trying to pull a very angry bull in the required direction. The child's face was puckered with irritation at the animal's intractability – not white with fear, as would have seemed more natural. We stopped to watch this drama; eventually the child won and disappeared down a side-street, the bull ambling amiably after him. Down another side-street we lunched in a primitive eating-house with long crude trestle-tables and unsteady benches and a huge mud-range in one corner. Ample helpings of rice and beans, and a little tough mutton, cost us 100 soles each.

A mile outside San Marcos, beyond a wide, almost-dry river bed, we found this roadside site where short green grass grows between small unfamiliar trees. The main attraction was a neighbouring field of well-grown alfalfa, some of which we hoped to buy. This ground looked like common land but as we unloaded the owner arrived – a lean, severe mestizo – and forbade us to camp. "Show him the Prefect's chit!" whispered Rachel. So I did, and all was well. Rachel can be useful on occasions; without her prompting, I would never have produced that vital document. Later, the owner's charming adolescent son gave Juana such a generous helping of alfalfa that she couldn't finish it. He indignantly refused payment – "You are our brave guests from Ireland!" This is my chief objection to using chits and letters of introduction; people then feel obliged to subsidise one, which is fine in the First World, where almost everyone is richer than oneself, but to be deprecated in countries like Peru.

As we set up camp a group of friendly little boys gathered to watch and offered to help Rachel groom Juana. Leaving them together, I went to bathe my lacerated foot in the murky remains of the river amongst droves of gigantic tadpoles. On the far side rose a sheer grey cliff, mottled with dark green vegetation. A path ran along its base and I watched colourful lines of campesinos returning from the market, almost all leading pigs of various sizes and hues. Then a solitary woman appeared, wearing a wide, ankle-length red skirt and a bright blue cardigan and leading an enormous bull with eighteen-inch horns and testicles almost to the ground. She was carrying a plastic bag of toffees and looked abstracted and worn; after puberty, most campesinos seem *old*. Directly opposite me she suddenly paused, helped herself to a toffee – and presented one to the bull. He accepted it gratefully, she scratched him between the horns and they went on their way. I begin to see why these Indians have a reputation for great kindness to animals, a most unusual trait among hardship-driven peasants. Again, like the Tibetans.

Our enjoyment of the sunset was curtailed by swarms of stealthy midges and shrill mosquitoes who recked nothing of insect repellent. Not so long ago, San Marcos was known as the Gold Coast of the Andes and abortive attempts were made to resettle its inhabitants on higher ground.

Camp in Field by Irrigation Channel. 11 September

A day of such splendour that this evening I feel drunk on weak coffee.

We were up before 6 – luckily, for an irrigation channel had just been opened to flood our site (hence its green grass) and the camp would soon have been awash. Juana was in a bolshie mood, perhaps suffering from indigestion, but by 7.30 we were climbing through the most fertile land we've yet seen. Maize and potatoes flourished on well-irrigated hillsides and sometimes our little path wound through groves of exotic trees and shrubs. As we emerged onto high pastureland we could see, away to the left, vague clouds wisping around a mighty heap of mountains – like square granite blocks. Diminutive sheep were being herded by spinning campesino women, sitting on boulder vantage points with their colourful skirts spread around them – slightly like gnomes on toadstools. A pueblo of neat little houses had – most unusually – a paved main street and a café-bar-restaurant which I thought it seemly to resist at 9.30 a.m. There was much animal traffic – the market was busy – but no trace of motor vehicles. Here we bought our lunch: ten bananas for fifty soles. Expensive by local standards, but we're far from banana-growing country.

Again up, the breeze becoming cooler, the pastures greener, the sheep more numerous. Looking back, we could see the mountains around Cajamarca and all the intervening wilderness of blue-hazed hills and valleys. Soon dark mountains came crowding close on both sides: no more sheep or shepherds. Suddenly we felt very conscious of our *smallness* – three minute creatures toiling ever upwards. "We're like ants on an elephant", said Rachel.

All unexpectedly we reached the pass and stood wordless, shocked by the immensity of the grandeur before us. This was the very quintessence of mountain beauty – a boundless glory of heights and depths, of jagged rock peaks far above and curved valley floors far below – of range thrusting up behind range in sublime and eternal disorder. Through crystal air the colours glowed as though all the world were a jewel: green, brown, ochre, navy, gold, purple, silver. Above was the strong blue of the mountain sky and filling our lungs was the keen air of high and desolate places – elixir air, that makes one feel it must be possible to leap from summit to summit. This was a memory forever, an indelible imprint on one's whole being. I hope Rachel, too, has received it.

No houses or pueblos were visible from the pass but for many miles ahead we could see sections of our red-brown track clinging to precipices. This was not redura territory; such sheer slopes permit no short cuts. The first stage of the descent took us to the edge of a 2,500 foot gorge. Along its sides were cultivated ledges and slopes, and a few hovels crouched at odd angles over staggering drops. The gorge floor was a dense tangle of trees and shrubs and very far above it towered a long purple-grey rock massif. The scale of this landscape is overwhelming.

Our track soon became a path, scarcely two feet wide, that hurtled downwards with a drop of at least 2,000 feet on one side. The surface was of loose dusty earth and round pebbles and here Juana more than atoned for this morning's misdemeanours. It would have been unwise to lead her so I went ahead and she nimbly followed – never faltering, even on the most vertiginous bends – while Rachel brought up the rear to watch the load. I had mercilessly tightened the girth at the start; on such a gradient the law of gravity can do dreadful things and a slipping load could have been fatal.

Descending this path, one felt *absorbed* by the Andes. None of the surrounding mountains bore a trace of cultivation, though campesinos will attempt to grow *something* almost anywhere. The slopes were of red-gold or pale grey earth, with thick patches of brown or green vegetation and occasional clumps of pink or blue flowers – chiefly lupins, which are, I'm told, native to the Peruvian highlands. There were several essential lay-bys: narrow ledges, or shallow caves in the rock-wall. Two burro trains civilly gave way to us. And we gave way to an awe-inspiring elderly-looking woman, bearing some bulky burden wrapped in a striped blanket, who came skimming upwards as though she were ice-skating. Personally, I found going *down* exhausting enough. My 'brakes' (thigh muscles) were throbbing by the time we reached a vast, parched river-bed of large, loose stones and stretches of fine sand.

Here grew an extraordinary variety of giant cacti – grotesque and oddly threatening, yet beautiful in their own cruel way. The real threat came from tall thickets of thorny bushes, leafless and vicious, which grabbed us agonisingly, drawing blood even from Juana. Small dead black bushes had thin angular branches that snapped at a touch. Strange, low, naked trees, with thick shiny silver boles, had an evil-coloured parasite cactus growing from the junctions of its branches. Other, taller trees had very beautiful crimson pods that glowed among olive green leaves like slender flames. Yet others were leafless but laden with royal blue blossom; these also had pods which, when stirred by the breeze, produced the only sound in all this sunny desolation – a thin, sweet, magical melody, coming from everywhere and nowhere.

When our path disintegrated into a plethora of ambiguous goat-trails Rachel said, "I *knew* we'd get lost down here! You just have a mania for going off into the wilderness." This indicated that she needed her lunch so we sat on a bottom-burning rock and ate five bananas each and drank pints of water. We were now down to about 6,000 feet and amidst such aridity the afternoon heat was stifling.

The river-bed, if you can call it that, had become rocky rather than stony and was broken by countless awkward little gullies, full of that malign bush with the fish-hook thorns. There was no way of avoiding those gullies, unless we turned back. I was relieved to find that turning back is against Rachel's principles – it seemed only fair to give her the option – so we struggled on, bloody and sweaty, in what I assumed to be the direction of the road. Though roads do such quirky things hereabouts one couldn't be sure . . . When eventually we found it there was one last snag: an almost sheer brick-red slope of crumbly earth, sans path. It was only about thirty feet high and we could make it – but could Juana? We decided to unload her if she said she couldn't. I scrambled up, with some difficulty, and lovingly called her. She looked at Rachel, who made encouraging noises. Then she shook her head violently, rolled her eyes, laid back her ears – and took the slope like an 18 h.h. hunter. As Rachel followed I flung my arms around Juana's neck and told her that she is the bravest, cleverest, most agile mule in all Peru: which was not flattery. She scratched her face on my hip and seemed to agree.

The road surface here was strewn with sharp stones. Far ahead we could see the green of a long, cultivated valley but we were immediately surrounded by bare, thorny, grey-black scrubland, palpitating in the heat, from which rose brown hills, low and round, with a solitary prickly-pear cactus squatting on one summit like some deformed sentinel. Rachel walked because of the atrocious surface, on which Juana occasionally stumbled.

At 3.45 we came to a road junction – a rare phenomenon in the Andes, for obvious reasons. Our road crossed the river-bed, now in a deep gorge, by a new metal suspension bridge – very long, very high, with very loose floor-boards. A freak wind roared up the funnel of the gorge, moaning most strangely through the structure of the bridge. Juana was appalled. The unnerving noise, the unfamiliar glinting metal, the rattling of the boards when I went ahead to coax her – everything about this monstrosity justified a mule being mulish. We surveyed the terrain, confirmed that the bridge was a must and blindfolded Juana – to no effect. Then we unsuccessfully attempted to back her onto the boards; if she could once be induced to set foot upon them all would be well. Next I unpacked our emergency rations and tried to tempt her with mint-cake; she snorted contemptuously, conveying that she wasn't in the business of taking bribes. We were close to despair. I crossed the bridge and called; Juana didn't budge. I returned, sent Rachel across, put my arms around Juana's neck and begged her, with tears in my voice, to follow her owner. When Rachel shouted to her above the wind I went briskly ahead, tugging hard at the bridle – and suddenly Juana was clattering behind me, breathing fast with fear through distended nostrils. She would have been worth 500,000 soles.

Now we were in that long green valley. Not far from the bridge was the first dwelling we'd seen since morning, a miserable road-side shack. But beside it grew a field of alfalfa and soon Juana was having her just reward: four kilos for forty soles. The one-roomed shack was a family home-cum-'shop', stocking only beer and Inca Cola (no chicha). The furniture consisted of a single bed, sagging

badly in the middle, a tin table and two wooden stools. When we
arrived a wretched young campesino woman was sitting spinning
in a corner of the yard, her toddler son lying across her lap tugging
at a flaccid breast. He is aged seventeen months but looks less than
a year. When Mamma went to cut the alfalfa she handed him to
me and suddenly I fell into a slough of despond. He lay passively in
my arms, his hair matted and nitful, his red little eyes oozing
yellow matter, his face disfigured by septic insect bites, his clothes
stiff with filth and reeking of urine. One of how many with no
future? The yard held small piles of adobe bricks, roof tiles and
planks. Mamma explained that her husband had been hoping to
build another room but prices have risen so sharply he can't.
They hope to sell those materials at a profit.

Juana now had a problem, described thus in Rachel's diary:
'When we took off the bridle to let her eat in comfort we found she
had a very nasty sore where the bridle had been rubbing against
her nose. It looked very sore and we knew we couldn't put the
bridle back so we just left the problem until we had been refreshed
by our drinks. Then I got her white leading rope and tide it to the
two rings and it made quite a good little bridle as long as *she's*
good.'

We continued up the humid, well-irrigated valley between
thriving crops of barley, wheat, potatoes, maize, sugar cane,
bananas, alfalfa. I bought another eight kilos for Juana's supper
and tied it behind the saddle, much to her frustration. Despite this
fertility the inhabitants look puny and ill-nourished and there
were no pueblos, only scattered dwellings or small groups of
hovels. Some fields were being ploughed by pairs of oxen drawing
wooden ploughs light enough to be carried on the shoulder. We
refilled our water-bottle from a roadside irrigation channel and
added a double dose of purifying pills. By then we were in a muck
sweat and this, mingled with thick white dust, gave us a coating of
mud like Punjabi chickens waiting to be baked.

Mulish needs determined our choice of camp-site and we are in
a small triangular grassy field beside the road. An irrigation
channel flows swiftly on one side; on the other, tall shady trees
conceal us from passers-by. About 200 yards away the roofs of two
little houses are just visible above cactus hedges and as I write
I can faintly hear the music of Indian bamboo pipes. There has
been much equine traffic on the road, including several women
cantering briskly, their infants' heads bouncing helplessly and

alarmingly from side to side. We have been observed only once, by a youth walking home, with his scythe over his shoulder, on the irrigation path. He paused briefly to admire Juana – "Muy bonito!" Most campesinos are extraordinarily incurious.

Beyond the irrigation channel lies flat wasteland dotted with tall bushes, leafless and black. On the top branch of the nearest bush an enchanting small bird – all cardinal red – sang his happy evening song, pausing at intervals to swoop through the air, making little clicking noises as he reduced the insect population. At 6.30 the long rolls of pearly cloud to the west briefly became gold, then rose-pink, fading to smoky blue. And quarter of an hour later the stars were out. While writing this I have drunk four litres of water.

Cajabamba. 12 September

One and a half people in a one-man tent on a hot night, when the entrance has had to be zipped up against insects, is not a receipt for sound sleep. We lay stark naked, dripping gently and scratching savagely. Yet neither of us felt tired this morning, as one would after a broken night at sea-level.

Further up the valley crops were replaced by goats and multi-coloured sheep – black, white, brown, grey – foraging on harsh slopes. Outside one shack we watched two women weaving a vividly dyed blanket, but they ignored us so pointedly that we soon moved on. Here the average family holding is under four acres and the children look like Oxfam posters. But at least they're not yet being eaten, as the Inca chronicler Huaman Poma reported some children were – and by their parents, too – during a ten-year pre-Conquest drought.

The Peruvian government, like so many others, is encouraged by First World countries to spend lavishly on armaments; yet it has no money to spare for even the most rudimentary public health service. Doctors' fees (when there's a doctor within reach) are so high that one illness can leave a family permanently in debt. The health-care scene was much better in colonial times; one of the outstanding Spanish virtues (following the Catholic medieval tradition) was concern for the sick. During the 16th century, eight hospitals-cum-poor-houses were founded in Lima and the largest and most richly endowed was for Indians. Many sierra towns also had hospitals, often staffed on a weekly rota basis by voluntary lay workers – members of religious confraternities.

In the yard of a large Co-op farm three campesinos were taking a tractor to pieces, or maybe trying to put it together again. The yard and buildings looked conspicuously uncared for and we were told this evening that the locals have been greatly disappointed by the results of Agrarian Reform. Previously they were not paid but given free shelter and seeds; now they have to find their own accommodation, buy their own seeds – and still they are not paid. A few haciendas have been returned to their hereditary owners at the campesinos' request. But usually the owner doesn't want his property back as it has been so abused that to restore it would cost more than he can afford, or at least is prepared to pay. Some haciendas were allowed to run down *before* their appropriation because their owners knew what was coming; others had been grossly neglected or mismanaged for generations. Peru, like many Latin American countries, is still suffering from a centuries'-old tradition of absentee landlordism. In colonial times – and the attitude has persisted – to *own* land was very important, to farm it productively much less so. Most haciendas have always been run by responsible – but rarely very knowledgeable – mestizo mayor-domos while the owners enjoyed Lima life, using their sierra estates merely as holiday homes. Yet the average campesino now considers the pre-Reform system to have been the lesser of two evils.

We climbed for miles towards a flat-topped, red-brown wall of rock. Then we lost sight of it, while taking a steep redura along a white, dusty, rocky cliff which led to an even steeper redura up the rock wall. By 12.15 we were in the main plaza of this enchanting town on a well-wooded plateau.

This is Juana's half-day off because here we are staying with a friend of the Calderbanks – Mike Garnett, an English priest who has been working alone in Cajabamba for the past ten years and has fifty churches in his parish. He lives in what was formerly a convent, an attractively simple building surrounding a patio ablaze with flowers. At present several young campesinos also live there, while trying to make up their minds whether or not they want to go to the Seminary at Cajamarca to study for the priest-hood. This is not an easy decision, nor is it easy for the Church authorities to decide whether or not they are suitable candidates. I've already referred to the Indians' radical 'adaptation' of Christ-ianity and the notion of a campesino priest is revolutionary.

Despite ecclesiastical Resolutions in 1697 and 1725, and a 1766 Papal brief ordering the admission of Indians to religious orders, they have always been excluded from the priesthood by the local hierarchy. And one feels that to encourage them into a seminary now is locking the stable after the horse has gone.

Before looking for Mike we had to look for alfalfa – which has now become 'Alf' in Murphy jargon. We wandered up and down neat, straight, Spanish streets, almost free of motor-traffic and full of friendly people. Alas! we were too late for Alf who only appears in the early morning when the campesinos bring in burro-loads from their fields. Remembering then how our Mexican pony had relished maize grain, we decided to give Juana a well-earned treat. From an astonished grocer we bought two kilos at (relatively) vast expense. But Juana spurned it. In despair we tried to force-feed her, shoving a handful into her mouth. With luck the centavo would drop and she would realise that here was some delicious though novel nutriment. Baring her teeth most comically, she spat it into the gutter. Whereupon an enormously amused bystander informed us that maize grain is *human* food which no Peruvian animal has ever tasted. (A starting point there for some essay on the comparative economies of Mexico and Peru.) Accepting defeat, we sought Mike, who in due course solved the Alf problem – and also the cobbler problem which was, as you might say, no less *pressing*. He incidentally informed us that a *white* flag over a doorway means bread for sale: a useful tip. But what really made my day was an encounter with an ancient man, redolent of chicha, who ended a welcoming peroration by describing Rachel and myself as 'two flowers that have sprung up on the pavement of Cajabamba'!

Camp on Ledge above River-bed. 13 September

Alf-trading starts early and not a leaf remained when we reached the marketplace at 6.30. As we gloomed over our problem – we couldn't start with an empty mule – an Alf-laden burro appeared out of a side-street, followed totteringly by an old man, bent and half-blind. After some hesitation (this was a daily order for a de Paso breeder) he sold us six kilos for sixty soles. (The standard price; off the tourist trails, no one in Peru tries to over-charge gringoes.) This was enough for two meals so we left Caja-bamba, after loading up on the church steps amidst a crowd of giggling children, with the surplus tied to my knapsack. We ourselves had been well fed on buns spread with avocado and salt, and a delicious drink of extraordinary gruel made from a local ginger-type root mixed with milk and cocoa.

Soon we were on a steep stretch of the Camino Real, where Rachel dismounted. Mike had told us that from Cajabamba to Huamachuco we could ignore the motor road as the Camino Real provides a shorter and more dramatic route; though given the form its drama takes, it probably isn't shorter in *time* . . .

Reaching level ground we paused to gaze down on the old russet roofs of Cajabamba, tranquil and timeless amidst groves of tall eucalyptus. Then on, the Camino Real only slightly undulating for miles, its stone paving just visible under a carpet of soft grass. This luxury was appreciated by all; Juana sometimes trotted spontaneously out of sheer *joie de vivre*. Yet on either side was sadness: field after field of maize, potatoes and wheat all withered and brown and mournfully rustling in the breeze. Many substantial two-storey dwellings were deserted; whole families have fled to Trujillo or Lima to escape famine, as they think. This unfortunately is nothing new. Because of the erratic rainfall, two out of five Andean harvests are poor – if not as calamitous as this – and there is a long-established tradition of migration to the coastal cities in times of drought. For much of the way the Camino Real was lined with tall shady eucalyptus, or bramble hedges. In a village of straggling hovels a red flag fluttered and I swilled the chicha avidly, though it was bitter and weak and full of interesting insect corpses. One is advised not to drink alcohol at these altitudes but I can't think why. Here a dozen unfriendly, jeering mestizo boys followed us for half a mile and tried to mislead us onto another track; but they turned back on the edge of the Rio Negra gorge, which lay some 2,000 feet below the edge of the escarpment. As yet no river was visible – just a vast width of pale stones, stretching as far as we could see to left and right, and beyond them an unbroken wall of soaring brown mountains.

"How does the Camino Real get through *that* lot?" wondered Rachel, dismounting. "We'll soon find out", I said cheerfully, tightening the girth. Here no Inca paving remained; the path was of loose stones or thick grey dust. Halfway down, gravity won; the load slipped forward and Juana (sensible girl) at once stood still. She had to be completely re-loaded though there was no room for us to stand side by side. I ended up tightening the girth squatting under her belly; luckily my relationship with those leather thongs and iron rings is now quite good. Towards the end of the descent it began to rain lightly; and far up the gorge, to our left, we could see solid banks of black cloud raining heavily – an odd phenomenon, like watching a waterfall that had started in heaven.

Down at last, we stood and looked around us. I was aware of an exhilarating isolation. Although a village was so near, we might have been – in the *feeling* of this desolate gorge – 1,000 miles from the nearest human being.

"Where's the Camino Real?" demanded Rachel. We scrutinised the surrounding stoney waste – all those miles of it! – and could discern no hint even of a goat-trail, never mind a Royal Road. I waved a hand in a vaguely westerly direction. "It must be down there", I said. "Why?" asked Rachel. "Why shouldn't it be up *there*?" – and she waved a hand in a vaguely easterly direction. "I just have a hunch it's downstream", I said, wondering uneasily if Rachel was right. "Hmm!" said she. Bitter experience has taught her that her mother, though allegedly an Intrepid Traveller, has no sense of direction. We looked at the map, but the relevant cartographer had chosen not to go into details about this region. No *camino*, *real* or otherwise, was marked. So we went downstream.

First, of course, we had to find the stream – still invisible. It proved to be narrow (some thirty yards) and only waist deep but with a bed of rolling stones and a powerful current. Fortunately Juana decided that this was fun and happily splashed across, Rachel acrobatically placing her feet on Juana's neck. I removed my boots and shirt and followed slowly, testing the river-bed with my stick. Then we wandered down the gorge for an hour and a half and never have I walked on a more exhausting surface: either round loose stones – very large – or deep soft sand. But that was a low price to pay for the austere magnificence all around us. On our right rose 2,500 foot cliffs of bare rock and vividly red earth. On our left were those brown, scrub-covered mountains, too close for their summits to be visible. And ahead was space – an infinity of blue sky. (The rain clouds were behind us, and dispersing.)

"*I* think we're lost", Rachel said at 3.45. "Could be", I conceded, "but it's worth it!" Then suddenly we saw a human, where the brown mountains receded slightly to allow a small patch of cultivation. The miserable little maize crop was dead and the equally miserable campesino, filthy and ragged, was herding five gaunt sheep amidst this worthless fodder.

"*Donde esta Camino Real?*" I shouted across the intervening wilderness of stones. The campesino came through a low thorn hedge and pointed to the ground we stood on. "*Camino Real?*" I yelled again, incredulously. The campesino nodded, then abruptly turned away and retreated inside his fence.

The river then played a nasty trick by swinging in to the foot of a sheer mountain, forcing us to ford it again. Beyond another long stretch of shifting, tiring sand we passed the remains of two ancient bridges, both of which had crossed now-dry tributaries just above their confluence with the Rio Negra. We were still on the wrong side of the river, which here was deeper and faster. As the gorge gradually widened we could see a long jumble of blue mountains against the far horizon. Now the red cliffs were lower and a gigantic rift appeared in the brown mountains – presumably the Camino Real's exit from the gorge. We could no longer postpone our third fording of the river and this time Juana was a little disconcerted by the strength of the current – a reaction I shared.

At the wide entrance to the tributary valley, amidst a wilderness of dense thorny scrub, we really did get lost. When I cautiously went ahead, to investigate what might lie beyond a particularly menacing thicket, Juana impetuously plunged after me and Rachel's left arm was severely torn by dagger-like thorns. Mercifully she ducked in time to save her face – these bushes were ten feet high – and characteristically didn't complain though spouting blood. This evening she noted in her diary, 'I got the whole of my upper left arm punctured by lots of slightly poisonous thorns when Juana dragged me through thorn bushes. You can't controll her at all with the home-made riens we had to make because of her poor sore nose.'

Briefly we rambled south, passing a sinister colony of ten vultures sitting flapping their wings in leafless trees. "They'll enjoy us when we've died of starvation", observed Rachel. Our hopes rose when we found an active irrigation channel but on trying to follow it our way was blocked by an impenetrable thorn hedge. So instead we followed a stream a few inches deep, with an almost invisible pathlet beside it. For lack of anything else, we decided this must be the Camino Real: tomorrow will prove us right or wrong. Here we were climbing again, following a river-bed no less stoney than the Rio Negra's. At 5.40 we came to this site, which is very beautiful but remarkably inconvenient from several

points of view. We could have continued for another half-hour in
search of grazing but my nail-hole was being tiresome. The Rio
Negra had long since removed its bandage and too many wettings,
plus sand in my sock, had not soothed it. So for this evening I
decided to put myself before Juana, much to Rachel's disapproval.

We are on a too-sloping ledge, some thirty yards by fifty and
about ten feet above the river-bed at the base of a mountain. Our
pathlet crosses this ledge and carries an astounding amount of
traffic; half a dozen campesinos passed before sunset, ascending to
their up-valley shacks. We seemed to frighten them, for they
quickened their pace to hurry by without greeting us. A few other
groups drove loaded burros up the river bed; green, red and blue
skirts, and striped ponchos, made gay flares of colour against the
grey stones. There is nothing here for Juana to eat – not even
withered weeds – so we firmly waylaid an old man, almost invisible under a load of dry maize stalks, and bought a bundle for
ten soles. I wanted him to take twenty but he refused: evidently ten
is the market price.

We've cleared the tent-space of sharp loose stones but could do
nothing about the bumps. The gradient guarantees that one of us
(Rachel) is going to roll on the other (me) throughout the night.
We ate rolls and sardines by brilliant moonlight while heaped-up
clouds to the north were still orange-brown in the afterglow. Our
pudding of some esoteric coconut-flavoured fudgey substance
(presented to us in Cajamarca) might have seemed inedible had
we not been so hungry. All was washed down by water tasting
strongly of pills. Rachel then retired and I settled down to write.
Here I feel a profound content, perhaps partly because of the
immutability of the scene around me. Few places today are safe
from 'development' but no one, in the foreseeable future, is going
to develop this defiantly inaccessible region.

Huamachucho. 14 September

When Nature called me at midnight the surrounding glory,
beneath a flood of silver radiance, kept me sitting entranced on a
rock for over an hour. Beneath our ledge the river bed glimmered
pale. Near and far, dark mountain silhouettes stood out against a
royal blue sky, faintly star-sprinkled. There was no stirring of a
breeze, no whisper of running water: the stillness was so unflawed
that it seemed the sovereign moon, floating high, must have put

a spell on our whole world. To me that perfection of stillness is the grace of the mountains, poured into one's soul. There is more to such experiences than visual beauty; there is also another sort of beauty, necessary to mankind yet hard to put in words. It is the beauty of freedom: freedom from an ugly, artificial, dehumanising, discontented world in which man has lost his bearings. A world run by an alliance of self-hypnotised technocrats and profit-crazed tycoons who demand constant, meaningless change. A world where waste and greed are accepted – even admired – because our minds' manipulators have made frugality and moderation seem like failure in the Acquisition Game. A world where *deliberate* cruelty to each other, despite a proliferation of 'humanitarian' do-gooding agencies, is tolerated – because who can stop the multinational conquistadores? What I'm trying to express is scoffed at nowadays – or simply not recognised – or if recognised made into an off-putting cult. But I *know*, and have always known, that we 20th-century humans need to escape at intervals from that alien world which has so abruptly replaced the environment that bred us. We need to be close to, and opposed to, and sometimes subservient to, and always respectful of the physical realities of the planet we live on. We need to receive its pure silences and attend to its winds, to wade through its rivers and sweat under its sun, to plough through its sands and sleep on its bumps. Not all the time, but often enough for us to remember that we are animals. Clever animals, yet ultimately dependent, like any other animal, on the forces of Nature. Sitting there in the moonlight, it frightened me to think of the millions who have become so estranged from our origins that many of their children believe architects make mountains and scientists make milk. These are people who live *always* with artificial heating, lighting and transport. People who have never *used* their bodies (is this why sex has become such an obsession?) but use only their minds. And often not even their own minds, but the minds of others who have produced the goods that make it unecessary for individuals fully *to live*. The Box epitomises it all – millions passively absorbing misleading over-simplifi-cations and being artificially stimulated by phoney emotions. Where are we at? The end of the road, perhaps . . . For we have travelled too far and too fast from the life the campesino still lives. And it may be that we are now meeting ourselves coming back – never a healthy encounter.

At Cajabamba, Mike remarked that one feels much happier

away from the Affluent Society: but then he is living and *helping* here. My own feeling of relief, at having escaped temporarily into the freedom of simplicity, could be regarded as selfish romanticism. Yet I'm not arguing that First Worlders would be better off living campesino lives. Extreme poverty is also dehumanising and here the local poverty permanently shadows my enjoyment – as it doesn't, oddly enough, when I'm travelling in India. Is this because the campesinos seem to lack that potent spiritual dimension to daily life which sustains even the poorest Hindu peasant? 'Escape' journeys like these are for me a necessary therapy. Whole areas of one's humanity could become atrophied if one remained always within a world where motor-roads are more important than trees and speed is more important than silence.

I'd just returned to my flea-bag when footsteps approached and a cheerful whistling man passed by. Here one feels no tremor of apprehension on such occasions, however unexpected a sound may be. The vibes are reassuring.

By 7 a.m. we were on our way – as empty-bellied as poor Juana, having recklessly eaten our breakfast last evening. One of several campesinos descending with unloaded burros confirmed that we are still on the Camino Real. Crossing a stream – tributary of the tributary – we watered Juana and filled our container. This was a toughish uphill walk, again on sand and stones, and I was sweating hard long before starting the real climb. There was no pueblo but where the valley narrowed we passed a dozen scattered dwellings, causing alarmed small children to flee indoors. Rachel eyed the towering mountains that now enclosed us on three sides, leaving only a slice of sky above. "How do we get out of here?" she asked. "Wait for it!" I replied. And not long after our path swung sharply left and leaped onto a precipice. Rachel dismounted and I advised her to lean well forward during this ascent. Up we went – and up and up and up – the path narrow and dusty between drought-sick scrub and massive boulders, some the size of barns. As the air became perceptibly thinner, I feared for the ill-fed Juana. But she plodded steadily upward, never faltering. We greeted three small groups of descending campesinos who firmly snubbed us, as though gringo mothers and children driving mules to Huamachuco were a daily and rather unwelcome apparition.

The climb ended unexpectedly, as such climbs do; flies on elephants can have no over-all picture of the terrain. Suddenly we were on a level ridge, separating two valleys of incalculable depth.

Looking back, we were also looking *down* on the summits of all the mountains we have so far traversed; we must have been surveying at least 100 miles of Andes. The conquistadores were not as keen on this sort of thing as we are. Pedro de Cieza de León, a soldier and enthusiastic chronicler who vividly described the Inca Empire as the Spaniards found it, recalled a similar ascent: 'Climbing great and rugged mountains, so lofty that their summits were lost in the cloud and the accompanying scud . . . I was so done in that it was very difficult for me to reach the top and on turning to gaze down, it seemed that the ravines reached into the bowels of hell'.

From this ridge our path, now grassy and comfortable, dropped briefly before climbing to within a few hundred feet of the true summit. Rachel, once there, found it frustrating to be *not quite* on top. So she went scampering off to complete the ascent as though she had not just climbed 4,000 feet on an empty stomach. Perhaps she was a campesino in a previous incarnation.

Meanwhile I sat on a rock admiring the view – in this context a ludicrous phrase. Here was no 'view' but a whole universe of mountains, gorges, spurs, valleys, peaks, ridges – the remotest crags disappearing and reappearing through half-transparent curtains of pale grey cloud. Beneath a darkening sky the colours were subdued: olive green, cinnamon brown, black, charcoal grey, navy-blue.

The terrain immediately ahead was too irregular to be called a plateau, too wide and withdrawn from the mountains to be called a valley. Much of the land was cultivated: long, low ridges with shallow dips between. Yet if transported to Ireland those 'low' ridges and 'shallow' dips would themselves seem a respectable mountain range . . . Our path sloped to level stretches of thirsty pasture and withered maize fields scattered with adobe hovels too far apart to be called a pueblo. A few campesinos were driving bony cows or ponies, or small flocks of sheep, to their non-grazing. From our height they seemed to be wandering aimlessly, toy figures emphasising the vastness of their world. When it rained heavily for twenty minutes we rejoiced – and shivered, for suddenly it was very cold. We often hesitated at path junctions but when we sought directions the campesinos looked blank or uneasy or sulky and nobody answered. Amidst all this drought and privation, we were moved to hear poignant bamboo pipe melodies drifting out from several hovels at 9.45 on a cold wet morning. The

Indians find much comfort in their music, which has remained almost totally 'pure'.

The next ridge took us above Rachel's summit and here I began to notice the altitude. Rachel, also walking, looked astonished when asked temporarily to forego the pleasure of human converse because I needed all my breath for climbing. Soon we had reached the Camino Real's highest point between Cajabamba and Huamachuco. A low cairn surmounted by a small cross marked the spot. High peaks were all about, quite close, with sun-broken clouds straying among them. As we rested a small boy on a burro, wearing a poncho almost large enough to envelope both, abruptly arose out of the valley ahead.

The first stage of that descent plunged us into two long, narrow gorges from the depths of which we again had to climb steeply. Beyond the second we cravenly considered a brunch of emergency rations. Then, pulling ourselves together, we admitted that this was no emergency and proceeded with rumbling stomachs.

During the next, easy, stage we scanned the enormous chaos of peaks ahead, wondering how any path could possibly find a way through. Shifting clouds produced a changing pattern of subtle nameless shades; and from our height we could relish the contrast between the immobility of the mountains and the restlessness of the sky. A few families were driving laden burros from Huamachuco and when the track became vague we sought the guidance of their footprints. Passing a tiny pueblo, with no one in sight, we realised that what had seemed to be a shed was in fact a church of sorts; crosses were painted on a door that looked as though it hadn't been opened for years. A large surrounding graveyard was enclosed by a seven-foot adobe wall oddly roofed with withered cactus. When the descent became violently steep Rachel dismounted, as another icy shower swept our mountain. We stopped for water at a clear spring; one loses an amazing amount of sweat at this altitude and our liquid intake had been spectacular all morning. As the sky cleared, we could see an elongated pueblo very far below in a narrow, tree-filled valley. This part of the descent was far more leg-taxing than the climb, though lung-resting. Our path changed to a rock-stairs for the last stage and wriggled its way past red-tiled shacks piled one above the other on a precipice. Crossing a puny river on stepping stones we stopped at the first open shop at 1.15 p.m., after six hours walking during which we had covered some fifteen miles.

Setting off from London

La Colpa church near Cajamarca

It was unclear why this biggish shop had remained open; it stocked only ten eggs and a few dozen beer, the latter now beyond reach of local purses. Row upon row of empty Coca-cola and Inca-cola bottles lined the shelves, uncollected as there is no re-stocking. A kind mestizo woman with an attractive oval face and large sad eyes saw Rachel's disappointment and insisted on giving us the remains of the family lunch: a small plate each of boiled potatoes, and maize stewed in some tasty juice – delectable, though scarcely enough to blunt the edges of our appetites. I bought two bottles of beer and four eggs but our friend would accept no payment for the meal. Her two sons, aged six and four, huddled fascinated in a corner, watching us eat. Their father migrated to Lima eight months ago, when trade virtually ceased in this pueblo, but he could find no work and now has TB. The four other pueblo shops have closed because there is so little cash in circulation. Yet Sanagoran is a sizable village with both secondary and primary schools. Its substantial adobe houses, often surrounded by large farm-yards, suggest modest prosperity; but now it has a disquieting atmosphere of life in abeyance. We left feeling sad for the locals and guilty about our still unfed Juana.

The Camino Real, here level and ten feet wide, continued through a sun-filled gorge between towering cliffs of jagged red rock or grey scrub-dotted earth. The river seemed quite full because confined to a narrow, deep bed. Stately groves of mature eucalyptus were swaying in the breeze, interspersed with plantations of silver-blue-green saplings – all quivering and shimmering. Beyond the gorge, our path rose gradually, following the curves of a series of red-brown mountains. By Andean standards this region is densely populated; its gentler slopes allow more cultivation, and enclose wider, more fertile valleys, than any we saw this morning. But we passed no pueblos and our hunger reached the 'acute' mark as the air became thinner and colder. I ate the four raw eggs, Rachel having declined to share them with me. Then the terrain was again uninhabited, as the Camino Real ran level along a sheer grey mountain wall of naked rock with a slit-like chasm on the left – its far-away floor a tangle of trees and shrubs. Ahead rose a bulky, forested mountain; and at last, between the trees, we glimpsed a few roofs. But another hour passed before we turned the shoulder of this 11,000 foot mountain, near its summit, and were looking down on a dense eucalyptus wood through which Huamachuco – at 9,300 feet – was just visible.

We stopped at the first hotel we came to, in a broad colonial street reeking of urine; scores of youngsters, some rather hostile and mocking, gathered to watch us unloading on the pavement. I then rushed off to fodder-hunt, leaving Rachel sitting on the hotel doorstep holding Juana. Mercifully I was in time to buy the last four kilos of the evening's supply of green oats (no Alf here) from a friendly campesino woman who has promised to put eight kilos aside for me tomorrow morning. Juana munched ravenously while the hotel proprietor, an amiable but rather ineffectual character, sent minions to look for a safe corral. Rachel took our gear up a narrow, steep stairs and down a long corridor to our room, which has a carved balcony overlooking the street, a clean single bed, a clean bare wooden floor for me to sleep on, a tiny locker for me to write on, a feeble electric bulb for me to write by (luxury after torchlight!) and even a chair for me to sit on. Pretty good value for forty-five pence. When Rachel rejoined me it was dark and crowds of men had collected to admire Juana and beg me to sell her; the Peruvians are far more interested in our mula than in ourselves! After a cold forty minutes sitting on the pavement under frosty stars we appealed to a passing policeman for corral advice; he shrugged indifferently and walked on. "Show him the Prefect's chit!" urged Rachel. But at that moment the mestizo draper whose shop is next to the hotel took pity on us and offered to corral Juana in his yard for two nights. We left her tethered beside a mound of withered maize stalks. Then to an eating-house for human fodder and so to bed, Rachel almost asleep on her feet as we crossed the deserted plaza.

The same. 15 September

At 12.15 a.m. two rifle shots woke me. Several more followed, and then a burst of machine-gun fire and a surge of angry shouting which ended in sudden total silence. When I enquired about the 'incident' today everyone was evasive. But it reminded us that while we are ecstatically ambling through the Andes the towns-people of Peru are enduring a period of considerable political tension.

By 7 we were back in the eating-house, ravenous again. We have spent much of today working on the camel principle and stuffing ourselves in preparation for lean times ahead. Our eating-house is a friendly establishment; its three dimly-lit, grubby rooms, leading into each other, have sexy trade calendars decorating the walls. Sitting in the back room, our view of the kitchen might weaken less robust appetites. Yet what comes out of that dire cubby-hole is delicious: spiced noodle soup and generous helpings of lomo saltado, a concoction of chopped goat's meat, tomatoes, onions, potatoes and peppers all in a most appetising sauce. And for breakfast we had giant tortilla verduras – omelettes with onions, tomatoes and chips. As we ate, half-starved dogs wandered in from the street and cringed in corners, watching their chance to clean up under vacated tables.

We've decided that the mestizos, with some memorable exceptions, are not physically attractive; in this respect the mix hasn't been a wild success. The Indians are far more pleasing to the eye, especially those with 'Inca' features who are usually, for some baffling reason, men. Sitting opposite us at lunch today was a tall man in a dashing embroidered poncho who had *white* skin. Peru offers every possible skin shade from almost white to darkish brown but a true white is most uncommon. Rachel observed that here, as in India, all the advertisements show pure whites.

After breakfast we sauntered through the market, where many stalls were ominously unoccupied. This seems an even less prosperous town than Cajabamba, though it's a provincial capital and nearer Trujillo. Along the edge of the pavement rows of impassive campesino women sat behind piles of bright fruits and vegetables – huge purple onions, monster pumpkins recalling Cinderella, red and yellow bananas, orange and green oranges, sweet limes, rosy apples, plump, grooved crimson tomatoes, countless varieties of multi-coloured potatoes. If Mamma temporarily disappears, tiny tots are left in charge – incredibly on-the-ball infants who know the exact price of everything *and* give the correct change.

Huamachuco lacks the charm of Cajamarca and Cajabamba, though it's another 'undeveloped' colonial town with spotless streets which seem to be cleaned every two hours by teams of sweepers. A hideous new cathedral dominates the fine main plaza, one of the biggest squares in Peru. We visited this blot on the townscape during a special service for a senior schoolboys' confraternity and noticed that the entire congregation was mestizo. The interior is a nightmare of vulgarity and affectation but how many billions of soles must it have cost? While campesino children die regularly, nearby, of curable diseases . . . This is the sort of thing the Liberation Church of Latin America is determined to fight, to the point of schism if necessary.

This afternoon we found six tins of sardines which I hope won't poison us; though only fifty soles each, they are rusty and thick with dust. We also bought half a kilo of noodles, which cook quickly on a camp fire, and in the morning we'll buy two dozen fresh rolls. Yesterday taught us that however modest one's demands it is not now possible to live off the Andean land.

We visited Juana four times today, laden on each occasion with green oats. Not the best diet – Alf is more balanced – but much appreciated. Señor Antonio's large corral (yard) is approached through a small patio with a primitive baño in one corner where a handsome young man was vigorously soaping his torso this morning and looked comically taken aback to see us. In the yard a miniature black sow (like an Irish piglet) was quarrelling with her only child in a spacious clean sty. Elsewhere a tethered nanny-goat was enthusiastically consuming what looked like the remains of a bonfire. A small Alf-patch, visible over the wall, had died. Children swarmed, but only two of them were Antonio's. During the afternoon his wife – thin, haggard, a trifle obsequious – invited us into the parlour and gave us her gynaecological life-story. Two boys aged nineteen and twenty are now at university in Trujillo. The next two babies were stillborn, the fifth died in infancy. Then there were four miscarriages before the two youngest arrived: now aged seven and nine but about half Rachel's size. Rachel lives in a state of constant astonishment at finding herself already taller than so many adult campesinos; and it seems the growth genes – if there are such things! – of the Indians have won through and affected the average mestizo stature.

This parlour was a sad room: long, high-ceilinged, mud-floored, furnished only by eight tin and plastic camp-chairs ranged along one wall, a sewing machine in a corner and a few bits of 'best china' on a rough wooden shelf. Señora Antonio crochets woollen saddle-covers and tried to sell me one for 1,500 soles. When I looked at it with insincere admiration and murmured "Too much!" she at once dropped to 1,000 soles. "You *must* buy it to help this family!" Rachel whispered vehemently – "Think of all *they've* done to help Juana!" And I didn't resent this rip-off; after all, Señor Antonio is determined to accept no corral payment. The thick warm blanket, of black, red and blue squares, will add a touch of luxury to our equipage and may ease Rachel's seat during long weeks in the saddle. (Though actually she's been out of it, so far, as much as in it.)

Long before the Incas arrived Huamachuco was the administrative centre for one of the larger Andean tribes, some of whom were quite advanced. The Incas wished however to seem the sole creators of all worthwhile culture, so their propagandists manipulated oral history to obliterate all traces of the regional cultures which they had used as 'foundation stones'. Because the Andean peoples were without writing that propaganda still works. At the time of the Conquest, Huamachuco and its surrounding province seem to have been a lot better off than they are now. Pedro de Cieza de León reported: 'Huamachuco was in ancient times thickly settled. There used to be great lords in this province who were highly respected by the Incas. With the past disturbances and wars, many of the people of this province have disappeared. Its climate is good, cool rather than warm, and it produces abundant food and other things needful for human life. Before the Spaniards entered this kingdom, there were in the lands of Huamachuco many flocks of llamas, and in the highlands and unsettled regions a still greater number of wild flocks, called guanacos and vicuñas . . . In the valleys of the plains the natives plant cotton and make their clothing of it, so they lack for nothing . . . But the wars the Spaniards waged against one another were like a plague for the Indians and the flocks'.

Pizarro and his men rested for four days at Huamachuco where they debated which route to follow to Cuzco – for here, unusually, there was (and still is) a choice. As John Hemming has explained: 'They decided not to take the main highway through the Conchucos to the east of the Cordillera Blanca because of its many hills. They descended instead into the deep valley of Huaylas . . .' We have decided otherwise, because today the Huaylas route leads eventually to an embryonic tourist area. Later, beyond Huánuco, we may have to tolerate motor-roads of a sort – 'But not yet, oh God!'

Today we wrote many letters which seem unlikely to arrive at their destinations. The Post Office is a dusty, dingy barracks where there were no other customers and the startled clerk – elderly and taciturn – took eighteen minutes to adjust his scales and calculate the rates to Ireland, of which he had never previously heard.

This evening I stood myself a non-treat of a bottle of Peruvian non-wine – the most nauseating grape-derived potation I've ever tasted anywhere. "What better could you expect for *ninety pence*?" said Rachel.

3

Familiar with the Clouds

Camp at Foot of Mountain. 16 September

Poor Rachel was bug-struck last night – that kitchen! She vomited copiously three times from our balcony, which I thought showed commendable presence of mind if not much civic spirit. But by dawn the thin dogs had tidied up.

While Juana had a last feed of Huamachuco oats we breakfasted hugely; Rachel has mysterious powers of Instant Recovery. We'd hoped to be able to carry lunch for Juana but this morning's fodder supply was so poor that the vendor, rightly putting regular customers first, rationed me to three kilos.

Today the Intrepid Traveller, now for all practical purposes off the only available map, demonstrated yet again her inefficiency and led the expedition wildly astray. Rachel has just distilled the essence of our morning – 'We found a track that Mummy thought was the right one but after about an hour of going quite steeply up we found it ended at a farm. We hunted around a little for something but didn't find anything apart from a tiny track that we thought looked like a goat track, really, but took for fun. It ended in a tiny little piece of grass that we could see a bit of our road from and that we tried to battle our way down too, but we couldn't because the crupper came off and we had to load all over again. Then, after another little escapade, we retraced our steps untill we came to a track leading off the one leading up to the farm which we dicided to take.'

The 'little escapade' over which Rachel has skated froze my (not easily frozen) maternal blood. When we turned a sharp corner to find our goat-track broken by a landslide Rachel had to dismount on the edge of a fearsome abyss and perch on the landslide while I backed Juana, as always astute and cool in a crisis, to a safe turning point.

This afternoon our track climbed gradually across uninhabited heathland – rough, brown, rock-strewn and flecked with green

patches of bog. When an icy wind brought driving rain and hail
from the sharp, high mountains to the east poor Juana was
shocked and dismayed; probably she has never before experienced
the like. An hour later the force of the gale ripped Rachel's cape at
the neck but happily the rain/hail/sleet eased off soon after. We
were climbing ever higher. Now occasional hovels crouched on the
bleak moorland, far back from the track, and in fenced-off areas
sheep, cattle and horses were huddled together with their backs to
the wind. "Juana must envy them," commented Rachel, who had
had some difficulty keeping her steed facing into the gale. At 4.30
we found this sheltered stretch of level, slightly boggy ground
between a long, high, smooth-topped ridge and a much higher,
jagged mountain. Short green grass grows between tall clumps of
coarse brown ichu grass – which last, perversely, Juana seems to
prefer. In the soft bogginess it was difficult to find a reliable spot
for the picket. The clouds spat warnings at us as we got the tent up
but we were safely tucked away in dry clothes, eating buns and
sardines, when the next deluge came. How to dry my sodden
bush-shirt and jeans is tomorrow's problem. I've no idea where we
are this evening but the setting sun confirmed that we're moving
south, which is the general idea.

Camp on Verandah of Casa on Mountain-Ledge. 17 September

A slightly uneasy night, wondering if Juana would lift her picket
– which I changed twice, to facilitate grazing. It rained hard until
midnight and one of the challenges of this life-style is how to pee in
such weather while remaining dry. Fortunately our medium-sized
saucepan makes an adequate chamber-pot.

By 5.45 we were breakfasting off buns and sardines while a
ghostly light seeped into our glen through the clouds that sat on
the mountains. Juana was then close to the tent and I moved her
because she likes to investigate everything as we pack up. Ten
minutes later Rachel noticed that she was loose – and grazing
towards the track. We advanced cautiously, but she reached the
track first and there the sound of the picket rattling behind her
on the hard ground sent her galloping, panic-stricken, towards
Huamachuco. (Just laugh at anyone who tells you mules can't
gallop.) We also began to gallop, no less panic-stricken, but soon
discovered that at approximately 11,000 feet *walking* and *galloping*

are two quite different activities. As Juana disappeared over the hill I ordered Rachel back to guard the camp and trotted in pursuit – being quite overwhelmed, despite my anxiety, by the beauty of that dawn. To the west a long rock mountain was suddenly pure gold, while the rest of our world remained green-brown bog below and pale grey cloud above.

Ten minutes earlier, a campesino boy in a maroon poncho had galloped up the track on a palomino pony – and now, from the crest of the hill, I saw him tethering Juana to a low bush. I paused for a moment, panting painfully and almost sick with relief. Then, as I hurried on planning a suitable reward, the boy vaulted into his saddle and went cantering up a mountain-side without a glance in my direction – not even waiting to be thanked. Although I shouted my gratitude he never once looked back before vanishing into a cloud. He was the only human we'd seen since noon yesterday; had he not chanced to pass, who knows when (if ever) we would have been reunited with our mula bonito? It distressed me that I'd not been allowed even to *thank* him. And his melting into the mist, when I so desperately wanted to communicate, somehow symbolised the elusiveness (and disdain for outsiders?) of the campesinos – just as his altruism recalled the disinterested courtesy and generosity with which the Incas received the original conquistadores.

An excess of oats, as everyone knows, is *bad*. Despite the stinging cold of the morning air I was dripping sweat when I rejoined Rachel; Juana had fought me over every yard of that mile-long walk. While I completed the packing-up, Rachel attempted to soothe Her Grumpiness by grooming her fondly. But this applied psychology didn't work and I was kicked in the ribs while loading. Luckily a feeble kick: those ribs have been broken four times over the years and must by now be rather fragile. When we set off at 8.10 I was still wearing my pyjama/husky-suit and carrying yesterday's casualties in my knapsack.

Where we turned onto the high mountain that overlooked our site a grass-thatched stone hovel, with two tiny windows on either side of the low doorway, reminded us both of an Irish peasants' cabin of times past. Presumably our knight had come from this dwelling. Sheep were baa-ing within stone outbuildings, also thatched, and a fat, pompous-looking grey rabbit was hopping around the yard on excellent terms with three dogs – who, strangely enough, did not remark our passing.

These Andean days tempt one to disregard all literary propriety and let loose a flood of superlatives: the highest, deepest, broadest, longest, narrowest, steepest, wildest, most precipitous, most rugged, most varied, most difficult, most silent, most barren, most isolated, most exhausting – and most beautiful. Undoubtedly today was the most superlative-provoking of all; at 8 p.m. I'm still 'high' on the glory of it. During our ten-hour walk we saw three people ('most isolated'). At one point my nerve almost failed me on Juana's behalf ('most difficult'). And all the other 'mosts' may be applied, freely and literally, to various stages of the day's progress.

Stage One took us up a long, shallow valley – an easy walk, except where the path dropped into mini-ravines with steep sides of loose boulders which taxed Juana's surefootedness. We were not on the valley floor but above it, ascending steadily a series of mountains. We were hesitating at a junction when a man came trotting down-valley on a sturdy pony whose hoof-prints we followed towards a pass excitingly visible in the distance – a short, straight line on the horizon, between two gaunt, grey peaks.

When the sky cleared at 9 I put on my rain-laden shirt and spread my jeans across the load. On the far side of the wide valley we saw one stone shack with a solitary tree standing beside it and grey sheep grazing nearby – at first we mistook them for boulders. A small boy in an ankle-length poncho was herding four cows by our path; when we greeted him he shrank behind a boulder. Nearby some patches of grass had been burned to improve the grazing. Several strange Alpine cacti fascinated us, especially a deceptively velvety-looking grey-green cushion, perfectly round, speckled with minuscule pink flowers. For once I needn't feel inferior about not being able to name flowers noticed en route; the classification of Andean flora is still incomplete and there is no field-guide. Today we also saw more bird-life than elsewhere: the Andean lapwing, the partridge-like tinamou and the caracara – a large black and white carrion eater, with orange legs and a red face, which in the good old days provided feathers for Inca head-dresses. Without the invaluable Bradt 'Backpack' guide we couldn't have identified any of these. Rachel is disappointed that we haven't yet seen a condor but it seems these are now much commoner along the coast, where the pickings are easier.

The last half-mile to the pass was steep and my lungs told me we must be at about 12,000 feet. Then we were up, standing with thudding hearts looking at our first Andean snow-peaks: a remote, jagged line, white near the fierce summits. On our right, far, far below, a wide valley – all broken by chasms and hills – held a scattering of hovels and a few clumps of trees. Beyond that stretched a blue-hazed ocean of angular peaks, smooth ridges, humped shoulders, sheer escarpments. "Are we going through *those*?" asked Rachel. "Not exactly', I replied evasively, in truth not having much notion where we were going next. But I felt we should try to keep that valley on our right.

Our path now joined a rough jeep-track; the map didn't mark it and we couldn't imagine where it came from or went to. Then, as it hair-pinned down between great banks of five-foot high Andean lupins – like scraps of sky fallen on the pink cliffs – we found a clue: good-quality coal scattered among the track's many stones. All around were signs of recent landslides (or an earthquake?). Thousands of tons of gigantic, sharp-edged hunks of mountain lay below the track, which suddenly ended on a wide ledge among small piles of coal and a few rusty wheel-barrows. From this abandoned seam we turned back to a faint path that descended into a broad, grassy bowl, all sunny and silent, before climbing a smooth green ridge. We were puzzled by smoke billowing from a summit near the mines, away on our left; its quantity and location seemed to rule out a campesinos' 'fertilising' fire. Is there a baby volcano here?

This ridge proved to be the rim of a long deep valley which reminded me of Agustín de Zarate's description of Inca strategy – 'Their strategy was to allow the Spaniards to enter a deep, narrow gorge, seize the entrance and exit with a great mass of Indians, and then hurl down such a quantity of rocks and boulders from the hillsides that they killed them all, almost without coming to grips with them'. This valley would have been ideal for such a massacre. We scrutinised its far side through binoculars, but our path's continuation was invisible. Yet we had no alternative but to descend to river-level, where we found three faint upward trails. The first petered out after fifty yards. The second had recently been cut by an impassable landslide. The third and faintest took us half-way up the mountain, and around its shoulder, before dying below a narrow ledge supporting a stone hovel – from which sprang three ferociously barking dogs who almost caused Juana to bolt over the precipice. We seemed to have arrived at the cul-de-sac to end all cul-de-sacs and were about to retreat, reluctantly, when an elderly man leaped off the ledge and beckoned us to follow him. Without showing the least curiosity about our origins or destination he helped to get Juana up a stone stairway, led us across the ledge-farmyard and pointed out the continuation of our path – here so narrow, vague and disintegrating, and overhanging such an abyss, that even Juana was soon unnerved. I then endured half an hour of tummy-tightening anxiety, the first since leaving Cajamarca. "I'm not surprised the conquistadores didn't come this way", said Rachel, peering straight into the most profound chasm we've yet seen. As she spoke a bit of path just behind us came loose and dribbled down towards the shadowy, scrub-smothered depths thousands of feet below. The tiny noises of sliding or bouncing stones seemed to tear at the smooth stillness. Glancing back, I noted that the path was now non-negotiable from Juana's point of view. (It had been almost so before collapsing.) So if we came to another damaged section we'd be caught between the two . . . When we turned the next corner, after a lung-busting climb, our path was visible for miles ahead: now level, edging its way along the *almost* sheer brown slopes of two more mountains, not far below their *perfectly* sheer silver-grey peaks – colossal splinters of rock probing the dark blue sky. From here the canyon below seemed so far away one illogically gave up worrying about falling into it: it belonged to another world. Also, the path was a few inches wider here and, being level, one didn't notice the altitude. During the next hour this Andean drama reached a crescendo. The eye could hardly take in those heights and depths and widths. I felt that tingling, reverent exultation that can also be the reaction to great music. One has to be a mountaineer to penetrate to the equivalent core of Himalayan majesty; humble trekkers can reach the inner Andean sanctum.

As we were turning the shoulder of the third mountain, leaving the canyon behind, our path became so hesitant that we paused for another binocular survey of distant possibilities. The scene below us was of total topographical disorder: an immense expanse packed with broken mountains, half-hidden valleys, ridges that suddenly became peaks, unpredictable gorges, flattish ledges, ravines into which the nearest mountainside had recently spewed ten thousand boulders. The whole looked as though some giant had been modelling a mountain range but got bored half-way through and impatiently pushed his materials aside. To the south-east rose a spectacular escarpment, soaring high above everything else within view and strangely symmetrical – like damaged pillars from some ruined Greek temple, all tidily stacked together.

Descending, we marvelled to see minute shreds of cultivation on near-vertical slopes. There was even one small field of shimmering barley, looking incongruously domestic – almost demure – amidst the surrounding violence of nature. In this area the past year's rainfall has been adequate, though not normal. Soon our path spiralled up yet another precipice, then wandered across gently undulating green pastureland. A large potato patch surrounded the first house we had passed since receiving guidance several hours earlier. Another stone dwelling was conspicuous ahead, on a grassy ledge directly below a long wall of jagged cliff; to its left, ending the ledge, a detached mini-mountain looked like a magnified grey-green plum-pudding. Our path led us onto this ledge, which is bisected by a swift stream, and Juana drank while we considered the cliff-wall. It is on the far side of a bridgeless ravine and we could see no alternative path off the ledge apart from the one we'd come on. "Here endeth the track for this day", observed Rachel. It was only 4 p.m. but we'd covered some twenty miles of rough stuff and Rachel had walked at least half that; more and more, Juana is becoming a pack-mule. If the campesinos didn't object to gringoes in their garden, this was an ideal site: grazing for Juana, water for all, resiliant turf on which to sleep. No firewood so no hot supper, but you can't have *everything* . . .

I was about to approach *la casa* when a middle-aged woman appeared at the door, twenty yards away. She stared, then came towards us looking puzzled but friendly. She is more Spanish than Indian looking, with fine features and lively, intelligent eyes: not the sort of person I'd expected to encounter here. She couldn't be persuaded that we are self-sufficient and only wanted permission to put up our tent and graze our mule; obviously she's never before heard of a 'carpa'. We must sleep on their verandah, she insisted, as her husband (Carlos) and daughter – equally surprising – arrived. They all pointed to swollen black clouds gathering above the 'pillared' escarpment and said it will get very cold tonight because we are at 11,400 feet: and anyway the ground is no place to sleep. Carlos firmly led Juana to a slightly higher ledge of beaten earth, surrounded by buildings, and pointed to our 'bedroom' – a spacious verandah, some six feet by twenty, outside a storeroom-cum-bedroom where a married son sleeps with his wife and small baby. When Juana was back on the grass, Carlos shouted to his fourteen-year-old son (the youngest of six children) to give her chopped barley straw and oats. Even from our distance, we could sense her delighted astonishment. For us, too, this has been an astonishing evening. We're not used to such outgoingness in the Andes – though it has its limitations, which interest me. We've been lavishly entertained on the verandah, yet not invited into the family dwelling. Why?

When Carlos asked if we needed food I said no but suggested a little hot water for coffee. This request soon produced a large saucepan of boiling *milk* which enabled each of us to have three big mugs of *café con léche* with our buns: an unprecedented treat. By then it was very cold and raining slightly and thunder was roaring from peak to peak. When the eldest boy, aged twenty-six, arrived home from Huamachuco driving three laden donkeys (one with foal at foot) I wondered how he'd got his animals across the broken path. Answer: he'd mended it. This monthly journey takes him twenty-four hours – what a trip to the nearest town! He quickly unloaded the donkeys, piled sacks in a corner of the verandah and without a moment's pause was away on the next task: driving two of the donkeys to fetch enormous sacks of newly-lifted potatoes from the foot of the steep green slope below the ledge – a 1,000 foot drop, at least. Every day, this family of nine has potatoes and cows' milk for the two main meals (morning and evening) – again like Irish peasants not so long ago. The surplus potato crop is exchanged for noodles, kerosene, salt, sugar, matches, clothes, household needs. It does one good to be among adequately fed Andean citizens who don't need to chew coca. Comparing this mestizo family – mentally alert, not shy of gringoes, well-mannered, well-built, well-dressed, well-organised – comparing them with the average Indian family one again glimpses that shadow of doom over the native campesinos. After all, Carlos & Co., living on this ledge, could hardly be described as enjoying any unfair advantages over Indian farmers.

As the sky cleared, towards sunset, we climbed the little 'plum-pudding' mountain and watched the family going about its evening ritual. On the steep mountainside nearest the house, Mother was milking five small reddish cows which she'd just fetched from their pasture *very* far below the ledge. Before milking, their near and off legs were tied together, and then their forelegs were tied to their horns – a complicated procedure. "Why don't they build a milking-stall?" wondered Rachel. But somehow it's impossible to imagine anything ever changing on this ledge. Daughter-in-law collected the milk in two small churns and looked like a maiden in an eighteenth-century engraving as she moved across the mountain with a churn balanced on each shoulder and wide skirts swaying. Further off, the youngest son was herding twenty-eight sheep and several new-born lambs across a near-vertical brown scrub slope to their stone pen within the yard complex. And meanwhile Aunty (who is one short of the shilling but rather sweet) was competently and affectionately shooing hens and cocks and turkey-hens and cocks into their respective houses where they roost on wooden beams beneath thick puna-grass thatch. Another son had vanished behind the house; he soon re-appeared driving a small jet-black sow and four jet-black piglets – all giddy and vociferous as they rushed around the yard trying to avoid incarceration. Then the eldest son also re-appeared, rising out of the depths with his two potato-laden donkeys, plus three ponies who had been grazing on the potato stalks. These were tethered near Juana, with a dog tied nearby for the night to give warning should a puma threaten. The three donkeys share a stable; Carlos told us they can't safely be left out all night in these temperatures.

We descended from our hill as the last of the chilly, greenish light drained away behind chunky black summits. Mother was helping Aunty to feed the poultry while the boys were chopping enough wood to cook the supper. The greatest local supply problem is fuel: each branch – each twig – is precious. It all comes from that wooded ravine we'll be tackling in the morning; without those low trees and fast-growing scrub the two families who now live so comfortably here couldn't survive. But of course there is nothing to spare for space heating so everyone goes to bed after supper.

All evening Father did little but stroll around supervising his work-force; he has the air of a country squire rather than a peasant smallholder. While the meal was being cooked he and his sons stood on the verandah talking with us by moonlight, wrapped tightly in their ponchos. There are three other teenage children at school in Trujillo: two boys and, astonishingly, a girl. Money made by Mother on the Huamachuco poncho trade pays the fees. As in Mexico, isolated families ambitious for their young have to forego the joys of parenthood and their children's help around the farm. But it must be unusual to find such ambitions as near to the middle of nowhere as you could get. This family is virtually self-sufficient. A spacious stone building at one end of the yard holds an ancient loom on which Mother weaves all the family's ponchos and skirts and blankets, from the wool of their own sheep. It's interesting how much of the Indian life-style has been adopted by these mestizos: most noticeably in the women's hair-dos, clothing and baby-care.

At supper-time Carlos provided us with two low 'nursery' chairs and a diminutive table which he placed in the most sheltered corner of the verandah. Then he himself made three trips to serve us, carefully carrying plates across the wide, neat yard where there isn't a stray feather or dung-pellet to be seen. That was a meal to remember, eaten by the brilliant light of an icy full moon with mountains looming everywhere along the horizon, like fabulous monsters that might suddenly move in the strange colourless light. And indeed they might move, literally, here. Carlos warned us that earth-tremors are frequent and we mustn't be alarmed if the verandah shudders during the night. The ghastly 1970 earthquake, which killed tens of thousands on the other side of the Cordillera Blanca, also did some damage in this area.

We were given plates piled high with small, delicious potatoes boiled in earthy skins, accompanied by a saucer of extremely hot chilli sauce and a dish of scrambled turkey eggs with chopped chives, followed by brimming plates of noodle soup. Seeing me peeling my spuds with a bone-handled camping knife, drawn from a leather sheath on my belt, Carlos's eyes glazed over with a childish sort of covetousness. When he later asked if it was for sale I presented it to him and his face lit up: it's nice to be able to give so much pleasure so easily. Before saying good-night he inspected our flea-bags, laid out on the earthen floor with space-blankets wrapped around them. He then produced a thick 'double-bed' straw mat woven by his wife – such as the campesinos sleep on, curled up in their ponchos. What between hot food and soft floors, we'd go decadent if we stayed here long.

My linguistic feebleness has been seriously frustrating me this evening; I'd have liked to discuss Carlos's philosophy but could only gather that he despises urban (i.e., Huamachuco!) life and considers himself lucky to be able to live well on his remote ledge, with his happy, healthy, co-operative family. I wondered at one point if he could be a drop-out, but no. He was born on this ledge and hopes to die on it.

The eight feet

Going to market

Our route between San Marcos and Cajabamba

Camp in High Valley between Summits. 18 September

We discovered during the night that Carlos's five large dogs, with whom we were sharing the verandah, do *not* love each other. Several times their bickering woke us and when it developed into something more serious they twice rolled over us in a snarling mass. Eventually one of them – the largest and most pacific – took refuge from the on-going fray by curling up between Rachel's and my sleeping-bags. His hyper-active fleas were soon eagerly exploring foreign bodies and relishing gringo blood. (They continue to do so this evening as I write.) When the dogs were not being canicidal, Grandson (aged eight months) was yelling inconsolably just on the other side of the door outside which we lay. When Mamma failed to quieten him, she put on a wedding gift 'trannie' to drown his yells; so we had Peruvian jazz (better than most) till 1.30 a.m.

By 7.40 we were off, into a crisp, clear, joyous morning, after a 'treat' breakfast of very sweet *café con léche* and buns (the latter now beginning to taste elderly). Carlos accepted 100 soles for Juana's fodder, after only a token protest, but would accept nothing for human fodder. Daughter-in-law, accompanied by her three-year-old son, led us to the edge of the ravine and pointed out the path which can only be described as unreasonable. Our flea-merchant friend rushed ahead, down the precipice, and Daughter-in-law said cheerfully: "He will show you!" Then she firmly turned back, having wished us all sorts of blessings and good luck – which I reckoned we'd be needing at once. Juana now put on a classic and totally understandable display of mulishness. She stood with legs braced, ears flattened and eyes rolling expressively towards the depths of the ravine where a torrent foamed noisily between cottage-sized boulders. I had to lead her down, applying a judicious mixture of wheedling and abuse, depending on how appalling our immediate situation was when she chose to be bolshie. "Actually she's *not* being bolshie", said Rachel, who was slithering along behind. "She's just being sensible. This isn't a *mule* track." I remained ever-ready to spreadeagle myself against the cliff-face should she stumble, or suddenly decide to leap ahead. But we arrived at the bottom together and intact (at least physically: our nerves may have been a little frayed). Surprisingly, Juana made no fuss about fording the torrent by an unsteady stone causeway some eighteen inches beneath the water. We feared then that she might try to rush up the overgrown path opposite, as is her wont, but this slope curbed even her urge to get to the top as quickly as possible. Here, almost certainly, we were on an Inca road – a path which disdained effete zig-zags and retained many stretches of stone steps, to Juana's dismay. But she gallantly jumped, where necessary, and was not deterred even by dense, overhanging vegetation pulling at the load.

I was pleasantly surprised by my own condition today: no breathlessness, even on that climb. Evidently adjustment proceeds apace. It takes a month or so to complete, this being the time needed for the manufacture of the required increase in one's red blood cells. Two-thirds of the way up we had a breather on a broad ledge from which we could see human specks moving about Carlos's yard. Here a shepherd's stone hut, reminiscent of early Irish 'beehive' houses, stood in the middle of a night-pen with high stone walls. A flock of brown and white sheep, no bigger than fortnight-old Irish lambs, was being tended by a young mestizo campesino woman (our friends' neighbour) and her small son. We were again climbing steeply when she came bounding after us, shouting that we were on the wrong path. I'd seen no other, but she led us towards the crest of the mountain along a faint goat-trail. Before turning back she sent the flea-merchant home, to Rachel's grievous disappointment. He'd been ingratiating himself with us en route and obviously longing to get on the Murphy bandwagon.

The last lap was easy. We had left the cliff-face and its vegetation far below and were on gradually-sloping, brown-green puna at about 13,500 feet. Standing on the crest in warm sunshine, we faced an invigorating wind and noted the virtual disappearance of our path. The configuration of the landscape allowed an illusion of being on top of the world; there were no higher mountains nearby, only vast widths of puna bright beneath an infinite blue arc. One felt a sense of achievement none the less satisfying for being rather absurd. The clarity of the light gave a magical distinctness to every distant boulder and clump of spiky ichu grass. The quality of the silence was holy and healing. The purity of the air made one tingle with energy, as though one ran on electricity. Somehow that place and time induced an elated awareness of *freedom*. Everything that might tie one to the superficial and superfluous had been shed like a snake's skin and nothing mattered but the immediate moment.

Rachel said: "If we can't find a path, where are we going to get food? Those buns are nearly gone. And anyway they're stale. And they were never very filling."

Within an hour the only path we could find had led us astray by plunging down, then swinging north along a sheer grey mountainside littered (as was the path) with huge lumps of shattered rock. We stopped to 'binoc' the situation and could just discern, across the valley on our left, a broad track climbing south towards the 'pillared' summit. But how to reach it? We retraced our steps, looking in vain for a way down. Gloom was setting in when a couple approached us, driving two burros, and pointed out a path so faint our untrained eyes would never have detected it. This was even worse than the earlier cliff-face descent; many boulders seemed loose, as though recently deposited and poised to go rolling again with little or no encouragement. And the load, despite rigorous girth-tightening, began to shift before we were half-way down.

For a few miles our new track was bliss to walk on: a soft green carpet curving around the rim of a circular wooded valley with sheep grazing between the trees; at intervals the faint notes of a bamboo pipe rose on the wind. Then the surface became rougher and for three hours we were climbing steadily through golden sunshine, while charcoal grey clouds piled themselves around the summit above.

The base of that escarpment – a great black fortress, rising straight from the track – must have been close to 16,000 feet. In three directions we were overlooking hundreds of miles of convulsed Andean splendour – a sort of madness of mountains, possessing the earth to the farthest horizons. "Everywhere is *below* us!" exclaimed Rachel. Moments later a cruel puna wind was driving sleet into our faces and making my dust-bin-sack rain-cape look rather silly. But this squall was brief.

An hour later we turned a corner and were on the brink of a chasm that stopped the heart – a long, narrow, shadowed abyss immeasurable by the eye and almost frightening in its extremity. Beyond it, facing us, was an unbelievable vastness of sheer black rock-wall – a mountain (I suppose one must call it) miles long, straight as though Inca-built, with rags of grey cloud shifting langourously along its jagged crest.

"Where do we go from here?" asked Rachel sternly. And now the Intrepid Traveller's poor navigational powers were relentlessly exposed by her daughter, whose diary best describes the sequence of bumblings: – 'I think this is the best day we have had yet, though every day seems to get better and better. Up close to the top of one of the mountains we came to a junction. Mummy insisted on taking the upper one even though it seemed a lot less used than the other one. I was sure that there was another junction that we couldn't see and that the lower road was the right one. The stones along this road, which are mostly little pieces of marble, have got lots of different colours in them. When we had gone on for about half an hour the road started to get very dilapidated. There were lots of quite big cracks that must have been made by the 1970 earthquake and nobody had bothered to repair them. Round a few more corners we came to what I had expected, a dead end. Mummy was still persistint about this track being the right one. But we discovered it was a miners road that had been disused, propably because the mining holes had been made dangerous by the earthquake. The clouds had cleared away and the sun was blazing down. We had a sit down in the beauty and majesticness of the great mountains while we thought about what to do next. Mummy wanted to go up the mountain on a little miners track because she pretened that she thought it was a short cut but I had the strong feeling it was just because she wanted to climb up to the top. I refused firmly, and I am sure if Juana could have talked she would have thoroughly agreed with me. So we took the lower trail which was very exciting and soon we could see a little group of miners houses that had obviously been distroyed by the earth-quake. It was a very sad sight. All the roofs had fallen in and most of the walls had collapsed. A little further on we came to a disused but big mine hole with lots and lots of lovely crunchy iron ore around it. I wanted to pick it up to see how it felt but Mummy wouldn't let me. We got very confused on which road to take. The only one going in the right direction looked as though it was just a track to a disused mine and it stopped at a very old building that had been wrecked by the earthquake too. Mummy left me at the foot of the hill and went to explore a track. If I was to follow her she would whistle. I sat on the rock and let our very good Juana graze. At last Mummy whistled but half way up the hill Juana went firmly on strike. After I had pulled for a long time and Juana still wouldn't come I whistled to Mummy as we were supossed to in an emergency. Mummy came and dragged Juana up the hill to her little track which suddenly died out in the middle of nowhere. It had started to rain heavily so I put on the cape again which was almost useless with all its ripping and tearing. Juana was being obstinate so Mummy had to use all her strength to pull her along. The country was very desolate. We were walking through lots of big stones. At last we found a track which we followed.'

Alas! this track also died out, quite soon, while we were still in the middle of nowhere, with low, torn cloud hurrying past the nearby summits, adding mystery to their grandeur. The immediate scene was of peaks sharp or shoulders rounded – of slopes gradual, grassy and boulder-strewn, or precipitous, barren and grey – all swept by an icy wind that stung our faces with a mixture of hail and rain. For a moment I considered this aesthetically pleasing but practically unpromising panorama. It seemed wisest to go to the top of the next mountain, a gradual climb through high clumps of puna grass from which Juana plucked mouthfuls as I led her upwards. Rachel followed, trying to keep her disintegrating cape together and wondering (she later told me) why *she* had to have a lunatic mother who *enjoys* prancing to the tops of mountains in violent hail-storms . . Actually I didn't much enjoy that bit of today. I don't mind not knowing where a path is going, but in such terrain it's more soothing to be on *some* path, however indeterminate. At the summit our view was blocked by another mountain – no surprise. From the top of the second mountain I could discern, about 500 feet below, a path crossing a long, low ridge. While waiting for Rachel I sheltered behind a solitary boulder, massive as a two-storeyed villa. Rachel was unimpressed by this new path, which clearly went to nowhere of any consequence – certainly nowhere with a food shop.

Beyond the ridge we descended gradually through tangles of scrub scattered with wondrous flowers, mosses and lichens. By 4.30 we had reached the floor of a slightly sloping, vividly green valley where we drank quarts from a crystal-clear torrent: a treat for Rachel, who is revolted by pill-water. The rain had stopped but already the air was fiercely cold; here we are at about 15,000 feet. From above, this valley floor had looked a tempting site; in fact it is a bog.

We climbed again, steeply, seeing no trace of cultivation or habitation and no possible site. By 5.45 we were ascending into a cloud that was beckoning the dusk. Then a stretch of grass-land appeared just below the path. We scrambled down, praying that it wasn't another bog. Fifteen minutes later the tent was up and we were huddled within, devouring buns and squidgey sardines that looked extraordinarily like guano droppings. (Peruvian tinned sardines do not come intact and oiled.) Even had it been dry we couldn't have made a fire; there isn't a particle of fuel for miles around. This site is almost a bog; whenever we move the ground beneath makes rather rude sucking noises. As we munched we stared out at a limited twilit scene. The isolated sharp peaks on either side of us, and not much above, were obscured by a waterfall of rain and we could see only a small area of open brown moorland sloping up from our site.

Suddenly we heard thundering hooves and down this brown slope two lively ponies came galloping, followed by a mestizo campesino woman in long, wide, scarlet skirts, black shawl and Panama hat. Evidently this is the ponies' regular pasture and they charged Juana with squeals of rage. She retaliated by rearing up, trying to bite, kicking out. When one pony scored a most palpable hit Juana skidded, was checked by the picket, rolled on her back – and as she scrambled up was kicked again. Rachel burst into tears of alarm and sympathy and then a huge black dog – a sort of Andean mutation of the Hound of the Baskervilles – came racing towards the tent showing his fangs and barking hysterically. Luckily neither Rachel nor I has any real fear of dogs and our reactions usually deflate even the most apparently ferocious of the species. This creature was followed by his owner who peered at us suspiciously through the thickening dusk. She cut short my efforts to explain in pidgin Spanish what two female gringoes were doing lying on a bog in a cloudburst at nightfall on uninhabited puna. And then she made it abundantly plain that we and our mule – particularly our mule – were unwelcome intruders. This I perfectly understand; here there's no grass to spare for touring mules. My first reaction was to pay for our grazing, then I realised that in these circumstances it might be unwise to display money before morning. When I had conveyed that we *couldn't* move on, even if we wished to, she called her monstrous hound to heel and drove her ponies away; one is a mare in foal and Juana had given quite an impressive display of equine Karate. In the morning we'll look for her casa and give her a present.

I was half-way through this entry and it was pitch dark and still raining hard when squelching footsteps approached. Two men called – "*Amigos! Olé!*" Their tone was less amiable than their words and I unzipped the tent reluctantly and shone my torch on (I assume) our adversary's husband and grown-up son – two hard-faced, harsh-voiced mestizos who spoke so rapidly that we couldn't understand a syllable. But we got the unmistakable message that they didn't at all care for our type. The Prefect's letter was indicated. They were squatting on the ground outside the tent, their ponchos spread around them like mini-tents, and Son read the letter aloud, haltingly and frowningly. But it worked. They stood up, handed it back, growled, "Buenos Noches!" and disappeared into the blackness. Their house must be near, though invisible. I like the way we are addressed as 'Gringa' and 'Gringita' (as though these were titles) by the campesinos – and others. Rachel is now asleep and the rain continues, violently, as I write. But in here we are dry and warm, unlike poor Juana. I feel apprehensive about her tonight. Has she been injured? Will she lift her picket, despite the mini-boulder Rachel and I placed on it? Will those hard-faced campesinos come back to steal her? Perhaps illogically, I wouldn't have this worry if they were Indians.

Camp in High Valley between Ranges. 19 September

Our first really grim day, after a grim night. I slept fitfully till about midnight when the rain stopped. Then out to rug Juana and change the picket, which took time because of the difficulty of coping single-handed with the essential mini-boulder. Back in bed, after that exposure, I was too cold to sleep and lay thinking longingly of our breakfast emergency rations. (The bun and sardine supply has at last run out.) But it wasn't hard to resist that temptation as the pannier-bags were outside. Meanwhile Rachel was rolling restlessly around, talking in her sleep and sounding very unhappy – unprecedented . . .

As we struck camp dense cloud remained almost within reach overhead. Rachel said she wasn't hungry so I decided to conserve supplies and skip breakfast. More rain was likely and to keep my dry clothes dry I put on soaking jeans, bush-shirt, socks, boots – all crackling with ice as there's no room for wet clothes in a tiny tent. That was a demoralising exercise. (Rachel has spare dry clothes.) My agonisingly cold hands were half-useless when it came to loading and Juana was in a forgivably vile mood. Despite Rachel's heroic attempts to control her I couldn't get the crupper on and was afraid to persist lest a better aimed kick than usual might seriously disable me. Leaving it off seemed the lesser of two risks. Then I noticed that Rachel was looking pale, by her standards;

normally she looks like a technicoloured advertisement for the
Outdoor Life. She admitted to feeling not herself and this evening
has written in her diary:- 'When I woke up I was feeling a little
queer. As there was nowhere to tie Juana while we were saddling
and loading her I had to hold her. She seemed to be in a very bad
mood. Suddenly after holding her when she was being specially
bad I felt all horried and sick and dizzy. It was a really un-
discribeably horrid feeling. Mummy said it was soroche, or
altitude sickness and that I had got it because Mummy had been
sparing Juana yesterday going up all the hills. When I mounted
and we started off we found that Juana was quite baddly lame. We
could see no swelling on her leg, it was her near-fore, so we thought
that it must be something to do with her hoof. The minute we got
onto the big road it started to go up, not steeply but it was still
going up which made my soroche even worse. Everywhere was
cloud, you could only see about ten feet ahead then everything
became a swirling mist, which I am sure if you hadn't been
perfectly miserable and depressed, the feeling soroche gives you,
would have been nice but it only added to my misery. We went
round and round and up and up. When we stopped going up we
remained on the level untill at last we came down to a valley where
my soroche got better and Mummy was sure there would be a little
pueblo or at least a house. There was nothing.'

Children and adolescents are more vulnerable to soroche than
adults, but at least this was only AMS (Acute Mountain Sickness)
– not cerebral oedema or pulmonary oedema, which are killers.
Rachel's symptoms were nausea, weakness, severe headache and
acute depression – no disorientation, hallucinations or coughing.
But I felt stricken to see tears welling in the eyes of my gallant
companion, who so uncomplainingly endures every sort of discomfort. Just once she said pathetically, "I only want to lie down".
When I explained that this was impossible, because the sole cure is
more oxygen, she rode on in stoical silence with large, soroche-
depression tears occasionally rolling down her cheeks.

From a practical point of view, Juana's state was more worrying. Soroche is less serious, long-term, than a lame mule. At first it
seemed a helpful coincidence that the two indispositions had come
together, rest being the cure for both. But after an hour or so
Rachel became utterly wretched about Juana's limp and had to be
forcibly restrained from dismounting and trying to walk, despite
her own weakness.

As we moved off at 7.30 we looked unsuccessfully for the campesinos' casa. Dense grey cloud was swirling around the turrets of black rock just above us, yet gazing down over yesterday's route we could see clear blue sky and the sun shining brilliantly on the awesome terrain we'd covered – framed by the mountain "V" of our site valley. That was a vision I shall never forget. It inspired an odd feeling of having been through some initiation ceremony and now *belonging to* the Andes. Perhaps the altitude is responsible for such crazy thoughts . . .

Our path climbed gradually across rough moorland; then, on a steep stony slope, the sole of my left boot came loose. What Rachel has somewhat flatteringly described as 'the big road' is another miners' track which *could* take a motor vehicle, though all day we've seen no trace of humanity. On the moor we had passed a small, perfectly circular black lake. Now, looking down from the track, we could see numerous other tarns reflecting the distant blue sky and looking like a scattering of diamonds on the yellow-brown bog.

An hour later the wind tore holes in the clouds to give us many glimpses of cataclysmic heights and depths. There was a marvellously melodramatic beauty about those cloud formations and movements, as different layers drifted among or stood poised over different peaks and ridges, the wind sometimes briskly shifting them to reveal vistas of blue and golden valleys far below – or still higher and wilder ranges in the near distance, some snowy. Again I marked the difference between Himalayan and Andean trekking. In the Himalayas one usually treks *between* the mountains, worshipping the unattainable. In the Andes one treks between, around *and* over them (as often as not *over*, in this area), which is wonderfully gratifying to the mountaineer *manqué*! Also there is here an incomparable sense of space as the smooth puna sweeps from mountain to mountain for many miles, like a great expanse of golden velvet suspended between rock peaks black or red or grey – and of every conceivable (and inconceivable) distorted shape.

Our track continued level around mountain after mountain; usually we saw the next corner a quarter of a mile away as the condor flies, across a profound chasm, yet it was always three or four miles away as the Murphys walk. (Many of those chasms contained bubbling green or rust-red mineral springs.) Then a gigantic snow-dusted mountain wall appeared beyond what we assumed to be a deep (and therefore therapeutic) valley. But when the descending track revealed this valley it proved to be quite shallow. However, we must now be down to about 13,000 feet.

At 2.30 we set up camp on spongy ground – with excellent grazing for Juana – as fat black clouds gathered to the north and the wind on the puna grew colder. This is a strangely melodic wind; as it strums through tall clumps of stiff grass it makes weird and beautiful music – the signature tune of the high Andes.

Miners' Settlement in High Valley. 20 September

Both patients were much improved this morning though neither was fully recovered. Rachel slept well, probably less because of the lower altitude than because she's acclimatising quickly. After a savagely cold night the ground was all ice-crunchy when we rose at 5.50 to dress by the first light of dawn and the last light of a waning moon. At this sort of altitude I must never again leave my boots outside; they were frozen so stiff it was almost impossible to force my feet into them. We couldn't have a breakfast drink because our water was frozen solid. And the tent was so iced I couldn't get it into its bag; instead I folded it on top of one pannier, reckoning it wouldn't soon thaw. But alas! it did, to the detriment of *The King's Peace*.

Another mistake to avoid at this height is getting up too early. I was struggling with the load at 6.30, almost sobbing because of the agony of freezing hands, when the sun rose above the flat-topped mountain. Instantly there was warmth and everything began to thaw. Small wonder the Incas were sun-worshippers. Twentieth-century man may know exactly why that yellow dwarf star warms our planet but it still *feels* like magic when, within moments, pain is eased and life simplified. I was aware of a spontaneous reaction of gratitude and reverence as I glanced towards 'Inti', a red-gold globe swiftly rising (the movement perceptible) above that massive bastion of black rock.

By 6.45 we were away, chewing our breakfast (of Kendal mint-cake) on the hoof. Juana wasn't limping but Rachel insisted on walking to spare her. I rashly chose to use two reduras, which meant that when we rejoined the track near the top of a high ridge we didn't know which way to turn. Having sorted that one out (an expense of energy in a waste of reduras), we walked for three hours around a series of mountains as dramatic and exhilarating as yesterday's – and a great deal more enjoyable because Rachel, despite our rapid regaining of height, remained soroche-free.

Soon after 11, mankind impinged; we saw a solitary horseman riding along the skyline of a distant ridge. A curiously moving sight, amidst this infinity of desolation. Then we met an ancient man and moronic youth driving two heavily-laden burros; they looked at us with something approaching terror and were incapable of explaining where they were coming from. Round the next bend three coca-chewing campesinos were resting on rocks, their unloaded burros grazing nearby, and they indicated that we'd soon reach a miners' settlement. "Where do all these people *live?*" wondered Rachel. "It's only *six* people", I pointed out.

A few mountains later, we passed four deserted, tin-roofed miners' shacks standing starkly on the puna; disused workings scarred the slopes above. Soon after we began to feel we were getting into a built-up area: a row of a dozen similar shacks stood by the track-side. Most were completely derelict, a few were in a lamentable state of disrepair yet occupied by apathetic men, women and children who stared at us like zombies, seeming hardly to see us. What do these people live on? There were no cultivated patches, or animals, around their shacks. And anyway *why* are they there?

A mile further on we came to a junction. Our track continued level, visible for eight or ten miles ahead, winding around mountains as is its wont. Another track, equally big (or small) branched off to the left and wriggled steeply down into a huddle of brown mountains. We scrutinised its dusty surface, which bore many marks of human and animal traffic. The level continuation bore no such marks, so we deduced the miners' settlement must be *down* – a judgement confirmed when we overtook a group of campesinos. These were all mestizos, apart from one young man of very low stature but strikingly distinguished 'Inca' features who was leading a no less diminutive and comically shaggy pony laden with potatoes. Another young man was being led by a bloody-minded ram, magnificently horned. This animal's antics on the end of a long rope were causing general amusement; he seemed intent on taking his owner over a precipice in a sort of suicide pact. A small, intense-looking elderly woman and her son were driving three burros carrying empty sacks; two good-looking youngish men were riding ponies scarcely bigger than the burros; a small boy, heavily laden, was leading his almost-blind grandfather by the hand. Again we remarked that most campesinos – especially men – wear neat, clean clothes, however primitive the hovels from which they emerge. Our appearance on the scene provoked no questions, just the usual exclamations of admiration for Juana. Later today our host here informed us that few Indians live between Huamachuco and Chavín, an area never effectively conquered by the Incas.

The track dropped into a long, narrow, uncultivated valley between grey-brown mountains, their rock-summits jagged against a violently blue sky. Then we fancied we heard distant thunder: but it was the growl of mining machinery. From the next bend we were overlooking a few score tin-roofed hovels, surrounded by the incongruous technology of a copper-mine, all squeezed onto wide ledges where the valley ends as the mountains converge. Looking beyond the settlement, at the opposite precipitous slope, we saw an unbelievable road snaking upwards as though its destination were Heaven; our companions informed us this is a *motor-road* for transporting the ore. It goes to Trujillo, and on that journey trucks average 8 mph. As we descended towards a SHOP I allowed myself to realise how hungry I was and saliva gushed.

Despite the altitude (11,700 feet) this whole settlement reeks of no sanitation. School had just ended and all ninety-eight pupils silently followed us – at a little distance, looking apprehensive as well as curious – while we wandered along narrow lanes of humpy beaten earth, seeking THE SHOP. It was down three steep steps from the 'street' and at first we could see nothing; the children were filling the doorway and pressing close to the tiny window. The shopkeeper – a mestizo miner's wife, young and sad-faced and gentle – explained that we were her first gringo customers and was heart-breakingly apologetic about her stock. She had only sugar and noodles for sale. Rachel's keen eye then discerned a solitary slab of chocolate, but on being opened it disintegrated. Nor was there any cerveza, only rum and coke. Rachel had two cokes; I had two treble-rums and the effect was sensational on a totally empty stomach. I tentatively wondered about torch-batteries . . .? A large box was taken from a top shelf but when opened it contained only one unrecognisable mangled lump. Those batteries, like the chocolate, were the victims of age and damp. Miners on £5.28 a week don't buy such things. As we drank, Señora disappeared for a moment and returned with her daughter. Our eyes had then become used to the gloom and we were quite overwhelmed by the beauty of this toddler, a Dresden ornament sitting on the edge of the counter gravely regarding us with lustrous brown eyes. Her mother responded to our reaction by suddenly looking happy.

Back on the street, the children surged around – bolder now, having had time to establish our humanity. Then a weedy young man appeared and introduced himself as one of the three teachers (here three to ninety-eight seems impressive). He comes from Huamachuco – which to us now seems a million miles away! – and asked if we wished to buy some bread. After school he's a bread-merchant and from a plastic sack in the corner of his cramped bedsitter he sold us twenty antique buns (teeth-breakingly stale) for ten soles each – four times the Huamachuco price, which is fair enough. Then he lost interest in the gringoes and we ambled on, each gnawing a bun, in search of a site on the unpromising, near-vertical slopes around the settlement.

As we passed a saw-mill, where eucalyptus trunks were being cut to suitable lengths for pit propping, someone shouted "Olé!" We turned to see a squat, astonished-looking man wearing an orange pit-helmet and an air of authority. He beckoned, and as we approached him his broad brown face broke into the most charming smile. He is Luis de Léon, the mine manager – one of the kindest characters we've met in Peru, with a deliciously subtle sense of humour.

Our sudden change of fortune has quite overwhelmed Rachel: from lying soroche-stricken on the icy puna, not knowing where the next meal is coming from, to lying on a soft mattress between snowy sheets beneath thick blankets, with electric light (albeit very dim) to read by, and with a full belly and the certainty that *three hot meals* are assured for tomorrow. The loo and bathroom leading off our bedroom are slightly irrelevant as there is no running water here and never has been. Clearly this is a declining mine. Our wooden chalet is one of a row of twelve built on the edge of a precipice for clerical staff; only four are now occupied. And many of the little shacks that line the squalid laneways are also empty.

Juana, having stuffed herself with puna grass on the slope below our suite, was stabled at sunset with a bale of barley-straw. Then Luis and his three senior colleagues escorted us to the group of bungalows where they live with their families. In the largest a long dining-cum-recreation-room is furnished with a ping-pong table and chess and draughts sets. Magazine pictures of nude women decorate the walls and a tar-barrel serves as wood-stove. The settlement's policeman also lives here and was sitting beside me at supper, talking in rather an odd way about drug-smuggling from the selva. I had the impression he hoped I might be a customer. He and Luis are obviously not soul-mates; it must be difficult to 'manage' awkward relationships in a community as limited and isolated as this.

Never have I enjoyed a meal so much: potato, noodle and crubeen soup, with a crubeen each to be sucked; enormous helpings of rice and fried potatoes with moderately hot chilli sauce and *very* tough hunks of beef; blissful lemon tea. The surrounding mountains support only a few burros, ponies and sheep – no cows or goats, so dairy products are never on the menu. Fruit and vegetables are also rare, apart from potatoes and eating-apples.

The same. 21 September

A restfully uneventful day, apart from three big meals which seemed to us like Major Events. For breakfast: Nescafé, two huge slices of thick fried bread and a soup-plate of that exotic concoction we had at Cajabamba, made of fine maize porridge, chocolate and a gingery root. For lunch: same as supper last evening. For supper: beef soup, rice mixed with chips, fried tomatoes, onions and chopped stringy goat-meat, an apple and lemon tea. Our 'humps' have been sufficiently restored to keep us going for the next week.

Mining is one of the three main pillars of the Peruvian economy and has been an important feature of Andean life since long before the Spaniards came. This little community, under Luis's benevolent dictatorship, is probably luckier than most. It certainly isn't ravaged by disease, violence, drunkenness and homosexuality, as so many of the larger settlements have been in the past – and still are, in some areas. Keeping families together helps a lot. At present a pall of depression and poverty hangs over this place but its difficulties are part of the national crisis, rather than occupational hazards.

Camp in Mining Area near Pampas (we think!). 22 September

Several plates of steaming maize porridge counteracted this morning's grey raw cold and we left our friends at 8.15 feeling pampered and grateful. The pass above the mine is over 14,200 feet so Rachel walked. Occasionally we paused to look back at the settlement; when last we saw it, still directly below us, Rachel said, "It looks like a Lego town!"

This has been our Day of Lakes and we saw the first pair on that climb, each about a mile across and close together – yet one orange-red and the other inky black. On the pass the sun was brilliant and ahead stretched a sublime prospect like the aftermath of some cosmic quarrel. Soon we were looking down on another pair of lakes – shimmering and blue-black (one round, one oblong), set in an amphitheatre of mountains with smooth brown crests. On those mountains I was somewhat unnerved by Juana's obstinately keeping to the outer edge of the track, though the drops could almost be measured in light years. Here we saw several eagles, and many hawks and small song-birds.

Then came an extraordinary visual phenomenon. From an immense height we were looking straight down a long, narrow, grey gorge. And at its end, four or five miles away, we could see through our binoculars a section of another world – a golden sunlit landscape, dotted with eucalyptus groves and fertile fields. In the middle of the picture was a little red-roofed pueblo on a gentle slope: the first town or village we've seen since leaving Huamachuco. "Are we going there?" asked Rachel eagerly, thinking of her next hot meal. "Who knows?" I replied. "We certainly don't *seem* to be" – and I pointed to the next section of our track, curving decisively away from the pueblo before climbing high to the snow-line. Yet the map suggests that this little town *is* Pampas. If so we should reach it tomorrow, having done a horseshoe circuit.

Up and up and up, stopping at 1.45 for a picnic of the teacher's stale buns, flavoured with kerosene. We must then have been at about 15,000 feet yet the sun felt hot as we sat on a mossy rock, sheltered from the breeze. On three sides mountains enclosed us and above their gaunt peaks round white clouds sailed high. The bare golden-brown puna was strewn with massive silver boulders and behind us Juana was picnicking off tough grass and sweet herbs. Her happy munching, and the grinding of our own teeth as we wrestled with those buns, were the only sounds. And one fancied that here there never had been any other sound – and never would be . . .

Again up and up and up, round and round and round; at one point we could see three matching blue lakes below us, one far above another, on 'steps' of the mountains. Then came a vast area of shattered rock, where thousands of tons of dislocated mountain lay above and below the track. There was something atavistically frightening about this evidence of Nature's instability. Looking up at the fractured peaks, now only hundreds of feet above us, one could see from where, *exactly*, a particular cathedral-sized chunk had fallen. As we approached the pass a whole line of new rock-peaks came into view, one retaining a dazzling sweep of snow just below the summit. And on reaching the pass we saw just below us a long, wide, vividly green valley, its far side curving up to merge into a wall of grey-black mountains riven by brilliant, pure, flawless glaciers. On the valley floor glowed a round jade lake, surrounded by several jade lakelets – like chips off the original jewel. Not far away two other lakes – black and glossy – stretched to the base of the mountain wall. And every colour had that extraordinary throbbing vitality peculiar to these heights. "This is a special place", said Rachel.

We longed to camp there, but couldn't for lack of fodder. Slowly we walked along the rim of that valley, gazing down at a few thatched stone cabins and sheep pastures scattered between the lakes. Rachel said: "It's sad to think they probably don't appreciate where they live, their lives are so hard." Here the mountain-wall beyond the valley was a mighty triangle of naked rock, too smooth to have retained any snow. Ahead we could see our path disappearing into a jumble of boulders the size of skyscrapers. We paused to look back, reverently, at that wondrous valley. Then we entered a narrow, descending corridor, walled by rugged brown rocks, which led to another world.

An hour later we were in a longer, deeper valley, full of the soft gold light of late afternoon – a valley that ran between smooth-crested mountains and seemed gentle and warm after the beautiful cold harshness of the pass. Soon we could again hear mining rumbles and a lake like an inland sea slowly became visible on our left. Across the water rose a conical snow-draped summit. Now we were overlooking hundreds of wretched tin hovels (tin walls as well as roofs). This was a far bigger and newer mine than Luis's, with much more complex and intrusive equipment which hideously disfigured the landscape. The few inhabitants we glimpsed looked sullen, hungry and dispirited. Having established that neither food nor fodder was available we hurried through this dismal place.

Then Juana suddenly went lame again and Rachel dismounted as the track continued to drop. In its upper reaches this valley is an arid wilderness; lower down, the river that flows from the lake, and which we had to ford three times, is used to irrigate scattered fields. At 6.15, as I was worrying about darkness falling before we found a site, this level strip of stony ground appeared on the right of the road at the base of a towering cliff. There is no grass here but luckily Juana relishes the available bushes, to one of which she is tethered because the ground is too hard for the picket. (The tent looks so insecure it may not stay up all night.) Those bushes have also made a fire possible and the teacher's buns are much more manageable eaten with soup and coffee. After supper Rachel played her fideog and we sat and talked by firelight and starlight, watching ghost-like clouds drifting palely around the nearby summits.

Stoveless trekking in the Andes spares the mule but tantalises the human. Fires are never possible when most needed – at 15,000 feet or so, after marching for hours through an icy downpour. Yet the pleasures of a camp-fire, as compared to the dreary utilitarianism of a stove, are well worth waiting for. Apart from the creature comfort of hot food, the beauty of an evening fire – orange-red flickering flames, pinky-red trembling embers, blue smoke plumes wavering into a black, gold-spattered sky – is the perfect ending to a day such as this has been.

Our descent from the jade valley was so continuous and steep we must now be down to about 11,000 feet. A jeep has just passed, jolting slowly towards the mine; here we are back on the fringe of the motorised world. But the map indicates that between Pampas and Chavín we'll be able to evade motorable tracks almost everywhere.

4

Lacabamba, Pomabamba,
Indians and Mestizos

Juana's limp seemed better this morning but Rachel walked all day, just in case. Near our camp we came on another squalid miners' settlement, even more depressing than yesterday's, and not far from that was a long-established mining-town which stank of piss'n'shit. Everything looked decrepit and sleazy, including several newish eight-storey blocks of jerry-built flats. It was then 7.45 a.m. but few people were about and there was no food, drink or fodder to be had. It took us over an hour to get through this town, which is built in tiers on an unreasonably steep mountain-side overlooking a gorge so deep we couldn't see its floor. The road fell from one tight hair-pin bend to another in as remarkable a display of engineering genius as ever I've seen. When we paused to gaze up at it from the base of the mountain it literally *did* look like a corkscrew. A truck-bus arrived just then from Pampas but made no attempt to ascend the 'main street'.

Our road wound level around the bulging mountain that here overhangs the gorge and we had to cross the remains of several gigantic recent landslides, before coming to the *most* recent – which had happened since the arrival of the Pampas truck-bus. Earth and pebbles were still streaming into the bottomless pit on our right and Juana was acutely unhappy about venturing onto this horrid slope of loose rubble. While she and Rachel rested I con-trived to stamp out a level pathlet for her. (*"Don't* lean against the cliff!" I yelled neurotically at Rachel.) Juana had crossed when four miners arrived with shovels to clear a way for the truck-bus's return journey.

Soon after, we noticed (set plumb centre on a monolithic grassy mountain) what looked like the world's most insanely inaccess-ible dwelling. From the shadowed depths of the gorge a thread of a path leads up to a minute stone hovel, seeming no bigger than a brick and semi-encircled by eucalyptus trees seeming no bigger than wall-flowers. Who lives there? An eccentric? An outcast? A hermit? Or merely a shepherd? The climb from river level to the front door must be no less than 3,000 feet.

At the end of that gorge we were looking up another, which was oddly familiar: we'd been looking *down* it when we first saw Pampas twenty-four hours earlier. The embowered town now seemed close but we didn't arrive till 10.15 though we took every available redura up and down various mountains, stopping frequently to remove layers of clothing. By the time we reached Pampas we were dressed as though for mid-summer in Europe – yet sweating, and being savaged by the gnat equivalent of the hordes of Genghis Khan.

Pampas relaxes on the lower slopes of a cultivated mountain – an attractive little town of narrow cobbled streets winding between tiled, two-storeyed adobe houses with carved wooden balconies and overhanging eaves. No two houses are exactly alike yet each blends with the rest: soothing after the mass- (mess-) production of modern Europe. On our way to the Plaza, Rachel and Juana simultaneously noticed a bundle of Alf (six kilos) displayed outside a shop; to Juana's excited delight we bought the lot. No external sign indicated that this house was a shop and empty shelves lined the dusky interior. In the large Plaza we sat on stone steps in the shade of a wooden arcade and happily watched Juana eating; it upsets us both when we know she's being underfed. A friendly crowd gathered: schoolboys and a dozen young men – all mestizos. Most Peruvian children are outgoing and well-mannered – or rather, most mestizo Peruvian children. Nobody could describe the Indians, of any age, as 'outgoing'. The majority of these Pampas children looked alarmingly undernourished yet all were clean and neatly dressed. One young man pointed to a shop across the Plaza where I *might* be able to buy food and drinks. It stocked only a few kilos of rice, sugar and noodles, four bottles of Fanta and one of beer. Crates of empty bottles were piled ceiling-high. I bought half a kilo of sugar and noodles, two Fantas and the beer. As we drank, many more amiably curious adults joined the throng and asked the usual questions. They seemed vague about the locations of Cajamarca and Cuzco; Trujillo was the city they were aware of as a 'real' place.

Yesterday afternoon my left boot again fell to bits and I decided I must be reshod. A charming ten-year-old boy led me up a steep street to the town cobbler, an elderly, taciturn man who makes boots for the campesinos; but he had none to fit me. He scowled contemptuously at my Mexican non-masterpieces, then set about doing complicated things with different sized nails. I sat unsteadily on a feeble home-made chair that had lost most of its cane bottom. The workshop was dark and Pampas has no electricity. When crowds blocked the doorway the cobbler fiercely whispered something that instantly dispelled them. He seemed to know what he was doing with my boot, but refused to accept payment.

Back in the Plaza, I asked if we could buy bread, or milk, or eggs. But no . . . A group of youths then held a muttered consultation before one of them led us to a minute eating-house. He looked at us anxiously when he had pointed it out and mumbled something about its being 'very poor'; obviously he and his companions had been worried lest we might spurn the local restaurant. But our reaction must at once have reassured him. As there was nowhere to tether Juana our young friend held her while we wolfed brimming plates of mutton soup thick with noodles and potatoes, followed by heaped plates of rice, chips, raw onions and smoked fish. Rachel was fascinated by a vividly-coloured wall-chart of the human body that hung above our table and the mestizo-campesino proprietress explained that her son worked as servant for a doctor in Trujillo. As we were leaving, she warned us to beware of the local miners – "bad men who drink too much".

From Pampas we climbed steadily between low cacti hedges enclosing pathetic fields of failed crops. This too is a drought-stricken area: which seems extraordinary to us, remembering all the rain we've endured on the nearby puna. Two-thirds of the way up this mountain our path vanished without trace on a grassy ledge. So down we went, to the nearest junction, and up again more steeply than ever for forty minutes. Juana insisted on several rest stops – the gradient was brutal – and this suited me as I was beginning to feel the effects of an unwontedly large meal at the fatal hour of noon. If moderation can't be achieved, then it's easier to walk through the Andes with too little rather than too much in one's belly.

The descent from that summit, on a path of loose stones, was also trying for Juana. (Our own thigh-muscle brakes are no longer bothered by such tests.) When we had dropped to the cool, shadowed level of an unusually extensive eucalyptus wood we were overtaken by an elderly man and a beautiful young mestizo

woman, both riding tiny, thin ponies wearing gay cloth pannier-
bags. They stopped to offer 30,000 soles for Juana, which provoked
Rachel to sudden gloom. "One day", she said, "we'll *have to* sell
her!" "*Don't!*" I begged. "That's too far ahead to be grieved about
now."

A small pueblo was packed onto a ledge near the foot of the
mountain. In the sunny cobbled Plaza the little whitewashed
church was closed and there were only two visible inhabitants – an
ancient, shrivelled grandad sitting on the ground by the church
door with a pensive-looking toddler on his lap. He told us that a
German priest visits occasionally and pointed across the deep
wide gorge of the Rio Conchucos to another mountain where,
half-way up, a few red roofs amidst eucalyptus green mark a
pueblo. There the German lives, alone; he never sees another
gringo and our informant thought we should visit him. The pueblo
was scarcely two miles from where we stood, as the condor flies.
But the trek to it would take at least two days, beginning with a
return to Pampas. We decided the German *hated* meeting other
gringoes.

The rest of that descent took us to the head of a valley where it
seemed one could touch the mountains on either side by standing
with outstretched arms. We forded a trickle of a stream, then
climbed onto a slope where our path levelled out amidst astonishingly fertile fields. It rounded two more mountains and passed
through a still smaller pueblo (a 'shamlet' in Murphy jargon)
where the substantial adobe houses looked well-kept and the
natives were friendly. But they had no food for sale, though in this
area intensive irrigation has conquered the drought. We were now
at a junction of three valleys, where the Rio Conchucos bends
sharply to flow from our wide valley into a gorge so awesome that
we had to throw our heads back to see its edges, away up there
against the sky. And behind us was the third valley, from which we
had just emerged.

A mile before reaching it, we could see a long tree-trunk foot-
bridge over the Rio Conchucos; so we began to soothe and flatter
Juana in advance. Actually she took this challenge rather well,
after an initial display of shock and horror. The tree-trunks were
close together, and only about ten feet above the racing café-au-
lait river, and the afternoon was windless. Had this contraption
been swaying, we might all have found it more difficult to
negotiate. Rachel wanted to camp on the far side, in a eucalyptus

grove by the water; I reminded her that one never camps at
river-level – even during a drought. The drought has to end one
day (or night). Also, the flat riverside fields were dotted with
stagnant pools. So for the next hour we climbed steeply and at
sunset reached this ideal site, an artificially levelled threshing-
floor – the only level space for miles around – with ample (though
not very sustaining) fodder for Juana and lots of firewood. By 6.30
lunch seemed many hours and climbs away and our noodles,
simmered with a Knorr chicken cube, tasted like some fabulous
Cordon Bleu invention. Unfamiliar trees cover the slopes directly
above us and fill a nearby ravine, where a hidden stream is noisy;
yet we have a spectacular view of the surrounding heights and
depths.

We must be near Lacabamba, though since crossing the river
we've met nobody. Now that we're back in inhabited, cultivated
regions, I'd expected to meet more fellow-travellers. Yet what
would be the locals' motives for travelling, when there are so few
goods to be sold or exchanged? One's judgement of distance alters
here; I've given up thinking of miles or kilometres – instead I think
of so many summits and valleys between Point A and Point B.

Occasionally this evening I have to stop writing to gaze at the
massive dark majesty of the mountain just beyond the ravine – and
then to look up at the sky, where fiery golden sparks burn in a
coal-black infinity. One pities the travellers who stay always in
hotels.

From what little we've seen of the mestizos of this area, they are
exceptionally alert and friendly. What are their origins? Have they
some of the blood of those tribesmen of the Conchucos area who,
during the Second Inca Rebellion of 1537, rallied to the Inca
general Illa Tupac? From these mountains that tonight are all
around us, the Conchucos poured down by the thousand towards
the new Spanish city of Trujillo, slaughtering all the Spaniards, or
Spanish-supporting natives, they could capture en route. They
then offered their victims to their tribal deity, Catequil. One gets
the impression those tribes were more spirited and vigorous than
the average Inca subjects. Pedro de Cieza de León reported:
'Among the Conchucos the natives are of medium stature. They
and their women go clothed, with their ribands or insignia about
their heads. It is said that the Indians of this province were
warlike, and the Incas had trouble subduing them, although some
of the Incas always tried to win the people over with kindly acts

and friendly words. These Indians have killed Spaniards on several occasions, so many that the Marquis Don Francisco Pizarro sent Captain Francisco de Chavez out with a force of Spaniards, and the war they made on them was fierce and horrible, for certain of the Spaniards tell that a great number of the Indians were burned and impaled . . . The houses of these Indians are of stone with a thatch roof. Even though evil has had great power over them, I have never heard that they were guilty of the abominable sin of sodomy. To be sure, as happens everywhere there are bad among them; but if the practices of these are known, they are despised and looked down on as effeminate, and they treat them almost like women . . .'

The Incas were in agreement with Mr Ian Paisley on 'the abominable vice'. When they found that sodomy – both private and ceremonial – was popular and accepted in certain areas, they set about liquidating whole families in their unsuccessful efforts to clean the place up.

Camp at Head of High Valley. 24 September

A late (8.45) start. At 5.30 I moved Juana to a patch of green grass, lest there might be no Alf at Lacabamba; this patch was so perilously placed that it would have been risky to leave her there unsupervised. It rained lightly last night and was still cloudy and humid when we began to climb through thick groves of trees with delicately scented rose-pink or violet blossoms. Our path sometimes became a rock-stairs and we were all sweat-drenched when we arrived in the deserted Plaza, which faithfully follows the Spanish pattern universally imposed on these Andean settlements. Soon we were noticed by a stocky, cheerful-looking young woman with a kindly-bossy manner who broke the news that here we could find no Alf, oats, noodles, tinned milk, eggs, tinned coffee, sugar, bread, rice or beer. "Chicha?" I asked wistfully, more out of habit than with great expectations. But *yes*! – there was chicha! It surprised our friend that a gringo would drink it . . . She knocked on her neighbour's door and after a few moments it was opened by an old, old woman in a black shawl (recalling the Irish 'mountainy' women of my childhood) who wonderingly but graciously invited us into her twilit and bare-shelved shop. She drew forward a low stool for Rachel and a rickety chair for me, then provided two litres of watery chicha fascinatingly diversified by scraps of floating vegetation. ("Better than insects", commented Rachel, peering into my glass.)

During the next ten minutes, a heartwarmingly concerned crowd – of all ages – gathered outside the shop. The two local teachers entered; both spoke a little English. There are over 100 pupils in the primary school but it's hard to teach them anything as no equipment is provided by the present government and parents have no cash to spare and are too far from anywhere to exchange potatoes and eggs for notebooks and pens. Soon others took courage and entered the shop; most of them looked pinched and underfed, everyone deplored the present State of the Nation, yet no one seemed *personally* depressed. But it's misleading to use that phrase 'State of the Nation'. To what extent can the Peruvians, even now, be considered a 'nation' in our European sense of the term? One gets no feeling of a link between these people and the Lima government, not even the link of resentment or hate or anger. Nor do they seem to relate their regional problems to those of the miners, or of the sugar and cotton workers on coastal haciendas – or of the migrants in urban barriadas, most of whom come from the sierra. Many of them don't know, or care, who now leads their country. Political fatalism is endemic; whether ruled from Madrid or Lima, the Andean peoples have passively endured centuries of misgovernment. At present things are worse than usual, yet the positive indignation that would be evident in a democracy is absent. No channel exists for constructive anti-government thinking and feeling. Even under ostensibly democratic administrations, no one believes that elections are fairly conducted or that 'elected representatives' are ever likely to put their country's interest before personal gain. The exception we've heard of is Fernando Beláunde Terry; this morning several people referred to him as though he were a saint rather than a politician.

A sack of barley-straw was brought for Juana by a beaming, wrinkled little man in a patched poncho who steadfastly refused cash but was at last persuaded to accept a packet of cigarettes. Our shawled hostess then asked if we were hungry. I thought it tactful emphatically to say "No!" though my supper of noodles felt very remote. But Rachel equally emphatically said "Yes!" and was given two cups of milk and a brown bun. The food shortage is becoming critical; I had no idea it would be so hard to find the basics. Now I regret not having bought a kilo of noodles at Pampas, but seeing only a few kilos in that shop I didn't want to be greedy. Had we pleaded for supplies in Lacabamba, I'm sure *someone* would have rallied with *something*. But then they would have had to go even hungrier, for our sakes, which isn't good enough. Had they had anything to spare, they would certainly have offered it; they were deeply worried about our welfare when we left them.

The tough climb out of Lacabamba soon had us sweating hard. By noon the little pueblo – its red roofs widely scattered among green groves – looked like a wooden Toytown I had as a child. Our path was then rounding a colossal rocky bulge (a sort of mountain hernia) and it seemed one could drop stones onto the diminutive roofs. The teachers had told us how to find the way at this point but somehow I missed the junction they had so carefully described. For half an hour we rambled to and fro across a plateau divided by dry stone walls into small, parched fields. Here the dirge-like rustle of dead maize sounded loud and we grieved over the unrewarded labour that had gone into the cultivation of these crops. Eventually we plunged into a narrow green valley and began a gruelling, climb through thorny scrub onto another plateau, higher and more rugged. From here a shadowy path, overhanging a sensational abyss, led to a distant craggy summit. I rejoiced, but not so Rachel. "That's only for *goats!*" she snorted. We climbed through vicious thickets of spiked cacti and poisonous thorn-bushes which one didn't dare dodge because that crumbling path left no room for manoeuvring. Then the gradient became even more severe, amidst a wide, forbidding wilderness of large dark boulders. Finally the going got so rough that I went on alone to investigate, just as the puna wind drove an opaque sheet of sleet in our direction. Tiresomely, Rachel was right again. It would have been impossible to get Juana over the top; I found the climb difficult enough and if she missed her footing the drop would be onto a disarray of boulders a thousand feet below.

From this summit I could see another faint path which we tried next. On the way down to the valley floor we sheltered from a hailstorm in an enchanting grotto just high enough for Juana to enter and with a natural stone 'bench' along one wall. This conveniently placed cave is evidently much used by local shepherds.

After an hour's climb, our new path entered a narrow rock corridor where a saucepan stuck, ripping off one of the pannier-bag straps. (An elementary misjudgement on my part; having had only two litres of weak chicha since supper-time yesterday I was beginning to wilt.) Here we were looking up another long, broad valley, magnificently blocked at its head by a sheer grey-black mountain wall which seemed to take up half the sky. "I hope you don't imagine our path goes over *that*!" said Rachel. I didn't; but possibly the path might find a way out to one side of the wall. However, when it became a maze of pathlets on the boggy valley floor I realised that we weren't going to get to Conchucos, or anywhere else that might have food, before nightfall. Even for Juana the prospects were poor; this region has recently been drastically over-grazed. Making for the head of the valley, we crossed and recrossed a network of streams. I went ahead, testing the ground for dangerous bogginess. High on the mountain to our left goats and sheep were being tended by children whose shouts rang uncannily clear in the thin air though we could see them only through binoculars. With every moment we felt colder, wetter, hungrier, tireder – and higher. Then suddenly we were on a wide, clear track leading to tolerably good grazing just below a mass of loose black broken rock at the base of the mountain wall. Here I again left Rachel and Juana and climbed hopefully towards the southern summit; but the path petered out on a wide ledge where new grass was growing through burnt cacti. At one time it went over the top; now an almost Inca-perfect wall has been built to block it, probably because earthquake damage left it too dangerous for use.

I looked down at Rachel, sitting on a rock inscribing her latest poem in her notebook with Juana grazing beside her. It's a relief that my fellow-traveller has become a poet; literary endeavour occupies her en route in a silence blessed for me. During our trips in Coorg, Baltistan and Northern Ireland, when she was aged five, six and seven respectively, she was far more dependent on Mamma for entertainment. Now she and Juana looked mere dots; the climb I'd done since leaving them would take one half-way up any Irish mountain, yet here it's an afterthought at the end of the day. The scale of this landscape makes it much harder to find one's way; e.g., what seems from a distance a 'slight depression' turns out to be a deep valley. I shouted to Rachel "No go!" and asked her to begin unloading: it was 6.15 and would soon be dark. Before descending I gazed down the valley towards a blue-green ocean of sky – which curiously seemed to be far below me – where a few thin streamers of carmine cloud floated just above a long ridge of purple cloud and beneath a flotilla of pale gold cloudlets. Already our valley was dusky, which made this sunset seem like something on a cinema screen.

A Scotch mist enveloped us as we rushed the tent up and we were just tucked away when the next downpour started. Rachel had the last tin of sardines for supper and while writing this I've eaten a whole slab of mint-cake, which in an odd way restores one's energy without satisfying one's hunger. The rain has stopped now, the stars are dazzling and it's *very* cold – I've just been out to change the picket. We must be at about 13,000 feet.

Conchucos. 25 September

At 6.15 there was much ice on tent and gear. Poor Rachel looked rather wan: she was obviously hungry and cold, yet uttered not a word of complaint. Her account of the Road to Conchucos is more graphic than mine:

'Juana doesn't seem to be a bit lame today even though we had such a rough day yesterday. We went steeply down a slippery slope and at the bottom it took ages to make Juana go across the little stream. There a hummingbird suddenly whizzed out of nowhere and hovered for a second in front of Mummy's nose. He was bright emerald green and had a long beak, like all humming-birds. The hummingbird must suck the nectar from the beautiful bright sometimes blue and sometimes pink cacti flowers. I would not have thought hummingbirds could live so high up for we must be about thirteen thousand now.*

'After we had crossed the stream again we started hunting around for a track going up. We followed lots of goat tracks untill we came to quite a main looking one that we hoped went some-where. We came to a rock with wet slippery moss on it and Juana slipped and went down on her knees. I was quite scared while she was floundering up because there was a drop that could be dangerous on one side, but we managed perfectly. We came to a

* 'It seems remarkable that more species of hummingbird live on the chilly slopes of the Andes than any other bird family, but these little birds show a remarkable adaptation to their habitat. The Andean hummingbirds, such as the hillstar and the giant hummingbird, feed on insects as well as nectar. The body temperature of the tiny hillstar may drop during the night to 15 C, from its normal daytime 39.5 C.' From *Backpacking and Trekking in Peru and Bolivia*, by Hilary and George Bradt.

little flat spot that was quite grasy and there was a really lovely view. I would say that you could see for about a hundred miles as the crow flies. Way over on the horizon you could see the pointy cone shaped mountain that we passed quite closely on the way from Cajabamba to Huamachuco. I walked for a while because it was getting chilly. We started to go down steeply and there were lots of little jumps for poor Juana. We can see a big pueblo a bit bigger than Pampas that must be Conchucos. It is about four miles away. There is a lovely smell of thyme in the air. There are lots of thyme bushes dotted all over the hillside. We went down a steep nasty piece of earthquake damage. At the bottom I mounted but had to dismount soon again for another rift. There were the lovely ball shaped flowering cactuses and another nasty type rather like spear cactuses except that they weren't so long and a lot slimmer, of a redish greenish colour. I kept getting stung as I bashed about, it was most unpleasant I can assure you. I think Juana hated it too.

'At last we got out of the beastly mess onto a quite respectable looking path going up parralel to the village, almost. It went up steeply for awhile and then all of a sudden Mummy began to have suspicions about wether the path went to the village at all, suspicions I had had all along. So Mummy left Juana and I resting and went on up to investigate. In a few minutes I heard her shouting, "Wrong track, it just goes out onto the puna" all what I had expected. When Mummy got back we sat down and wondered what to do. After looking at the opposite hill for a while Mummy said that we should go back untill we came to a little track that branched off our track and went down steeply. So that is what we did. I think Juana was enjoying today apart from the steep rough part. I feel a hundred persent now. It wasn't very long before we started to go down. Then we came to a place where the earthquake had torn up the track. From a little way off it looked impossible for Juana but close up it was very simple as long as I dismounted. Juana went over it like a lamb. Conchucos looks temptingly close now but we still have the fear of not being able to get to it today because of a block that we couldn't get Juana over. Soon we came to a landslide that Mummy thought we couldn't get her over but we dicided to try and Mummy got her over. Then we came to a very big rocky landslide that Juana just wouldn't go over. While Mummy was trying to get her to turn round her stick slipped out of my hand and went sailing down a landslide slope.

Mummy needed the stick to go down the steep path so I had to go sailing down after it in a mini landslide which was most painful indeed. When I had got the stick I had to get back up the slidy slope. It was very hard work and Mummy was in an exceedingly impatient mood but at last I reashed the top.

'Meanwhile Mummy had seen another little track going down to the road which she thought was better. I led Juana and Mummy went behind with the stick. Juana didn't need much persuasion but if she had known what was coming I am sure she would have. There is a horrid little cactus on theese slopes. They are always oval with long stabby things. Thease diabolical things have got the disgusting habit of breaking off the body so the minute you brush against a prickle the whole section comes off and sticks onto you very firmly. They really hurt when you pull them out and often leave the tip of the prickle behind. Juana got two on her hocks, one after the other. I got one on my leg and Mummy got one on her hand. The path got worse and worse until at last it disappeared and we were left sliding down a landslide slope in the midst of lots of little stones rushing along. I got Juana over to Mummy and I went behind her with the stick. With great difficulty we got off the slope and managed to stay on two feet just to the end. There we had a little rest before I mounted and we continued on to the village. On the way we saw a bloated donkey lieing dead on the road. The vultures hadn't got her. How glad I was at last to get somewhere where I was sure there would be food. Remember our friends in Lacabamba had said there were thieves here but I wouldn't have cared how many thieves their were if there was food. Whatever the people said, I think it is a very pretty place, at least in looks. Just as we were going into the village we saw a group of men sitting by a stream. They told us a great many pleasing things. There was a hotel, Alf, and drink and food. Mummy looked delighted. One of them asked if Juana was my pony. Imagine thinking a mule was a pony. We went and had on my part three Inca-colas and twelve nice savoury biscuits which to me was blizz. Mummy had two big beers and eight biscuits. We got eight small tins of fish for the puna. There was no bread and no coffee. One of the men who had told us the good things came into the shop and asked all the usual questions. Then we went to look for the hotel and a coral for Juana who is limping again. We found the hotel which was really a posada. The nice woman had room for us and for Juana around a cornor. It was a very nice room with three beds in it. The walls were nicely white-washed and there were lovely pictures of different parts of Peru pasted on. We unloaded Juana and I gave her a quick grooming, then the woman showed us where she was to go. It was a secluded little kind of yard. There was a nice white pony tied to a tree eating straw. We tied Juana to a stump and she was given a fair amount of straw. The nice woman would accept no payment for it. She said we would be able to get Alf later on. When we had seen Juana organised we went out to look for some food for ourselves. We found an eating house but they didn't serve main meals untill seven. We had coffee and delicious buns. It was very cheap. Then we went out for a dander and a look at the pueblo.'

Conchucos stands at a junction of three valleys, where a tributary of the Rio Conchucos joins the main stream. All these little pueblos seem very quiet; here the loudest noise is of water racing and gurgling through three-foot-wide channels that flow by the side of most streets – channels in which people wash dishes, clothes, meat, fleeces, vegetables and children, and from which they collect water in buckets for human consumption.

The same. 26 September

A relaxing day, during which the emphasis was on eating. After a blissful breakfast of innumerable fried eggs, buns and mugs of coffee with tinned milk, we set off up the tributary valley with towels and sponge-bags and found an ideal pool of deep, clear, icy water, semi-private below huge boulders. But alas! this valley harbours the most vicious Peruvian insect we've yet met: a minute black fly whose bite causes enormous Instant Blisters. And today's bites were past reckoning ... My left hand and wrist were attacked with particular ferocity and this evening are grossly swollen and extraordinarily painful.

Conchucos has an unusually large and bare Plaza, a vast, oblong expanse of cobbles with no shrubs, seats or statues. The south side is dominated by a biggish church startlingly painted red, green, gold, purple – not unlike a Tibetan temple. Quite a contrast to the white-washed or pale brown adobe façades of the dwellings surrounding the Plaza. No priest regularly visits Conchucos but four Peruvian nuns open the church at 5 every afternoon and from within play jazz records, hideously relayed on amplifiers all over the town. This is supposed to attract the young to Christianity. At 6 p.m. a nun leads the rosary over the amplifier but neither the young nor the old pays the slightest attention. Inside, the church smells mouldy and the otherwise bare walls are decorated with valiant attempts to fan the embers of local faith – hand-drawn charts and diagrams, ingeniously relating biblical texts to the daily life and work of the campesinos. A dark-skinned crucified Christ hangs over the unused – but pathetically flower-bedecked – altar. Another, smaller crucified Christ, in a locked glass case, wears a jewel-encrusted kilt stiff with gold thread. The nuns twittered with excitement on hearing that we come from Ireland – to them a Garden of Eden, pullulating with priests, where everybody goes to Mass every Sunday and empty churches are unknown.

On the eastern side of the Plaza an imposing wrought-iron gate, under a fine stone archway, opens into a spacious yard where the eating-house is a solid lean-to. The restaurant-cum-kitchen is cramped but congenial with a wood-burning mud-stove warm and bright at one end. People sit around three little tables on wooden benches that wobble because of the bumpy mud floor. Whole pigs' livers, and bloody hunks of mutton, hang just above the tables – and hungry campesinos, who have walked who knows how far, carefully choose exactly what they can afford. The washing-up is done in the channel outside the gate.

As eating has been our chief occupation here, we've got to know the restaurant owners pretty well. Grandad is courteous and quiet-voiced, with long sensitive hands and an open mobile face – sometimes sad and thoughtful, sometimes merry as he tries to cheer up those customers who are finding the burdens of life too heavy. His own burdens are heavy enough because his eldest son migrated to Lima seven years ago and bigamously remarried there, leaving Grandad to cope with daughter-in-law and four small children. The eldest, Pilar, is now fourteen – a cheerful lass with a broad Indian face, though Grandad looks very Spanish. Rachel envies Pilar because she owns an ebullient half-grown lamb, called Dado, whom she sometimes carries in a striped blanket on her back, as though he were a baby, and sometimes releases onto the restaurant floor where he skips around baaing demandingly and pucking customers' knees in quest of a finger dipped in coffee which he sucks ecstatically. Pilar's mother works at the stove from dawn to dusk, chopping wood when she isn't cooking, and she's such a loving person that she severely upbraided me for dragging a starving nine-year-old across the icy puna day after day. "But I enjoy it!" protested Rachel loyally. (And truthfully – I think!)

Our posada hostess, Rosa, is a lively young woman who yesterday afternoon, when she heard on the grapevine that we had been too late for lunch at the eating-house, invited us into her own living-room and gave us each a cup of coffee, a boiled egg and a little plate of plain biscuits. Her ten-year-old son is also envied by Rachel; he has a pet cock – fully grown and magnificently plumaged – which he carries around in his arms, caressing it gently and murmuring sweet nothings in its attentive ear.

This 'hotel' was opened two years ago when a weekly truck-bus-service from Lima began and it seemed possible that *tourists* might find Conchucos. So far they haven't. The large, two-storeyed, brightly blue-washed structure was built by Rosa's menfolk, with the assistance of eighteen relatives and friends. Our room opens directly onto the pavement and has a tethering hook outside the door. The floor is of beaten earth and the two unglazed windows are heavily barred. As I write this – by very dim electric light, which goes off at intervals for ten or fifteen minutes – half the adolescent population of the town seems to be crowding around the door and windows. They are a noisy lot and Rachel wants to get to sleep so I am now going to hang space-blankets as curtains.

Camp on High Puna. 27 September

As we left Conchucos at 8.30 everyone waved good-bye and wished us luck; even the schoolboys on their comically sloping soccer pitch stopped a game to cheer. Two hours later we were back on the puna where we still are. All day we met only two young men, driving a pottery-laden pony around the shore of a wide black lake shadowed by a sheer grey rock-peak. Here we picnicked off buns and sardines while admiring a pair of glorious Andean duck: the male scarlet with a blue bill and black head and tail, the female rust-coloured.

Having scrambled down a treacherous slate stairs that taxed even Juana's agility we were again climbing, to higher and still higher expanses of sunny, wind-swept, green-gold puna. We saw several tinamous, and shrill Andean lapwings, and splendid Andean geese with white heads and bodies and black wings. At 2 we passed today's only dwelling, a thatched stone hut such as one might have seen on that same spot 4,000 years ago. Three ponies were grazing nearby and two dogs, sitting by the door, barked half-heartedly: but no one appeared. As there was neither culti- vation nor any sign of flocks, we assumed this to be a latter-day tambo; the pony-man was doubtless asleep within. Travelling was much easier for the Inca troops than it is for the half-starved Andean peasants of today. Pedro de Cieza de León recorded: 'Every four leagues there were lodgings and storehouses abun- dantly supplied with everything to be found in these regions. Even in the uninhabited areas and deserts there had to be these lodgings and storehouses, and the representatives or stewards who lived in the capital of the provinces took great care to see that the natives kept these inns or lodgings (tambos) well supplied . . . And all the roads in this Conchucos region were very well tended, and where the mountains were too rough, they built them on the hillsides, with terraces and flagged stairways, and so strong that they endure and will endure as they are for many ages'. Probably that slate stairs near the lake was a relic of one such road.

Soon after 5, a sharp ascent took us onto the very summit of a flat-topped rock mountain that had been conspicuous across the puna since 1.30. My lungs told me that this was our highest point yet in the Andes and the map suggested we were not far off 16,500 feet. We stood, all three panting, and gazed across a turmoil of ravines and valleys at Rosco Grande and Rosco Chico – aloof, chunky snow peaks apparently on a level with our summit. We were tempted to rest here, savouring our equality with those gleaming princes of the puna, but we dared not. That final climb had sweat-drenched us and at such a height, in the cold evening wind, hypothermia could strike.

The terrain ahead appeared to be all shadowy chasm, looming cliffs and rock-ringed lakes. By the path grew what looked like two-foot miniature pine trees – delicate Japanese intruders on this rugged scene. Some way off rose a perfectly oval, grassy summit, symmetrical and slim – "Like a giant's tombstone!" exclaimed Rachel. Eventually we found ourselves at the base of this 'tomb- stone' where we rejoiced to see a long stretch of soft, juicy, green grass – super-de-luxe grazing, beyond the dreams of Juana's avarice. This site overlooks a 2,000 foot gorge but its sides are comparatively gentle; if we roll over the edge we certainly won't be killed though we might have some difficulty not rolling to the bottom. The tombstone so effectively shielded us from the evening gale that we were able to sup outside. At these altitudes the skyscape is no less overaweing than the landscape; and when they combine, as this evening, the slow-motion ballet of sunset clouds around high peaks leaves me almost (but not quite) too excited to eat my sardines. I'm still lying out on the grass and Rosco Grande and Rosco Chico are glimmering in the distance, their snows quietly radiant by starlight.

Sihaus. 28 September

At dawn a misty rain-cum-fine hail was hissing on the tent. Unzipping, the view was as from a boat: we seemed to be floating on a slowly shifting grey ocean. The gorge below us and the shallow valley immediately ahead were both cloud-filled: only Juana and the tombstone remained visible.

When we set off at 8.45 the mist was still thick and the air painfully cold. We lost our descending path on the edge of a sinister green-black marsh, then found it (we hoped) when the cloud partially lifted. Soon after we passed an Arthur Rackham lake: dark and still and somehow spellbound, in the half-moon embrace of a silver-black cliff.

Then our path became precipitous between bare rock-walls that seemed as though they might at any moment lean together and turn us into fossils. By early afternoon we were down to stream-level and in boggy trouble: Juana *hates* bogs. We could only solve the problem by walking *in* the stream for a mile or so, thus avoiding the unpredictable marshy patches on both banks. (How will my boots react to that?) Beyond this hazard, non-puna vegetation rioted in the gorge on our left. Here were meticulously built Inca stairs, and walls of smooth slippery wet rock down which poor Juana slid miserably but without protest. By now she seems to have accepted that life with the Murphys is a Fate Worse Than Death about which nothing can be done. It frustrates us that she spurns sugar, which is relatively plentiful; we can reward her more heroic endeavours only with cuddles and sweet words.

The afternoon was spend descending a long, winding, culti-vated valley: often our path dived into rocky river-gullies, or climbed steeply to cross untidy outcrops of mountain. Even on its highest slopes, this was the most fertile Andean valley we've seen. In one settlement two billy-goats were 'jousting', their whole performance (much of it on their hind-legs) curiously ritualistic and dignified. The clashing of those formidable horns echoed across the valley and at last a bent old woman came hobbling out of a hovel to shriek at them and stone them. As they separated, she suddenly noticed us – and hastily crossed herself!

Later we met much traffic and our impression was of surly, rather decadent folk – all mestizos. An impression this town does nothing to contradict . . . The old people look utterly wretched, their faces dehumanised by decades of hunger, exertion, cold and oppression. Many of the young look no less miserable – and sly with it, or just plain bad-tempered.

Approaching Sihuas, the track ran for a mile or more through a stately plantation of giant eucalyptus. The placid Rio Sihuas flowed nearby and beyond it, on a level grassy bank, small boys were playing pitch and toss in the gentle evening light. Monotony is not a problem in the sierra; within hours one moves from an extremity of desolate isolation to tranquil domesticity.

Sihuas – sandwiched between high mountains on the banks of its Rio – is our biggest town by far since Huamachuco. It is devastatingly earthquake-ravaged; thousands were killed in the 1970 disaster and much of the older part of the town has now been abandoned. People feel safer on higher ground away from the river. (Nobody seems to know *exactly* how many were killed; in nearby Yungay, the death toll was over 20,000.) Our hotel was partially rebuilt after the 'quake; it's an oddly unwelcoming place, where we sense covert hostility. The restaurant is a long, high-ceilinged, mud-floored, crudely built structure with wide un-glazed windows, a tin roof and rows of tiny tin tables and chairs. We were so hungry we ate two suppers; a) excellent potato and mutton soup, followed by boiled potatoes with chilli sauce and scraps of roast guinea-pig; b) chips with fried egg and chopped goat-meat. It was raining hard as we ate, sitting in a freezing draught between gaping windows. "We'd be better off in our tent", observed Rachel, "except for the food." But Sihuas offers an abundance of Alf and Juana is now happily corralled, with four tethered ponies, in the back-yard. Happy the region where hotels need corrals, not car-parks!

Camp on Mountain-ledge beyond Sicsibamba. 29 September

When we left Sihuas at 10, with four kilos of Alf tied to the load, the sky was overcast and the air cool: perfect walking weather.

Scores of yelling (sometimes jeering) children followed us to the edge of the town where we found a new, gradually descending carretera – a dry-weather motor-road to the selva. Today its muddy surface bore no tyre marks. Here an almost-dry river-bed took up the whole floor of a yellowish-brown valley bearing many earthquake scars. No vegetation grew on the fissured cliffs, which at intervals were still collapsing onto the track. No fields or dwellings were visible until we came to a small wooden shack by the roadside. From this, as we passed, Ramón emerged – a neatly-dressed, diminutive young man with uncommonly dark skin, a trim black moustache, very bad teeth, Indian features and a smattering of English. He shyly appointed himself our guide and led us down to the river-bed, through the Rio by an approved ford and into a narrow, vividly green side-valley filled with the noise of a leaping, gleaming, foaming torrent. Twice we had to ford this tributary, getting soaked to the waist. Lest we might be swept away, I hung on to Juana's neck and Rachel hung on to a strirrup; it would have been too risky to ride across, so unstable were the rocks underfoot. After the second fording we were on a fearsome Inca path, overhung by thorny scrub, which went *straight up* from about 8,500 feet to 11,400 – the sort of climb Juana, being a Peruvian, likes to tackle briskly. One of her abrupt upward rushes almost knocked poor Rachel over a precipice, so Ramón smiling-ly took the leading-rope and he and Juana disappeared, moving companionably at the same unnatural pace. Even trying to keep up with them (not that we tried very hard) totally exhausted Rachel and me. By gringo standards we've both acclimatised well but we don't have the Indians' physiological adaptations; their lungs and hearts, in conspicuous barrel chests, are not at all like ours.

From the top we descended, on a golden-brown mountain, to the outskirts of Sicsibamba – a small, scattered red-tiled pueblo built on different ledges of a steep spur, with many cultivated fields above and below it. Here Ramon pointed to a group of adobe hovels on a ridge above us – and without even an 'Adiós!' sprinted out of our lives. Then I felt again the sadness of the gap between us and the Indians. Ramón, having moved into the mestizo-dominated world of teaching, had been more forthcoming than most. But in any other country I know, our encounter would have led to an invitation to visit his home and meet his family. Are most Indians hyper-self-conscious about their poverty? Or do they simply regard social intercourse with gringoes as impossible and/or undesirable?

All morning it had been April weather: alternate hot sun and drenching showers. We were visibly steaming as we wandered along a rough street where Rachel's food-orientated eye discerned what seemed to be an eating-house, some thirty feet below street level. Four urban-type men were sitting at a rickety wooden table in a farm-yard, drinking home-made spirits while awaiting a late lunch. Noticing the gringoes, they yelled cheerful "Olés!" and beckoned us. Soon Juana had been tethered amidst pigs, hens, dogs, goats, turkeys and guinea-pigs – all swarming around the yard seeking what they might devour but apparently on excellent terms with each other. When presented with her luncheon Alf, which it had greatly inconvenienced me to transport thus far, our mulita bonito spurned it. "Not fresh enough for Her Highness", deduced Rachel; which was probably true, though I saw it being cut at dawn this morning. The proprietress – a handsome, charming mestizo campesino – then detected her pigs trying to steal our Alf and rushed to rescue it; but I said the pigs could have it. In exchange, we were given a free lunch of excellent soup to which one added barley-mash according to taste from a big dish in the centre of the table, followed by potatoes with rich gravy and a tiny leg of roast guinea-pig. (At home I'm both a vegetarian *and* a devotee of guinea-pigs; walking through the Andes, such sensibilities become atrophied. Here one would eat one's grandmother, even if she weren't very well cooked.)

From their own supply our urban friends stood us two cokes and two cervezas; they were studying the prospects for Agrarian Reform in the Sihuas area and had come well-stocked from Lima. One was a negro, black as coal, who must have been six-foot-four in his socks and, beside the tiny Peruvians, looked like the representative of some Superhuman Master-race. He and his three mestizo colleagues seemed a good deal more interested in the two daughters of the house than in Agrarian Reform. These strikingly beautiful lassies each wore two brilliant flounced skirts, all minutely hand-embroidered, and tight llama-wool bodices. They flirted boldly – almost brazenly – with the four men and their mother seemed to approve. (The visitors may of course be regarded as possible future husbands, or at least worthwhile 'protectors'.) One wonders how useful a report on Agrarian Reform in the high sierra could be produced by a coastal negro, two Lima-born civil servants and one young army officer from Trujillo.

Nowadays our plans are largely determined by the fodder situation. At 3.15 it was raining again and a dark cloud-lid pressed on Sicsibamba. Had Alf or oats been available we would have spent the night there; as only chopped dried cactus was on offer we pressed on. (Dried cactus is said to be a highly nutritious mule-food but the pernickety Juana won't even sample it.) We were followed by the entire juvenile population which had been in delighted attendance on us ever since our arrival. These high-spirited youngsters shouted encouragement as we struggled through their pueblo's muddy complex of steep alleyways. It seemed wise to ignore their advice, since each direction contradicted the one before it, and we might never have found the Pomabamba track but for the army officer who, feeling uneasy about our welfare, had hurried after us. He set us on a treacherously muddy path, overhanging a fearsome drop, and suggested that Rachel might be safer walking. This was our first Andean encounter with the peculiarly unpleasant hazard of slippy mud.

The grazing on this ledge is only moderately good. And it's too wet for a fire, though there's lots of wood lying around beneath nearby scrub. It's damp-chilly now, but not really cold; here we can't be much above 9,000 feet, if our American Geographical Society map is to be believed. But is it? The army officer, having looked at it, sneered. It's dated 1941, which perhaps partly explains why we get lost so often.

Camp on Mountain-ledge overlooking Pomabamba. 30 September

A cloudless morning, warm by 7, with the wide, rainwashed world below our ledge all sparkling and green. As we packed up we were watched intently, for about ten minutes, by two barefooted, expressionless mestizos (aged thirty-ish) who stood silently only a few yards away, their frayed ponchos wrapped tightly around them. Our greetings brought no response and it is extraordinarily disconcerting to be studied as though one were an *object* rather than a person.

Half an hour later we joined a carretera but during the next seven hours saw only one honda and one mini-truck, both near Pomabamba. We had climbed steeply from our ledge to the carretera and could see it winding for miles across bare brown puna to an 11,000 foot pass. In one dip, we were startled to see our barefooted friends standing outside a derelict shack, looking towards us; evidently they had used some hidden redura. For the first time on this trek, I felt a twinge of apprehension. Meagre as our possessions are, by First World standards, to those two they must have seemed like fabled treasures of the Occident: padded flea-bags, husky suits, space-blankets, a tent, binoculars – not to mention our mula bonito . . . And the four of us had the puna to ourselves; no dwellings, or shepherds, or horsemen were visible. As we drew level, one man stepped forward and abruptly asked for money. We stopped, and I explained that we had none – that's why we were sleeping out on the mountain – we couldn't go to a hotel without money – we were hoping to get some from a friend in Pomabamba . . . Both faces remained unnervingly impassive, but they must have believed me for they said no more. My story was plausible; we could hardly be mistaken for rich tourists, with our weather-blackened skins, sweat-stiffened hair, filthy clothes and disintegrating boots. Bidding them a cheerful "Adiós!", we continued at our normal pace. After a moment they began to follow us, so closely that we could hear their muttered arguing. "They're probably deciding where to throw our bodies", said Rachel with a macabre grin – the child reads far too many thrillers. I felt more relieved than I would admit when, at the pass, they turned west.

Soon we too found a redura and rounded mountain after mountain, steadily losing height. By 2.30 we were approaching the T-junction meeting of two valleys and could see ahead a wild chaos of peaks and spurs, with waterfalls flashing down creeper-draped cliffs and frothy torrents racing between jumbles of barn-sized boulders. Here the carretera had to turn due north, and creep along the base of a rock-wall richly emblazoned with flowering shrubs. We were almost at the head of the Pomabamba valley when at last we could cross the infant Rio Pomabamba (here a very noisy infant, in a steep-sided cradle of black rock) and again turn south towards the pueblo.

This new valley soon became domesticated, with intensively cultivated slopes beyond the Rio. The carretera remained high above the widening valley floor and we were looking down, as we walked, on a microcosm of campesino life. Red-roofed adobe farmsteads were scattered on either side of the river, very far below. Men and oxen were struggling to plough near-vertical fields which looked as though they might at any moment slip off the mountain. A couple were flaying a sheep that hung from the eaves of their home. Women were spinning while tending their flocks. Toddlers were playing with kids and lambs, cuddling them and tumbling with them on the green turf. Older children were chivvying a turkey flock away from the river's edge. Girls were fetching water in battered kerosene tins. Youths were unloading burros just back from the market. Pairs of old grannies were weaving poncho-cloth. Sleek horses were grazing on lush pasture. About this pastoral pageant – observed from a thousand feet up, so that one felt ridiculously like a spy – there was an aura of permanence, order, peace, security.

If Atahualpa had come back to accompany us, he would have noticed few changes in that valley. And what has Progress – our brand of Progress – to offer such people? Medical care, improved seeds, AI for the cattle, sanitation, literacy, birth control . . . But then a troubling thought: how can we give *our* goods without destroying *their* goods? Probably we cannot. Everywhere peasant communities have their own particular and precious integrity. And it seems to be virtually impossible merely to modify such cultures, so that the peasants can enjoy the 'suitable' benefits of modern civilisation while retaining what *we* deem valuable in their own culture. We can't say: "Keep on weaving – that's *good*! But you mustn't take your water from the river – that's *bad*!" As soon as Progress impinges, a community's special integrity goes; and do we think enough about its intangible value before we go marching in to smash it? Our simple faith in hygiene and literacy and contraceptives and 'the profit motive' perhaps blinds us to the more subtle benefits, for the average peasant, of his traditional culture. Its structure and pattern and rhythm provide a framework within which the individual (who usually doesn't think of himself as an individual in our sense) can find contentment. How will things be fifty years hence in the Pomabamba valley? If Rachel's daughter were to ride then along that mountain, what would she see? Not, I fear, what we saw this afternoon. We are lucky. We can still just reach the fringes of the past, by leaning far out over that chasm created in human history by the earthquake of Progress. And this is important, if we are to remain whole and real human beings. We couldn't live permanently like the campesinos – and wouldn't want to. But it's essential to remember that for tens of thousands of years, and until comparatively recently, that is how *everyone* lived. And the time may come when the survival of our species will require some of us to revert . . .

Spreading eucalyptus plantations heralded Pomabamba, a pleasant little pueblo of straight Spanish streets and welcoming people. There was no fodder available, but we were told of good grazing on the high path to Piscobamba. So after an excellent though hurried meal, in a clean, friendly eating-house, we crossed the Rio again at 5.15 and climbed *very* steeply to this acre-wide ledge from which we are directly overlooking Pomabamba. As I write, its scattering of tiny, twinkling lights are like a constellation fallen into the black depths of the valley.

It was so windy when we arrived here that Rachel had to help me control the tent, before turning to her usual evening task of collecting firewood; but the wind dropped as the sun set. We were then joined by Luis (aged ten) and Carlos (aged seven) who live in a nearby isolated shack. They are an enchanting pair, their curiosity and excitement beautifully tempered by courtesy and sensitivity. The local fuel is poor and our fire was a problem. So they rushed off, returned with armfuls of aromatic grass, stuffed it between my stones, expertly wielded their panama hats – and within five minutes our coffee water was boiling. They were very concerned lest Juana might be stolen while we slept and advised me to put the picket down *inside* the tent!

Pomabamba. *1 October*

I woke at dawn to see Luis advancing across the ledge, bent double under a load of maize straw. Carlos soon followed, accompanied by their mother (aged twenty-six!) who firmly refused payment for the straw but accepted three Irish stamps with solemn gratitude. A daughter died between Luis and Carlos and she has three younger daughters. She assumed Rachel to be my grand-daughter and was tongue-tied with embarrassed pity when I explained that she was my only child. All three squatted on the ground and watched – rivetted by the whole process – while we packed up. I could quite understand their fascination; to me this seems a daily miracle of fitting a quart into a pint pot. When one surveys the camp in all its glory – tent up, bags unrolled, food, clothes, books, maps, saucepans, notebooks and tack strewn everywhere – it seems incredible that within thirty minutes Juana will be trotting off carrying what then seems a negligible load.

For three hours we climbed steeply, traversing not a yard of level ground. During one rest pause, Rachel spotted a two-inch stick insect, thin and angular, his brown and green colouring perfectly matching the striped leaves of his perch. When we looked carefully, we detected several more in that area. This climb was a real lung-buster but the reward was proportionate to the effort – an incomparable view of the Cordillera Blanca when suddenly, after many 'false summits', we reached the ultimate puna and were facing the highest mountain range in Peru. Across a wide, shallow valley rose the snow-burdened mightiness of a long line of serrated summits, the two highest peaks just below 20,000 feet. All morning we had met no one and here on this immense sloping plateau – sun-warmed and snow-cooled, vividly green beneath a strongly blue sky – I had the illusion of having actually *left* the inhabited world, as though we were now on another planet. Behind us, the vastness beyond the Pomabamba valley – which had so awed us during the climb – was hidden by that long rock-wall through which our path had just found a way.

We brunched here, before climbing still higher on boulder-stairways which inspired Juana to circus-trick nimbleness. Now we were weaving our way through – and could literally touch – those tremendous crags, which saner mortals see only from a great distance as 'the mountain tops'. By noon I was suffering from such acute summit euphoria that I'd quite forgotten we had a destination.

Half an hour later we were startled to find ourselves again looking down, from a new angle, on the red roofs of Pomabamba. Yet we didn't at once lose hope: many Andean tracks are forced to be eccentric. Only when we could see this path continuing to descend, and heading north, did we pause to consider our alternatives: a return to Pomabamba and a fresh start tomorrow ("On the carretera", suggested Rachel), or a return to an unpromising previously considered thread-path. We both voted for the thread-path, only to lose the main track twenty minutes later, on the plateau . . . (It's misleading to refer to it as a 'main track'; at intervals it vanished completely for half a mile or so.) For the first time we were truly lost – unable to find a way forward or backward – though not alarmingly lost, with Pomabamba so close. Yet it can be quite difficult hereabouts to get *off* a mountain, as we'd learned on the way to Conchucos. "This is a dotty day!" exclaimed Rachel. And it was soon to become dottier.

We eventually found another distinct path, curving around grassy shoulders, but it dwindled to nothing on a long ledge where we passed the day's first dwelling – an empty stone cabin in a potato patch. From there Pomabamba was invisible, nor did we glimpse it for the next forty-five minutes while we were slithering down a slope of crumbly red-brown earth to a level path broken by deep gullies which required Juana to do some stylish jumping. Traversing a partially cultivated mountain, we saw below us a circular valley in which women were shepherding and men ploughing. When we shouted a plea for directions they pointed to a faint diagonal path crossing the steep upper slopes of their valley. That restored Pomabamba to view, but now rather further away; despite all our efforts, we'd been inexorably pushed north by the intractability of the terrain.

This path vanished on a rock-strewn slope above a sheer precipice. Rachel went ahead to recce and reported that by moving onto the next mountain we'd come to a gradient with which Juana *might* be able to cope. So we cautiously advanced, at every step feeling the loose earth shift beneath feet and hooves.

My first reaction to Rachel's route was that she must be feeling suicidal, matricidal and mulicidal. But here one gets used to attempting the apparently impossible. After only a momentary hesitation, we embarked on the most taxing manoeuvre of this trek. Juana was the problem. I led her and one false move of hers would have knocked me into eternity. (From that starting point, there was no other possible destination.) At the most crucial stage, when it seemed that neither Juana nor myself could ever again move up, down or across, Rachel called cheerfully, "I wish the camera hadn't jammed! You both look so *silly!*" "If that's how you feel, hurry on down and lead her yourself!" I yelled back savagely – before lengthening the rope and leaping across a mini-ravine onto a mound of earth that collapsed as I landed on it. Which was fortunate, for I slipped into a giant cactus just in time to get out of the way of Juana, who had too quickly jumped after me. Normally I don't enjoy cacti embraces, but this was preferable to *not* being caught . . . (It was a poisonous horror and tonight my throbbing scratches are turning black in a most interesting way.) As we continued our acrobatic descent, even the insouciant Rachel became slightly alarmed about the fate of her mulita and her mamma (probably in that order). But we suffered only one casualty when a thorn bush, with branches like steel wire, tore Rachel's mug off a pannier; we paused to listen to it rattling briskly to the bottom of the cliff. I don't know how long our ordeal lasted:

perhaps thirty or forty minutes, though it felt like a day. Safe at last in a precipitous stubble-field, we looked up at that most brutal of mountains and Rachel said, "Juana should get the VC!"

For the next hour we remained pathless, gradually working our way down and south across ploughland, stubble and wasteland. Then came an unexpected concrete irrigation channel which Juana resolutely refused to jump, though it was narrower than some of the gullies she had leaped over on the mountain. "She doesn't like concrete", said Rachel approvingly. We had to follow the channel to a footbridge from where a rocky path wound down for an hour between neat casas and shady groves. Here we bought six kilos of Alf and decided on a rest-day in Pomabamba to-morrow. I *must* have myself reshod; during our VC descent my left boot fell apart with an air of finality. When we again crossed the bridge over the Rio Pomabamba, on our way to the hotel, we completed a crazy circle begun exactly twenty-four hours earlier.

5

Fun and Forebodings

Our dottiest day had such happy consequences that last evening I was, regrettably, in no fit state to write my diary. Pomabambe celebrates its annual fiesta at this time (St Francis of Assisi is the patron saint) and it would have been churlish of me not to participate. So yesterday was spent in a haze of nameless alcohol. The occasion had something in common with an Irish wake, to the extent that during fiestas the campesinos see drunkenness not as an extravagance, or a joke, or a vice, but as – in some obscure way – part of the religious ceremony. This is an ancient and worldwide primitive tradition; at the dawn of Hinduism Aryan priests newly arrived in Northern India got ritually smashed on soma. I don't know what I got smashed on last evening but throughout the day I was given so many powerful potions that I ended up dancing with the campesinos in the Plaza – though dancing is not one of my skills. The fiesta spirit(s) so envelope(s) everyone that even the Indians, now thronging into Pomabamba, forget their 'thing' about gringoes. This uninhibiting effect of alcohol is the main reason why, for millennia, unsophisticated peoples have used drink and drugs during religious ceremonies; these free the soul to establish contact with whatever form of the immaterial is believed to exist beyond the confines and conventions of mundane life.

Yesterday Rachel observed that she had never seen or heard anything *less* religious than Pomabamba's fiesta, but today her attitude had changed. She said, sounding slightly puzzled, "Obviously the religious part does matter too". Often one can place more reliance on a child's judgement, in such matters, than on an adult's. Nine-year-olds are without our prejudices and have not yet lost their sensitivity to what may lie below the surface. To me the Catholic Church's cynical deviousness in Peru, and elsewhere throughout Latin America, is extremely off-putting. In *Indians of the Andes*, Harold Osborne explained: 'After 1650, many native practices which had before been the object of militant missionary repression came to be tolerated as harmless, if deplorable, superstitions and the way lay open for the advance of syncretic Christianity. Since that time it has not looked back.'

The Church in Peru had no alternative but to compromise, as the Buddhist pioneers in ninth-century Tibet had no alternative but to accommodate their teachings to the ancient Bön-po religion. But, unlike the Buddhist missionaries, the Church authorities never admitted that they had compromised and they still try to draw a veil of hypocrisy over Peruvian Roman Catholicism – a veil in which the Liberation Theologians have recently, to their great credit, torn some large holes. One is appalled by the sloth and greed of the native Peruvian clergy. *They* don't minister to the people of the sierra; that materially unrewarding job is left to foreign priests – Germans, Irish, Americans, English, Italian, Poles and Dutch. In fact not many Peruvians now become priests, but the majority of those who do cluster around the urban rich like bluebottles around bad meat.

In the Pomabamba area, during the past year, the whole campesino population, like most of the mestizo townsfolk, have been saving up to pay for this fiesta. It is believed that adequate rains, good harvests, healthy families and flocks, prosperous businesses and fertile wives all depend on the generosity of one's contribution to the fiesta fund. The campesinos look upon their patron saint as an ally of – or possibly another manifestation of – the aukis or mountain spirits, or the apus or place spirits. It would be wrong for the clergy not to accept the money thus offered, gladly, to insure against calamity during the year ahead. But the Catholic Church is a grossly rich institution which does not need the precious centavos of half-starved peasants and it should be possible discreetly to return fiesta donations to the community. Yet this is not often done. (Much of the money collected is of course spent on ceremonial booze; the Church only gets a percentage, which varies widely from area to area.)

Andean fiestas are the despair of earnest young American anthropologists who yearn to analyse in their theses the precise significance of every dance and costume and gesture and mask and musical instrument and coloured bead and ankle-bell and headdress. No coherent explanations are forthcoming, either from the locals or from Peruvian historians or folklorists. Here, the two educated mestizo families (a teacher's and a merchant's) who have befriended us, themselves know nothing of their fiesta's origins beyond the fact that similar celebrations were part of Inca and pre-Inca cultures and that the keynote is 'propitiation'.

In a small square, some distance from the main Plaza, we visited a delapidated little church with broken, grass-grown steps – a building clearly not much used throughout the year. In front of several statues and pictures of St Francis, campesinos were placing offerings of eggs, potatoes, fruit or flowers – and then prostrating themselves. Outside, in each corner of the square, as in many other parts of the pueblo, shrines have been set up (tradesmen's stalls, draped in coloured paper and lengths of bright cloth) and within each a statue of St Francis is surrounded by large dolls elaborately dressed in campesino style. Some are decorated with gold turnip watches, silver coins, pieces of quite valuable jewelry and cheap trinkets. The shelves beside the 'altar' are laden with further offerings: hideous china dogs and cats, plastic toys, plastic flowers, repulsive ornaments, gorgeously embroidered cushion-covers, antique tobacco pipes – any and every sort of household treasure or cherished family heirloom. These offerings are only on loan to their patron and will be retrieved at the end of the fiesta. It gives one a good feeling to know that even after dark they can safely be left on display in these open stalls – unguarded, unless one counts the statue of St Francis. This morning, the streets were crowded with women carrying silver objects to the church to be offered during that Mass which is regarded as the solemn (though not entirely sober) centrepiece of the whole fiesta. We were astonished by the quantity of good silver this pueblo could produce: goblets, plates, jewelry, salvers, ornaments, coins, crucifixes, rosary beads.

After Mass, four wooden platforms, handsomely carved and gilded and each carried by ten men, left the church to process around the town – a three hour ceremony, with halts at many shrines for drinking and dancing. On these platforms, under arches laden with plastic flowers, stood life-size statues of Saints Francis, Anthony, Peter and John. A woman's band preceded them, led by a man dressed in a pale pink track-suit who had the most blood-shot eyes I've ever seen; they looked as though they had just been gouged out and replaced. Evidently he was one of the thousands who had *no* sleep last night. (Rachel unkindly remarked that my own eyes didn't look much better.) Six women dancers accompanied the band, wearing pale blue ankle-length silk dresses, long black lace veils over their faces and complicated head-dresses surmounted by crests of peacock feathers. They intoned a weirdly beautiful Quechua chant while rhythmically beating the ground with seven-foot high staves topped by crosses from which hung tiny bells and clusters of red, white and blue ribbons.

The mayor – his robes gorgeous though frayed, his chicha content high – told me in English that this ritual predates the Inca Empire: which could be true, though I don't think *Quechua* was spoken in this area before the Incas took over. The dancing women were followed by two priests from Trujillo (who had celebrated the Mass), walking a few yards ahead of St Francis's platform with open breviaries and bored expressions. The Holy Quartet were followed by a motley crowd of musicians, dancers and clowns, who have been roaming the town since yesterday. Included were mestizo men inexplicably attired as 18th-century hussars; campesinos wearing leather leggings, black masks of hide and goats-hair, and Napoleonic brass helmets; campesino sword dancers with bells on their ankles; groups of men wearing comical or savagely glaring masks and elaborate cloth helmets bedecked with coins, buttons, shells, religious medals – all surmounted by coloured plumes that swayed as they danced, like a field of exotic blooms in a gusty wind. Another group wore tight scarlet trousers and short royal blue jackets with red collars and cuffs, the ensemble being completed by a Homburg hat, a (real) sword held in the right hand and a cluster of bells tied to the left hand. These gentlemen danced indefatigably all day and all night, to the music of violins and tall portable harps. Another group, also equipped with Homburg hats, swords and finger-bells, wore impeccable lounge-suits, complete with collars and ties, and their faces were hidden by blue-eyed masks. When they paused to imbibe, one saw that they were mestizo youths. In the more prosperous streets, flower petals and confetti were thrown over the statues from the upstairs balconies by pious ladies too genteel to join in the rough and tumble; and bouquets of fresh flowers, wrapped in cellophane, were lowered on strings and received by acolytes for the further gratification of St Francis.

As I write, firecrackers are still being let off every few moments; this has been going on for the past thirty-six hours and must be an expensive item on the fiesta bill. The scene had become uninspiring when we withdrew. Several ugly brawls were starting, as an oddly desperate atmosphere replaced the earlier gaiety – these things are hard to define, but one did feel that something potentially dangerous had been released.

We have much enjoyed this hybrid event, during which the most ancient of Indian traditions and emotions merged into the campesinos' idiosyncratic version of Christianity. Yet one cannot pretend that such a fiesta is a memorable artistic experience; there was nothing beautiful, skilful or subtle about the 'folk-art', and the general impression was of a static, stylised, almost moribund culture within which people feel no need to develop what past generations have handed down. (Apart from minor innovations, like the lounge-suited dancers who were mocking those Americans now controlling – in practice if not in theory – Peru's mining industry.)

Today Rachel acquired a new pair of walking-shoes but my own search for suitable boots was unsuccessful. However, the cobbler here seemed super-efficient, so again one hopes . . . Displayed in his workshop, as in several other places in Pomabamba and Conchucos, was a government-issued poster urging people to eat more potatoes and less rice because 'potatoes are as good as or better than rice'. Apparently rice has become the 'in' thing of recent years and potatoes are increasingly being despised as 'campesinos' food'. Food snobbery is unexpected in a country as poor as Peru.

Camp on Scrubland beyond Piscobamba. 4 October

My troops mutinied this morning. Rachel announced that she didn't fancy another Duke of York exercise and that she knew Juana was of like mind. So we stayed with the carretera for twelve miles as it climbed gradually to Piscobamba. In this region there is no reason to be alarmed by the term 'carretera'; today no vehicle passed us and there wasn't a tyre-mark to be seen on the rough stony track. Yet there was much traffic, of the sort we enjoy, as campesinos hurried towards Pomabamba where the fiesta will continue for another few days. Some raggedly dressed wretches were carrying buckets of chicha which they will sell for ten soles a half-gourd – what an effort to earn a few pence!

Between Pomabamba and Piscobamba the two-storeyed farmhouses seem unusually spacious and prosperous-looking – all freshly whitewashed, some even with glazed windows – and the land looks rich and well-watered. But the people were not as friendly as those north of Conchucos. At noon we rested in the shade of a eucalyptus grove where a damp grassy patch provided a mule-snack. Across the road, a young man was strenuously ploughing with one ox; his wife followed, scattering seed. When they paused for lunch, Mamma took her infant off the back of a small girl and suckled it while she herself was eating cold boiled sweet potatoes. Although we greeted this little family, and were sitting within conversation distance of them, they completely ignored us.

Piscobamba is another pleasant little pueblo now marred by an abortive (for lack of funds) water supply and sewage scheme. The torn-up streets had to be crossed on insecure plank footbridges which Juana hated, nor did she much like having to scramble over shiny stacks of sewage pipes.

Several steep reduras took us through a harshly infertile area of unexpected chasms, naked, rock-strewn slopes and isolated smaller mountains. All afternoon we passed only a few half-starved-looking campesinos who viewed us with some alarm.

This wide ledge of scrubland is well supplied with short grass and easy-to-light firewood. Not far below us, audible though invisible, is the Rio Pomabamba. I'm sitting now by a glowing pile of crimson embers, watching a silver sliver of moon sinking towards the black bulk of a sky-obscuring range we must cross tomorrow.

Camp in Field on Mountainside near San Luis. 5 October

By 6.30 we were skidding down to Rio level on a precipitous gravel path. On these river descents, one seems to be penetrating to the very bowels of the earth, so colossal and overbearing are the surrounding mountains. A jerry-built concrete bridge took us over the Rio Pomabamba for the last time; we all agree that we feel much safer on a well-made tree-trunk bridge. For two hours we were climbing steeply: first on a barren, rocky, thorn-bushy mountain too arid to feed even a goat, then on grassy, more gentle slopes where we passed a 'quake-stricken village with an abandoned school and two-roomed police-post. Three new 'quake ravines have severely disrupted the path and we almost went astray again while seeking ways to rejoin it. We brunched on a high, turfy pass, aromatic with herbs and overlooking a line of sparkling, distant snow-peaks. In the perfect stillness, sunny and windless, we could hear from far above the poignant, eternal music of a goatherd's pipe – to me the most enduring authentic link with the Andes of the Incas.

From here the carretera was again visible, a few thousand feet below. That descent, on a ladder-steep path much complicated by 'quake rifts, culminated in a tight-rope act when the path crossed the spine of a long, narrow, grey-black rock-spur with grisly drops inches away on *both* sides. My relief at getting off this horror was soon counteracted by the savage noon heat. We were now in a grim canyon of perpendicular rock-mountains with no trace of vegetation anywhere: not even a cactus grew on the walls of our oven. Crossing a dry, rocky river-bed, quarter of a mile wide, we rejoined the carretera and round the next bend beheld a motor – the rusting skeleton of a truck which added the final touch to this gloomy inferno.

I wilt within moments when exposed to extreme heat, which by my standards is anything over 75°F. Although the track continued level for a few miles, and we stopped often to drink our hot chemical-flavoured water, I soon felt more exhausted than if I had climbed 4,000 feet in a blizzard. Just then, as my morale reached zero, the Pomabamba cobbler – in whom I had tried so hard to believe – was revealed as a veritable charlatan when one of his nails suddenly pierced my foot to stigmata-like effect.

At last we emerged into a broad valley where the track began to rise along the flank of another dark, bare mountain, pulsating in the heat. Far below on our left flowed – we think – the Rio Yurma. (Here our map gives up pretending to be accurate and only a vague tangle of blue lines indicates the numerous local rivers.) Two hours later the track dropped steeply between outlandish grey-brown mud-cliffs that might have been moulded out of plasticene; when I poked my stick into one it easily made a dent. Now we couldn't hear ourselves speak above the roar of the river. Then suddenly we were crossing it, on a solid wooden bridge above a narrow channel so steep that the river here becomes a violently beautiful waterfall, raving into a white whirlpool between smooth but grotesquely eroded boulders. Leaning over the bridge – made deliciously dizzy by the clamour and force of the water, and dazzled by its translucent emerald brilliance – we were in a moment outside of time: part of an elemental everlastingness.

Soon after, a taciturn young mestizo joined us. He was determined not to communicate, yet he walked close beside us as the
road climbed away from the river to enter a broad valley – where we
could see the little pueblo of San Luis, on a distant mountaintop.
When we came to a road-side shack our silent companion,
pointing to it, considerately said "Chicha" – then scampered
away, up a mountainside. Never has chicha tasted so good. Three
soles bought at least a quart, in a huge gourd, from a filthy old
woman with an embittered expression. She squatted in her doorway, unsmilingly regarding us as we sat on stones surrounded by
turkeys, hens, striped piglets and spotted puppies. Repeatedly we
were threatened by a xenophobic turkey-cock of fearsome proportions who eventually saw us off his territory with a quite
alarming display of aggression.

We had difficulty finding a level spot for the tent on this steep
slope below San Luis. Then Rachel noticed a narrow grassy shelf,
just off the track on the edge of a newly harvested barley-field.
Soon we were drinking soup around a fire of incense-like eucalyptus wood and my lacerated foot, released from its boot, could be
forgotten as our exultant eyes beheld the King of the Cordillera
Blanca – Huascarán, at 22,180 feet the highest mountain in Peru.

Camp on high Puna. 6 October

By 7.10 I was limping up a multi-pathed redura, speechless
with pain. Rachel followed, leading Juana and looking anxious; I
could no longer maintain the fiction that my defective boot 'didn't
matter'. There was but a single thought in my mind: how to find
a cobbler. (By now I could write a substantial thesis on 'The
Cobblers of the Peruvian Sierra'; people have got PhDs for less.)
Soon we were mildly lost: we could no longer see San Luis. Then a
leprechaun-sized campesino noticed our mistake from afar, left
two heavily laden burros in the care of his tiny daughter and
insisted on walking back towards the pueblo to guide us onto the
right path. Predictably, he wouldn't accept a tip.

The cobbler was appalled, and we hope inspired, when I
showed him my mangled sole. While he hammered, I applied a
complex arrangement of padded plasters to the stigmata. San Luis
is a good foraging centre. For less than fifty pence, we bought four
packets of savoury biscuits, half a kilo of noodles, half a kilo of
sugar, five bananas and twenty *fresh* buns – bread less than a

fortnight old is a treat in these parts. A policeman, met in the bakery, told us that today's pass is over 14,500 feet.

When we reached this pass six hours later we realised that it is not, strictly speaking, a pass – there are no nearby mountains – but simply the highest point on the track. All around us stretched a vastness of puna. Behind us a dark array of sharp rock peaks rose above a long, low bank of blue-black rain-cloud – all the peaks of freakishly uniform size and shape, and all tilted slightly to the left as we looked back at them. Far ahead lay a succession of mighty ranges, some snowy – among them the Cerro de Vincos, which we must cross on our way from Chavín to La Unión.

It was 6.10 before we came upon this excellent grazing spot which is by far our coldest Andean site. However, the quenoa (a rare high-altitude tree) flourishes hereabouts and while I got the tent up Rachel, being very hungry, did her fuel-gathering bit with alarming enthusiasm. Once I looked around to see her two-thirds of the way up a tree that overhung a fifty-foot drop; she was breaking off dead branches and throwing them into the rocky gully beneath. So we have had the rare luxury of a fire on the puna – if you can call it a luxury. Because of the altitude we had great difficulty a) lighting it and b) cooking our noodles. Despite a steady wind I had to blow continuously to keep the water boiling and nothing was hot when served up; but we weren't in a fussy mood. When Rachel crawled into the tent it was already stiff and glistening with frost. Then I had to strip naked in the icy wind to put on my high-altitude underwear. There's no room in our tent for such manoeuvres, but though it may be cramped it's very efficient. While writing this I have thawed and am now all set for a comfortable night.

Camp on slightly lower Puna. 7 October

A worrying day, though I've tried to conceal my forebodings from Rachel. This morning poor Juana went very lame. By then we were in relentlessly rugged country and we didn't find this site until 10.30, by which time we'd covered scarcely six miles because Juana could only hobble. As neither of us knows anything about equine complaints we can't make a diagnosis – there's nothing *visibly* wrong with the leg or hoof. My fear is that she may not make it to Cuzco. And she has become such a beloved member of the team that neither of us, I suspect, would have the will to continue with another animal. This may sound sentimental, but when the going gets rough her unflappability gives us invaluable moral support. We wouldn't swap her for a thoroughbred de Paso.

This is a perfect hospital site: almost-level acres of soft, springy turf on which Juana reclined all day in warm sunshine, with Rachel lying beside her reading *The King's War*. Rachel is developing a heavy cold and would in any case have needed a rest-day; it's odd how their indispositions coincide. To the west, smooth brown puna slopes up to meet the sky. To the east – and quite close, beyond a grassy ravine – stretches a ridge of gently curved mountains. To the north are sharp, dark, sheer peaks. To the south are more distant but no less ferocious summits, many snow-flecked.

At first sight, this seems an unpromising 'fire-zone'. But if one persists the little bushes dotted about the semi-puna yield an adequate supply of dead-wood, though these thin twigs burn so fast in the lively breeze that cooking isn't easy. Nearby, a clear brown stream races down a gully from the high puna; it may be riddled with campesinos' bacteria but it looks so pristine that I've chanced not 'pilling' it – and so we feel we're living it up on the Andean equivalent of champagne.

The locals are pathetic. There are seven scattered hovels on this gigantic ledge, all crudely built of stones and tree-trunks, and roofed with tousled thatches of puna grass. These seem not human creations but part of the earth, like badgers' setts or foxes' dens. I toured them this afternoon in search of food, as we may be marooned here for days. Around each are a few minuscule fields, providing just enough potatoes and bizarre root vegetables to keep the population alive – but not kicking. The average IQ of these Indians is tragically sub-normal; clearly anyone with any spark of intelligence has long since migrated. It was hard to tell the animal from the human quarters, except that in the latter a few ragged spare garments were draped over low rafters and a few basic cooking utensils and tin plates were stacked in corners. I had thought nothing could be more poverty-benumbed than the remoter villages of Baltistan but the Baltis live like sybarites compared to these Indians. Nobody here understands Spanish and the tendency is to hide as I approach. But I had success at the fifth hovel. Outside it a small boy, with open sores on his face, was apathetically playing with a thin puppy and a half-grown golden-haired pig. The pup and two other curs barked hysterically at me. (Why do campesinos keep so many dogs, who often look better fed than their children?) The little fellow fled, whimpering with fear, and a moment later a woman wearing a stained black bowler hat, and carrying an infant on her back, rose out of the adjacent gorge – spinning automatically and surveying me expressionlessly. (From a distance she may have observed our setting up camp.) I tried to convey that my niño and I are stranded and need food – to wit, fifteen soles worth of potatoes. The woman wordlessly considered me and my proffered soles for long moments. Then she made a gesture inviting me to sit on a boulder in the yard, beside a tree-trunk pig trough in which a piglet was diligently working to scrape off a residue of dried food. Slowly she climbed an outside ladder to a locked attic room, excavated a key from the recesses of her variegated, filthy skirts, opened the door and disappeared. Ten minutes later she descended, with at least two stone of potatoes and Inca vegetables (I can never remember their names) in a wicker basket on her back. I held out an open bag, meaning her to give me fifteen soles worth. But she took the coins – looking at them rather bemusedly – signed to me to help myself and vanished into the house. Quite likely she had no idea of the value of fifteen soles. I took about a kilo of potatoes and vegetables and departed, being watched from behind a corner by the small boy.

These Inca roots have so many protuberances they can look like men, or birds, or beasts – or even red armadilloes with overlapping scales. We decided on miniature potatoes for this evening and I took them off to the stream to scrub them with Juana's dandy-brush. Because of their size and the concrete quality of their adhering earth, this proved a lengthy process. But sitting beside a waterfall, surrounded by tall shrubs with dainty pink flowers, I found this domestic chore quite congenial. And Rachel appreciated the result. Noodles are fine, but they're not characterful the way Murphys are.

As the sun set the temperature dropped melodramatically and I hustled Rachel – sneezing and coughing – into the tent. Then, for a little time, I sat on a rock, alone with a skyscape of pale delicate clouds interwoven with dark fearsome peaks. And, despite my worry about Juana, I felt a deep content.

Huari. 8 October

This morning Juana's limp seemed better but Rachel's cold was worse and threatening to go to her chest. So we decided to push on to Huari, where Juana could have medical attention and lots of Alf while Rachel rested in a hotel with three hot meals a day.

Soon it became apparent that Juana wasn't *really* better; she couldn't achieve more than an exhausting (for me) 2 mph. As every trekker knows, it is extraordinarily tiring to have to walk below one's natural speed (in my case 3½ mph at this altitude).

Huari stands on a 9,500 foot ledge half-way up a mountain semi-encircled by a river gorge. This being fiesta-time throughout the sierra, Huari too is making whoopee and, as we approached the pueblo, I was affectionately embraced by several reeling campesinos who mistook me for a gringo hombre. One of these men was being led by a Shetland-sized ginger pony with a coat of tight, negroid-type curls; Juana at once fell in love with this adorable creature and wanted to follow him. It had been a showery morning and we entered Huari to an 1812-ish fanfare of thunder and fireworks; luckily Juana is untroubled by both noises.

This is a squalid town. Its rough narrow streets, some 'quake-fissured down the centre, are strewn with litter and half-blocked by heaps of household refuse seething with flies and maggots. What was once an elegant main Plaza has been disfigured by a partially built ediface of singular hideousness, to replace an old 'quake demolished church. In all the Plazas, tall beribboned poles are aflutter with tawdry bunting; and decorated shrines glitter in every corner; and hundreds of colourfully-clad campesinos are dancing and drinking to the music of portable harps and pipes and drums.

My dream of Huari as a problem-solving pueblo has not so far come true. There is no veterinario and the Alf supply is poor because there are so many campesino ponies in town for the fiesta. Also, Juana has to share a corral with five obsessionally greedy pigs who, left to themselves, would gobble her supper within moments. So this evening I had to sit with her for two hours, reading Pedro de Cieza de León by torchlight and aiming frequent kicks at porcine marauders.

The same. 9 October

Our flea-infested Hotel del Sol is another brash, anomalous post-'quake building, tinged with plastic – one feels chrome and strip-lighting may happen any day now. It has delusions of grandeur and is comparatively expensive: 180 soles for a cramped and filthy single room with a glazed window that won't open. True, we haven't washed for a month (apart from that effort in Conchucos) and our clothes are stinking; but *other people's* filth is something else again . . . Today Rachel is so flea-bitten she looks like an acute measles case and I'm not much better. The waiters are welcoming and well-meaning but the food is repulsive. For supper last night we had luke-warm God-knows-what soup and half-cooked spaghetti with (in Rachel's opinion) minced motor-tyres. In despair I went out and bought a bottle of *vino* (good: rosé) for 300 soles. Today we ate among friendly campesinos in the covered market – a run-down Mercado, designed for more prosperity than Huari now enjoys. We each had five delicious meals (our camel trick again) for the price of one in the hotel. At almost every stall we passed, someone insisted on my sharing their gourd of fiesta chicha. I must by now have accumulated a representative selection of campesino bacteria; but for Rachel, there would be little point in 'pilling' our drinking-water.

Before dawn – I was out early to secure an adequate Alf-supply – the streets were littered with comatose revellers; and an hour later the beer-shops were doing a brisk trade in hairs-of-the-dog. Here we've seen many more men unconscious-drunk, sick-drunk and fighting-drunk than in Pomabamba. And many more Indians at the end of the poverty-tether, sitting slumped in corners – ragged, dirty, dull-eyed, chewing wads of coca and looking as though they might never stand up again.

During the fiesta, stall-holders not native to Huari sleep on the ground beside their merchandise, wrapped in ponchos, and before sunrise are displaying their wares. These include cheap shoes and· clothes and plastic kitchen-goods; locks and tools and brightly dyed blankets; exotic fruits from the selva and even more exotic witch-doctors' medicines – bark-strips, seeds, shells, stones, herbs, llamas' foetuses, snake and alligator skins, puma pelts, preserved toucans and other colourful jungle birds, tortoise-shells, armadillo carcasses and various unidentifiable pelts and heads and paws and tails. Rachel was particularly fascinated by books entitled: *Red Magic*, *White Magic*, *Green Magic* and *Black Magic*. Had they been in English she would certainly have bought the lot. Other pamphlets and slim vols, poorly printed on bad paper, dealt with various quasi-magical remedies both for physical disease and family problems.

Alf was elusive this afternoon. But at last a kind old Indian lady

sitting outside her house took pity on me and ordered her grand-
daughter to cut me fifty soles worth. Then I had trouble getting
into the corral. But eventually Pedro arrived, an eleven-year-old
who is the middle child in a family of fifteen and who entertained
me this morning while I was guarding Juana's breakfast. He looks,
as do his siblings, wizened with hunger. To admit me, he climbed
onto the twelve foot high corral wall, walked its length, jumped
down at the door and rolled back the stone that had been holding
it shut. A manoeuvre surely not beyond even an amateur thief
during hours of darkness . . .

Pedro's fifteen-year-old sister soon joined us. Teresa hopes to go
to Lima University – a hope unlikely to be fulfilled. She is an
attractive-looking girl (or could be if properly fed), but one is
rarely impressed by the Indians' IQ. Seventy years ago, the
Bolivian Franz Tamayo – son of a pure Spanish hidalgo father and
a pure Indian Aymara mother – wrote a passionate defence of the
Andean Indians. (He was their first modern champion). But even
Tamayo had to admit that 'historically the Indian must be judged
a small intelligence and a powerful will'. Many people blame
coca-chewing for Indian stupidity, apathy and ultra-conserva-
tism. (Already Teresa is chewing.) Others argue that only coca
enables the campesinos to survive hard physical labour at high
altitudes. Harold Osborne argued that 'the Indian has consumed
coca and chicha since the race was at the height of its glory and
they cannot reasonably be supposed to have effects so different
now from then'. But he was writing in 1951 and recent research
has shown that in Inca times coca was cultivated only in small
quantities, and for the exclusive use of Inca nobles, priests,
curacas and – exceptionally – long-distance messengers who had to
run up the sort of precipices we *crawl* up. This undemocratic ban on
general coca-chewing was probably wise, given its effect on the
unself-restrained peasantry. Some doubt if the ban worked, but
remembering the Incas' successful imposition of discipline at
other levels there's no reason to suppose they failed here. True, an
Inca noble, Huamán Poma, wrote towards the end of the 16th
century: 'Our rulers were undoubtedly responsible for the widespread custom of chewing coca. This was supposed to be nourishing, but in my view it is a bad habit, comparable with the Spanish
one of taking tobacco, and leads to craving and addiction'. By
then, however, there was a powerful Spanish pro-coca lobby –
racketeers who tried to influence the anti-coca Government

authorities by arguing that this addiction was an immemorial vice which colonial legislation could not hope to eradicate. Probably Poma believed this propaganda. The settlers' motives for encouraging coca addiction have been crisply outlined by John Hemming: 'With the fall of the Inca empire anyone could buy the leaves, and the habit swept the native population of Peru . . . Coca plantations lay at the edge of the humid forests, thousands of feet below the natural habitat of the Andean Indians. This did not deter Spanish planters and merchants who made huge profits from the coca trade. They forced highland natives to leave their encomiendas and work in the hot plantations . . . Contemporary authorities estimated that between a third and half of the annual quota of coca-workers died as a result of their five-month service . . . King Philip said in a royal decree that coca was 'an illusion of the devil' in whose cultivation 'an infinite number of Indians perish because of the heat and disease where it grows'. But the coca trade was too lucrative . . . Some coca plantations were yielding 80,000 pesos a year, and Acosta reckoned that the annual coca traffic to Potosí was worth a half a million pesos. Its protagonists defended the trade because it produced the only commodity that was highly prized by the natives. They argued that coca alone could inspire Indians to work for reward and to participate in a monetary economy'.

Coca may have been cultivated for use in the sierra as early as c.2000 BC, or so some people deduce from analyses of human faeces made recently by the Ayacucho Archaeological-Botanical Project. It was certainly in use centuries before the Incas took over in the 1470s. In the 2,000 year-old tombs and burial grounds of Peru's coastal civilisations, coca leaves have been found in small pouches tied to mummies – woven bags almost identical to those from which we have seen the Indians taking their next wad. The Incas allowed women to squat in front of the sacred bush and strip the lance-head-shaped leaves which grow in pairs along jade-green twigs. But the Indians further north, in what is now Colombia, were superstitious about the baneful effects of menstruation and only men were allowed to harvest coca. (The Incas also employed *only* the natives of the low-lying valleys to work on the plantations.) To this day coca is regarded as a sacred plant and is used in ceremonies that by no stretch of theological ingenuity could be given a Christian veneer. If you want to placate a supernatural power, of any grade, the most effective offering is a lump of llama fat mixed with coca and burnt at midnight inside a circle of dried llama dung – the ashes to be scattered, while still hot, on the surface of a stream. Coca also has many genuinely valuable medicinal uses, which were familiar to the Indians long before 19th-century European doctors discovered its anaesthetising properties.

Several friends have requested postcards describing the effects on me of coca as used by the Indians. But although one can buy coca here in any licensed merchant's shop, as one buys tobacco at home, I dare not risk another shackle – in addition to nicotine and alcohol.

Camp on Scrubland in Gorge. 10 October

When we heard that in Chavín there are two veterinarias and inexhaustible fields of Alf it seemed advisable to continue this morning, as Juana's limp was better (though by no means cured) and Huari's Alf supply is poor.

At noon we stopped for chicha outside a shack with a sheaf of dried wheat over the door – the local sign. Soon after, two valleys converged and our track followed a river; wide, fast, muddy-grey, its course marked by low trees. As we went upstream, flocks of raucous parakeets – the first we've seen – made emerald streaks against a cloudless blue sky. This was a hot, arid, uninhabited valley with pale grey precipices rising from the river. Looking back, our world seemed to be dominated by a mighty triangular rock-summit and, right up to the base of the triangle, someone had cultivated – on unbelievable slopes – several tiny, brilliant patches of barley. In the Andes Nature never repeats herself. Every turn of a path or valley reveals some original design exceeding the most outré imaginings of the most eccentric architect. When we were again facing the snows of the Cordillera Blanca we turned south, to follow the Rio Puccha to Chavín. On our left rose a sheer rock-wall: thousands of feet high, miles long, flat-topped, flawlessly smooth – one of the most spectacular geological phenomena I've ever seen.

We passed two shamlets, each with a small closed shop. An old man with a ghastly abscess on his cheek – the only person we met all afternoon – told us these had been closed for the past year. Towards sunset a solid tree-trunk bridge took us into this gaunt, river-noisy gorge where we began to worry about the total absence of either Juana-food or tent space. But soon we'd found this stony site, stocked with a brand of bushes which Juana eats when desperate. It was difficult to get the pegs in and as I struggled with them a sudden violent wind raged up the gorge and almost swept the tent away.

Chavín de Huantar. 11 October

An uneasy night for me, though Rachel slept throughout her own coughing. The tent was intolerably hot yet couldn't be unzipped because of mosquitoes. Juana repeatedly wound her rope around bushes and had to be disentangled four times. (The ground was too hard for the picket.) I was very worried about her injury. The heat was aggravating my multitudinous flea-bites. And – most unsettling of all – two bus-trucks passed, covering the camp with fine dust. Their unfamiliar roaring and rattling, re-echoing throughout the gorge for twenty minutes, seemed a monstrous desecration. Huari is at the end of a new dry-weather road that passes through Chavín.

We were off at 6.50, walking with a small boy and a large dog who had attached themselves to us as we were striking camp. When we came to an Alf field high above the road the boy requisitioned five kilos from his grandfather, who was cutting an armful for the family cow. Here the gorge had broadened and a few dwellings were visible. While Juana breakfasted we sat on a boulder showing Juan our maps, which he seemed to regard as some form of gringo magic.

Last evening, as we supped, a worried young man cantered down-stream with his small son on his pommel, clutching the pony's mane. He asked if we had noticed a straying donkey mare and foal; an hour later I was sad to see him returning by moonlight without them. Now he reappeared, on foot, and suggested that Juana should finish her Alf in his corral, while we breakfasted with his family. Javier is slim and dark-skinned, with strange green eyes, quick supple movements and a diffident smile. He worked for an American company in Lima until it withdrew from Peru ten months ago. Repeatedly we find that the most out-going campesinos are 'Lima-returned'.

The corral doorway, in a long, high mud wall, was just wide enough to take Juana's load. Inside, Javier's Lima-born wife, Maria – poised, friendly, good-looking – sat on a boulder in a

corner of the yard frying potatoes over a picnic-style wood-fire.
Javier's mother, younger sister and two older brothers were killed
in the 1970 'quake on their way back from market. His father –
squatting in a patch of early sunshine, aimlessly knotting and
unknotting a leather thong – ignored us. He hasn't smiled since
the 'quake, said Javier. In the inner corral the surviving brother,
who is slightly retarded, was struggling to milk an abnormally
large Friesan-type cow – all the time restless and kicking. Her
bawling nine-month-old calf was tied nearby and is still allowed to
suck twice a day in the belief that this stimulates the milk-flow.
Eventually Javier had to hold the bucket for his brother. Diagonally across the yard from the fire was a 'bee-hive' mud bread-oven,
similar to those we saw in Mexico. The hens lay beneath this, in a
space accessible only to children; Rachel found one egg. The yard
swarmed with life: hens, ducks, turkeys, several furry pigs, three
friendly dogs, a cat and four minute kittens, a dozen chirping
guinea-pigs. For breakfast we each had a small plate of fried
potatoes topped with a fried egg and followed by a cup of new milk,
boiled and heavily sugared. As we ate, Maria told me that her
parents had migrated to the coast from the nearby village of San
Marcos, where many of her relatives still live. She misses some of
the conveniences of city life but for the children's sake is glad to
have moved to the ancestral sierra, where at least a bare suf-
ficiency of food is available to farmers as 'prosperous' as Javier.
She fed the year-old with his egg: Javier, a doting father, fed the
two-and-a-half-year-old. Father and brother did not join us in the
tiny, neat dining-room, sparsely furnished but decorated with
tourist posters of Lima and Arequipa.

Javier emphasised what a splendidly rich and privileged
country Peru is – or could be, if well governed. An intelligent
young man, he has been grievously disillusioned by listening to
daily Lima gossip about government mismanagement and corruption. He informed us that ninety nine per cent of Peru's wealth
is owned by one per cent of the population: an exaggeration
horribly near the truth. I asked if he had ever considered joining a
political movement to help clean up the scene. He shrugged.
"There is no place in politics for an honest man. I was sad when
my job went because I would have got on and made nice money for
my children" – he kissed his elder son's head. "But maybe it is
better for them to grow up in the sierra where people are honest. It
is another world here. No one will trick you. And like Maria said,

we have just enough food if we have no big drought. And we will try to have no more children, so these two can have what there is. But here it is not easy to get medicines for that."

Today poor Juana is so crippled that the eight easy miles to Chavín took us four and a half hours. We stopped for a bowl of chicha in the little pueblo of San Marcos, also at present celebrating its fiesta with bunting and masked bands everywhere and dozens of drunks lying around at 11 a.m. Sitting imbibing on a doorstep, we attracted a group of friendly schoolgirls who had the usual heated argument about whether I'm a man or a woman. (The sartorial evidence and my deep voice both support the former theory.) Leaving the town, we saw one particularly gruesome fight. A pisco-maddened young man – we could smell the fumes – had badly beaten up his elderly opponent whose lower lip was split open to the chin-bone and pouring blood. As we passed, the older man's legs buckled and he sank into the ditch. Whereupon the young victor laughed and swaggered away, wiping his bloody fists on his trousers. A moment later a terrified campesino woman – wife of the vanquished – emerged from behind a dry stone wall and tried to stop the flow of blood. When we approached, intending to offer some disinfectant, she made it plain that she wished for no gringo interference.

From San Marcos, the white, dusty, stony track climbs gradually through a broad, rugged valley. Never have I felt so unhappy about an animal and so impatient to arrive at a destination. My eyes searched the broken terrain ahead, but it's never possible to guess where these Andean pueblos may be or how far away they are when first one glimpses them.

Then suddenly we were overlooking Chavín, tucked away at the base of a massive mountain, its red roofs straggling for a mile or so between river and cliffs, its Plaza green and well-kept – and many fields of Alf visible around the edges. This is an important archaeological site and the tourist authorities are trying to 'develop' the town, with little success to date as there is no reliable approach road. A steady trickle of gringoes arrives from Huaras by truck-bus during the dry season, but the majority are enterprising young back-packers rather than conventional tourists.

As we were coaxing Juana along a narrow street of two-storeyed adobe dwellings a pisco-drunk young man molested me, grabbing the leading-rope and demanding plata. I was feeling so on edge about Juana that I over-reacted and punched him unnecessarily, but he wouldn't release the rope and we were in danger of doing real mischief to each other when a prosperous-looking gentleman on a Honda intervened with threatening shouts. The many campesino witnesses had of course been assiduously ignoring the fracas.

A young policeman helped us to find the veterinario, to whom we both took an instant dislike. After a superficial examination this burly mestizo chancer said Juana needs only a few days rest and shoeing, which is nonsense; some serious damage has by now been done. Tomorrow morning we'll consult the second veterinario, who is 'out of town' today.

At 3.30 we had 'lupper' in the Comidor Chavín, an eating-house run by the local Co-op at one end of the Plaza. We sat where we could watch Juana grazing on a small patch of juicy grass behind the church, an ugly, oblong, grey building rather like a warehouse. This Comidor is bright, spacious, newish, cleanish and friendly. While we ate plates of delicious rice, fried with tomatoes, onions and chopped goat-meat, the young manageress brushed her teeth vigorously at a small hand-basin by the well-stocked bar and told us we would be comfortable in the Hotel Inca on the opposite side of the Plaza.

She was right. This is a delightful doss-house, with no pretensions to being anything else; our windowless, mud-floored room would probably be outlawed as a stable by EEC regulations. It is one of a row leading directly off a wide yard inhabited by the usual selection of animals, plus three litters of enchanting baby rabbits. And it has *two* beds. Admittedly, only one is supplied with a mattress, the other consisting of bare, rusty springs. On the far side of the yard, beside the al fresco dining area, there is a WC. But as it's permanently without W this cannot be reckoned a mod. con. And Rachel is not impressed by the overflowing container behind the door in which used lavatory paper must be deposited. "I think we'll go out to the mountain", she said rather faintly. Water for all household purposes comes from a deep well beside our room. There is a tiny outside hand-basin with a tap, but again that tap merely portends a more technological future.

So far all our Chavín contacts have been most sympathetic about poor Juana. (Except the one who counts – the veterinario.) She is now safely corralled on a patch of lush grass behind a little building in which the town's electricity is (or not, as the case may be) generated. The two men in charge of this delicate operation have advised us to soak her feet in *aguarras* (turps) twice a day. And one of them left his post to show us a minute shop down a side-street where we could buy this medicament.

Chavín is at 9,500 feet, with a perfect climate and hot sulphur springs nearby, in grottoes by the river, where we can wash ourselves and our clothes every day. We can think of nowhere more congenial for a rest-halt of indefinite length.

Interlude

We spent fifteen days in Chavín – nutritious and happy days, despite our Juana-worry. The second veterinario was an Indian campesino mellifluously named Felesforo Cadillo Sigueñas – Foro to his friends. He cheerfully admitted that he has no veterinario's certificate but claimed to know more about equine ailments than his rival. He certainly seemed to us both more expert and more caring. At once he confirmed that the patient's *legs* were sound, as we had hoped and believed, yet despite daily examinations he was unable to diagnose the trouble until 16 October. He then detected a foot abscess and hastened off to borrow a butcher's saw. I held Juana while he sawed halfway through her hoof, an operation which took seventeen long minutes. Foro worked very gently, his broad bronze face wrinkled with sympathy, all the time making soothing Quechua noises. He remarked on how strangely docile Juana was and we agreed that animals always know when they are being 'hurt to help'. But towards the end, as the pain worsened, she reared a few times, pawing the air. By then however I was feeling so relieved on her behalf that I wouldn't have cared had she trampled on me. We squeezed out more than a pint of vile pus, then came water and blood. She might have died but for Foro, since all this poison was lethally contained by the hoof. At home she would immediately have received a series of high-powered anti-biotic injections; here she was given only a perfunctory wipe with a dirty damp cloth and a lot of extra love.

Next morning the patient looked happier than she had done for a fortnight. Our spirits soared: crisis over. From then on we put her out to graze every day in a level five-acre Alf field just above the river bank; this field belonged to the hotel-owner and had recently been cut, but there was more than enough short Alf left to keep Juana happy.

By 19 October there was no trace of a limp, to our astonishment. But Foro wasn't surprised – "She is young and healthy and with the badness gone there is only a small wound to heal". Rachel said afterwards, "*Small wound* indeed! When her foot was nearly cut off!"

On 20 October Rachel rode Juana at a walk from the hotel to her pasture beyond the Plaza – and back again in the evening. As she never once stumbled, or seemed in any discomfort, Foro suggested a longer test next day. So Rachel took her for a bareback two-mile trot along the wide grass verge of the road to San Marcos. She moved beautifully and seemed actually to enjoy her outing. Rachel is sure that she missed us when left alone all day in her big field – which may be true. Mules are half donkeys and sociable in proportion. Foro then announced that she should be ready for shoeing on the 25th and 150 soles bought us a set of shoes from our hotel proprietor; hot shoeing is unknown here.

6

Plateaux, Precipices, and Pueblos on the Puna

Chavín de Huantar. 25 October

By noon a kindly crowd, anxious to provide advice and moral support, had gathered outside Foro's herreria (blacksmith's shop). The neighbouring baker, by now an old friend of ours, helped me to hold Juana's head. Foro and his amigo the cloth-merchant – Sinchi, who had closed shop for the occasion – held her legs. During hind feet shoeing, the relevant leg was tied to a rope that had already been firmly knotted to her tail: an ingenious kick-inhibiting device. She behaved well on the whole, considering how bewildering and alarming this experience must have been. Once she seriously attempted to kick out all round and escape, but when I fiercely berated her she immediately went quiet. The spectators were much amused to find that she has learned English. (Did they but know it, most of the words employed were pure Anglo-Saxon.) We were concerned to see her wincing as the nails entered the injured hoof but Foro thought this of no significance. That foot is naturally more sensitive than the others and will remain so for some time. His task completed, he fetched a small bowl of chicha and with the fingers of his right hand sprinkled Juana thoroughly – a ch'ura, to call upon her the blessing of Pachamama (Mother Earth, who is everybody's and everything's mother).

We are rejoicing to see our mula again looking so bonito; today she was described by an onlooker as 'el más bonito' – the pretti*est* mule he'd ever seen. She has regained most of her lost weight and shines like a chestnut after Rachel's twice-daily grooming. But of course she looked puzzled and miserable as she walked gingerly away from the herreria in her first set of shoes, not sure *why* the ground suddenly felt so odd . . .

The shoeing team then celebrated its notable achievement in the cloth-shop; Sinchi also sells cerveza. He climbed a tremulous ladder and handed the dust-laden bottles down from a high shelf above the bales. "Now people have no money for beer", commented Foro. "*Or* for cloth", added Sinchi sombrely. We sat on low wooden stools and shared a glass, as is the custom. I, being the hostess, filled it and handed it to Foro, the guest of honour, who poured several drops onto the floor – because Pachamama has to be served first – then quickly emptied the glass, shook out the froth and returned it to me to be refilled for my other guests. They also gave Pachamama her t'inka offering before drinking, as did I when my turn came. Nobody would accept a second glass. Outside fiesta time, the average hard-working campesino drinks only moderately, if at all. In our fortnight here we've seen no more than three drunks and all were notorious local cases, the chicha equivalent of winos.

We're looking forward to being back on the trail tomorrow, yet hating the thought of leaving Chavín where we've been made to feel like honorary citizens. Today many people hurried towards us to say "Adios!" and urge us to return soon – I wish we could! Rachel looks quite melancholy this evening; she is going to miss the many contemporary friends with whom she played football and hide-and-seek while I went on short treks through the nearby mountains. Apart from the other benefits of our stay here, it's done us both good to be away from mother/daughter for several hours each day.

Camp on wet Ledge of High Mountain. 26 October

Juana stepped out smartly today, already adjusted to her new footwear, and I was ecstatic in a perfectly-fitting pair of second-hand Peruvian army boots.

The path to La Unión presumably runs slightly south of east across this 14,000 foot Cerro de Vincos puna. I say 'presumably' because the map shows no path of any kind. However, we know by now that it tends not to be explicit in these areas and many of our Chavín friends assured us that a little-used trail does exist.

At the head of the Chavín valley we turned east into a ravine where curiously gnarled trees grew on cliff-faces between a variety of shrubs laden with blue, yellow or pink blossoms. Here we had the rare good fortune to see, right beside the path, a magnificent twenty-foot *Puya raimondi* in full bloom. This spectacular plant, found only in a few areas of Peru and Bolivia and now protected, is the tallest flower spike in the world and reputedly lives for a century, flowering but once before it dies. We paused, wonderingly, to examine it. The lower half resembles a giant green porcupine in a temper, and from amidst the yard-long, rapier-sharp leaves rises a thick ten-foot stalk covered with thousands and thousands of dainty yellow flowers – looking rather as though they had been stuck on, like Christmas decorations. According to the Bradts: 'This is the oldest genus of the Bromeliad family, a huge group containing over 1,600 species. Pineapples and Spanish moss are both Bromeliaceae . . . An estimated 8,000 blossoms grow on one stalk and attract the hummingbirds which probably play an important part in the plant's pollination. Other birds nest among the spiky leaves and some stab themselves to death on their doorstep'.

Higher still, on the edge of the puna, we saw several *rima-rima* plants with large bushy leaves and fragile bright red flowers – not unlike dog-roses, but bigger.

The sun shone warm this morning but by noon dark clouds were crouching coldly on the mountains above as we traversed a massive rock-wall with a sheer drop into a tree-filled canyon. Already this tricky path had been causing us some apprehension, because of our new-shod Juana, and when the rain started I found my fists clenching with tension. On the more or less level puna the path soon became a mud-rink and we all found it hard to remain upright. Here for the first time Juana slipped, completely lost control, went over on her side and for a moment lay floundering. As we helped her to her feet Rachel stated the obvious: "Lucky this didn't happen on the way up!"

By 2.30 it was snowing – not heavily, but enough to give the puna a new stern beauty as those vast bleak widths glimmered strangely beneath a pewter sky. It was intensely cold and soon the snow had turned to sleet-cum-hail-cum-rain. We marched on miserably, unable to see far, while the wind whined steadily through the stiff ichu grass. Everywhere the ground was impossibly water-logged – and anyway it would have been lunatic to unpack (unless forced to by darkness) in such dire weather. I hoped desperately that we might come upon a tambo shack, but humanity has made no mark on these desolate heights. Then at last our path rose still higher, taking us onto the shoulder of a cloud-wrapped mountain where we found a wide ledge, with abundant grazing. As the light faded the sleet eased off and the

wind dropped; so by working as quickly as numbed fingers permitted, and using unwonted ingenuity, we contrived to keep our
night-gear dry. We then huddled close in the tent, thawing each
other while eating an unhelpful supper of bread buns, frankfurters
that had frozen in their tin and water that was already iced. "I
think if we ever come back to the Andes we should bring a stove",
said Rachel.

Casa on Puna. 27 October

What an awakening! There is always some lavish compensation
for the incidental inconveniences of Andean travel. The temperature rose during the night and when I crawled out of the tent at
5.45 the clouds were dispersing. Turning towards Juana I saw,
seemingly on our own level, the southernmost peaks and ridges of
the Cordillera Blanca – mighty silver phantoms, floating in
an ocean of darkness. Pumpuyac, Quilcayhuanca, Barcapalca,
Jangya-Cocha . . . They sound as mysterious as they looked this
morning, in that pale pre-dawn light – their bases invisible, the
muted radiance of their summits a vision to be remembered
forever.

We moved off at 7.30, in brilliant sunshine. Across a narrow
boggy valley our path could be seen climbing again, to run level for
a few miles along the flank of a flat-topped ridge. Beyond that we
were overlooking a broad green valley, very far below, with a
solitary stone hovel on its level floor.

Around the next corner, we began a gradual descent into an
extension of this leg-of-a-dog valley. Half-a-dozen thatched cabins
were scattered towards the far end, which seemed to be completely
enclosed by an impenetrable semi-circle of fierce rock-peaks. We
could see no path going in any direction, apart from trails con-
necting the dwellings. But doubtless the inhabitants – from here
like crawling insects on a billiard table – would tell us of any
possible exit.

Not so, however. A young Indian woman in a flame-red skirt –
milking a cow near one of the hovels – stared at us, wide-eyed and
speechless, with evident fear. ("No wonder!" said Rachel. "Up
here we must seem like something off Mars!") Two men took
refuge in their corrals when we turned towards them and as we
don't know a syllable of Quechua we couldn't make reassuring
noises. So we wandered hesitantly on, soon coming to a swift

stream, no more than a foot deep, which inexplicably brought out the worst in Juana. It took us fifteen minutes to persuade her to cross and she continued in a foul mood for the rest of the day.

Now the rock peaks were close, beyond expanses of ichu grass interspersed with treacherous marshy patches and stretches of odd pseudo-bog. This weird phenomenon is peculiar to the high puna; it has a lethal appearance but is safe to walk on though it sounds hollow underfoot (very disconcerting!) and is criss-crossed by icy rivulets. It looks like a discreetly patterned carpet, being almost completely covered by tiny round green stemless plants, of a fascinating design.

Where the ground began to rise towards the rock barrier we met a many-skirted spinning woman wearing a bowler hat and driving a few score sheep out to pasture. Mercifully she proved less fearful than her neighbours; though she didn't actually stop to address us, and spoke only Quechua, she clearly conveyed that we were on the wrong path. I rather desperately repeated "La Unión?" – shouting after her, as she hastened away from us. She paused, half-turned and pointed to a black mass of serrated rock, towering against a royal blue sky on the far side of the valley. "I don't believe it!" said Rachel. "Unless there's some path going *around* instead of over?"

We climbed diagonally to the crest of a steep ridge that here ran across the valley like a gigantic embankment – and then we were transfixed. Below us lay a 'secret' lake, some four miles by two, so closely in the embrace of its surrounding crags – streaked silver and charcoal grey – that even from this morning's highest point it had remained invisible. The unexpectedness of this still splendour, wondrously combining different shades of green – jade green, bottle-green, emerald green, lime green – gave me a momentary dreamlike feeling. I stood motionless and bemused, as though this beautiful illusion must fade before I could move. Why do these remote, high lakes so powerfully affect one? Apart from their visual beauty, they have an extraordinary aura which is quite overwhelming.

"*Now* I can see a track!" said Rachel, indicating a faint path winding around the shore and disappearing at the base of that ferocious jumble of rock-peaks. At noon we came to a few clumps of ichu grass and stopped for snacks all round. Then the sky abruptly clouded over, increasing the drama of the lake's colouring. As we continued the clouds let go and that rain contained slender splinters of ice, instead of hail-stones.

From the base of the pass we could see, far below on the wide shore, an extraordinary geological phenomenon: a dozen oblong grey-brown boulders, of identical size and shape, sprawled like stranded whales magnified ten times.

Looking upwards, we felt renewed scepticism. Even by the standards to which we have become accustomed, it seemed absurd to expect any path to cross that wall. We paused to adjust the load and Rachel said: "This is like something out of a horror film". I could see what she meant, though in a mad masochistic way I was still enjoying the incomparable splendour all around us. But now it was a merciless and menacing splendour. The lake – so still when first we saw it – had been roused from its silken slumber and was half-obscured by speeding sheets of sleet, moving across the white-flecked surface as though someone were hastily drawing an endless succession of curtains. And through the eerie noon twilight jagged peaks loomed sinister, like the turrets of some Bad Fairy's palace.

It was unfortunate that our toughest rock-climb came so soon after Juana's first shoeing. There was no one obvious path up; it seems that the few who use this pass have varying views about the least suicidal route. Juana became more and more bolshie as the path did likewise. But no: that's unfair. Sometimes she was right, prudently to refuse stretches of smooth rock that were feasible for me but formed, in her estimation, a death-trap. Three times we were forced to descend hundreds of feet and start again in our quest for a mulish way over a particularly difficult bit. These alternative routes were atrociously dangerous in my view: of iced mud and preternaturally steep. But Juana much preferred them to the rock-slabs. Meanwhile Rachel had sensibly abandoned us and was finding her own way up by a route that from my distance looked more suited to an ibex than a biped. It certainly wouldn't have done for a mule – or an ageing Mamma.

When we reached the 16,000 foot pass my heart was hammering, my leg-muscles were throbbing and my lungs felt sore. Here the wind was like an icicle-tipped scourge and the sleet at once froze on my sodden husky-suit. (I had given up trying to use my space-blanket as a rain-cape, an impractical exercise when one is struggling up a precipice in a gale with a refractory mule.) Rachel was awaiting us, studying a chorten-like cairn that must have been in the making centuries before the Spaniards came. We paid our tribute to the local aukis, aware that we might soon be needing their assistance, and then considered the intimidating scene ahead. We were looking down a long, wide valley – though we couldn't then know how long it was because clouds restricted the view. Like many major Andean valleys, this had something of the Russian doll about it. On the pass, one was so awed by the immensity of the panorama that one couldn't take in the confusing detail of the valley floor, where mini-valleys between mini-mountains contained still smaller hills and hollows. The head of this valley was some 3,000 feet directly below us. Slightly to the left, as we peered down through the gloom, lay a perfectly circular, jet-black lake from which sprang a full-grown river – no puling infant stream, but a fiercely foaming adult torrent that raged away down the valley, disappearing into the mist. (This river is vaguely suggested, but unnamed, on our map.)

From the cairn, our path ran level along the narrow summit with low-seeming cliffs on our right, which in fact constitute the highest peak for many miles around. Then, where the mountainside became *not quite* vertical, we plunged down. This descent seemed interminable. Soon the zigzagging path became a racing stream and we were wading through icy water, slipping repeatedly on large, round stones. Here one had to keep one's eyes on the ground and we almost collided with a superb de Paso carrying a mestizo wearing an incongruous straw sombrero. An Indian was following a little way behind, having some trouble driving six laden donkeys none of whom seemed to feel that their journey was really necessary. When one has become attuned to total desolation, it is startling rather than reassuring suddenly to meet other travellers. We crowded perilously onto a ledge, to allow this improbable cavalcade to pass, and in response to my plea for enlightenment the mestizo curtly informed us that there is no set path down the valley: one simply seeks the most appropriate route for one's own purpose. I would have liked to know what happened next, beyond this valley, but our informant was not disposed to waste time on gringoes who plainly were loco. (Admittedly the weather was not conducive to leisurely chit-chat.) Rachel was scandalised to see a healthy young man riding up such a gradient. "Serve him right if he's thrown over a cliff!" she muttered furiously, with which unchristian sentiment I had to agree.

Our stream/path ended abruptly where the stream became a waterfall cascading down a precipice. We stopped to think. Here our 'pass mountain' merged into the long ridge that formed one side of the valley. It would have been foolish to descend to the valley floor, where we couldn't see what ravines, bogs, cliffs, marshes or impassable torrents might lie around the next corner. By 'walking high' we could more or less retain control of our destiny. So we stumbled miserably on, through dense brown thigh-high ichu grass which proved that – most unusually – no animals are pastured hereabouts.

Then the load slipped – no surprise, after such a descent. We turned our backs to the sleet while re-loading with numb fingers, on a slope so steep that our performance must have looked like a corny circus act. Juana registered her protest against the whole enterprise by moving at the least opportune moments, while I fought to tighten the girth, adjust the crupper, heave the load into place and securely tie the numerous essential knots. Poor Rachel did her best but is too small fully to control an exasperated mule on such a gradient; yet I could not possibly have managed without her assistance.

As we soldiered on the low dark sky, above the high dark mountain-walls, made it seem that we were in some fearful tunnel which would never have a light at the end. This is the sort of experience made tolerable only by 'switching off' one's sensitivity to the physical – cold, wetness, hunger, exhaustion – and letting one's mind go blank. Rachel asked this evening why we felt so tired when the actual distances and altitudes involved were not exceptional: we have often walked for ten hours and ended the day fresh. I can only suppose, in my unscientific way, that the extreme cold, and being wet through, required us to expend an abnormal amount of energy on that internal heat generation necessary for survival.

Gradually the valley floor became more comprehensible and at last we saw a foot-bridge not far below. Mercifully Juana crossed this meekly – I don't think I could have taken another battle – and then we were on a distinct path which continued down the wide, turf-grassy valley floor. Here Rachel mounted and I again wrapped up in my space-blanket. Soon we could see our valley joining another, to form one of those spectacular T-junctions that give aerial photographs of the Andes such a crazed appearance.

This new valley had minute fields on the lower slopes. Eagerly we looked for a casa, having long since decided to crave shelter in the first available shack. But none was visible. Which way to turn?

Here our path was one of many and in the vastness of this landscape the river had vanished. As we hesitated, a faint shout came from high on the mountain to our right, where a figure in a poncho was signalling to us to turn left. Waving our thanks, we struggled on. My numbed feet caused me to trip repeatedly and I had to hang onto Juana for support; she seemed aware that the situation had become pretty desperate and was back on the path of virtue. It was now 5.40 and the wind had dropped. Seen through a veil of pale grey rain-sleet, the slender, pointed rock-peaks towering close on both sides were like the background to some Gothic novel. Where the valley curved we rejoined the river unexpectedly and saw two square hovels not far ahead. Wisps of pungent dung-smoke rose from tiny, circular, igloo-type kitchen huts (half stone, half thatch), standing thirty yards or so from the dwellings. As we approached the first hovel a pack of five large snarling curs flew at us with bared teeth, which not infrequent occurrence doesn't bother us too much. Yet neither does it encourage casual callers and we were proceeding discreetly to the next hovel when the leader of the pack leaped on me and tore the end of my space-blanket. It was that sort of afternoon . . .

A rosy-cheeked small boy, clutching a pet lamb, observed our approach and ran terrified to his mother in the kitchen. She emerged, looking bewildered; a dumpy Indian woman, not much taller than Rachel, she speaks only Quechua. But the situation required no words. It must have been at once apparent that we were *in extremis* and no sort of threat to anybody. She pointed to the dwelling's deep verandah – virtually a three-walled room, thickly carpeted with puna grass – then turned back to her kitchen. Rachel collapsed in a corner, on a heap of cured fleeces, while I tried to unload. I was fumbling ineffectually, in a semi-coma of exhaustion and numbness, when husband arrived – a dark-skinned Inca-type who sought no explanation for this extraordinary invasion of his home but briskly unloaded, put our gear beside us and led Juana away to the corral. "Will she get anything to eat?" worried Rachel, through chattering teeth. I nodded emphatically, too cold to speak. No campesino would leave a mule fodderless at the end of a working day.

Rachel was too far gone to get out of her wet clothes. Somehow I unzipped a Diana-bag and helped her to change. Meanwhile several kids – human and animal, the latter in the arms of the former – had collected to stare. And our host was sitting on sheep-skins in the opposite corner, still saying nothing but looking kind. By now it was dark, intensely cold and steadily sleeting; the edge of the grass carpet merged into a morass of mud. While Rachel held the torch I slowly and painfully stripped to the skin, an astonishingly difficult task when every garment is sodden and one's hands are numb. Rachel – now thawing – had to undo my bootlaces and pull off my boots. At last I stood naked but for my briefs in the searing cold; yet once free of wet clothes I began to feel warmer. (Inhibitions about naked breasts are unnecessary here-abouts: and even if they were necessary I wouldn't have had them this evening.) Wife then called the family to supper and a few moments later husband returned with a heaped plate of boiled potatoes and two plates of watery soup. We fell on the hot food and I was aware of eating like an animal – devouring potatoes in their earthy jackets – yet the last few mouthfuls of soup were cold. I cannot recall ever, anywhere, feeling so frantic a need for food. By half-thawing me the meal made it easier to dress and I had just pulled on my Husky bootees when the family, having finished supper, assembled in the drawing-room, as it were. I wonder why? Although fuel is so scarce here, the kitchen must be warmer than the verandah. Elsewhere one might deduce curiosity, but not among the campesinos. Nobody tried to speak to us, or took any interest in our possessions. Also, why not add an outer stone wall to this verandah, thus making it into a small room? All building materials could be collected nearby. And why don't the family sleep in the inner room instead of in the open air at 12,500 feet (approx.) with blizzards blowing in their faces? Again, why were we not invited into the warm kitchen on arrival? Was there simply no room for us? Or is there some ancient taboo against this?

Although our host and hostess look so young they have seven children, from about twelve to zero, and father now directed the eldest (a pretty, cheerful, high-spirited girl) to bring us a saucepan of boiling water. We each gulped three mugs of coffee, which thawed us completely. I then hung our wet garments beside the few family rags, on sticks protruding from under the thatch, and stacked our gear in the corner. Rachel was much diverted by a pet lamb and pet kid, both spoiled rotten, who went bounding cheekily over everything and everyone until put to bed in the inner room with the three older children, whom we had ousted from the verandah. The room had to be tidied for them by the light of our torch; it contains a loom, stacks of sheep-skins and spun wool, mounds of potatoes and scores of empty Inca Cola bottles. Everybody sleeps on layers of sheep-skins beneath piles of old clothes and tattered blankets. Our host spread new sheep-skins beneath our flea-bags; then, obviously considering these bags absurdly inadequate, he fetched a newly-woven blanket – brown and white and silky soft like thistledown – and spread it over us. As a result, I have written this in an unbelievable glow of heat – unbelievable when one considers that we are lying in the open air in a below-freezing temperature. The human body is a marvellous bit of machinery; a few hours ago I was literally speechless with exhaustion, now I feel *too* lively after all that coffee.

By 7.30 the whole family was abed and the mountain silence broken only by the wailing of the baby, whose eldest sister had held him out in the sleet, bare from the waist down, and made appropriately encouraging noises, before handing him to his mother for the night. All these children are good-looking, bright-eyed, clear-skinned – a healthy brood, apart from a not incomprehensible communal cold in the head. They are naturally well-mannered and despite the trauma of our appearing out of the dusk they overcame their shyness quite quickly and by bedtime were beginning tentatively to befriend us. Before turning in, there was some lively conversation and argument between parents and children and one got the impression of a happy, affectionate family. But what will all these children do when grown up? Can this and the neighbouring valleys support an increasing population? And what are the prospects for illiterate youngsters forced to migrate to the coastal cities?

This has been one of the oddest evenings of my life. Even in the remotest hamlets of the Karakoram or Simien mountains there has been nothing quite like it – never such an absence of attempted verbal communication, combined with a most touching solicitude for our welfare. Probably we are this valley's first gringo trekkers. Yet our host and hostess have made not the slightest effort to solve the mystery that is us.

La Unión. 28 October

In the small hours I awoke and for an instant imagined that I was staying with some sybaritic friend and had forgotten to switch off my electric blanket. One couldn't sleep *indoors* on these sheep-skins. I looked out to see a dazzle of frosty stars in a cloudless sky. I wanted to stay awake to enjoy the blissful warmth but soon I was again asleep, having methodically scratched numerous flea-bites, from ankles to chin. When I woke next, at 5.20, the family was rising in that distinctive grey-blue light of pre-dawn in the high Andes. At once the five older children – all clad in scanty rags – set about their morning chores. The oldest girl, baby brother on back, hurried off with a small wooden pail (recalling a Little Grey Rabbit illustration) to milk two goats. She was followed by the boy who had first seen us, carrying his beloved kid from the inner room to its mother, for breakfast rations. Other children searched for eggs, fetched water from the river, fed the cuys, released a score of sheep from the corral behind the dwelling – and gave Juana a bucket of chopped barley straw. Then father was to be seen on the far side of the river, galloping hard on a sturdy pony towards a cattle corral at the base of the opposite mountain. Meanwhile mother was lighting the breakfast fire, but not wishing to be more of a burden than necessary we quickly dressed and loaded up.

I quailed at the thought of putting on clothes that had frozen solid. "You don't enjoy *all* of travelling, do you?" asked Rachel maliciously, watching me hammering the ice off my jeans before struggling into them. I maintained a dignified silence. Moments after putting on my boots my feet were numb again. But the sky was cloudless – soon we'd have Inti to the rescue.

We were off by 6.30. Our host, just back, would accept no money so I recklessly gave him three tins of sardines, trusting we could replace them in La Unión. (I was wrong.) He showed us a thickly iced pathlet down a steep slope to river-level. I then endured the first of my nine fordings of that river; as my jeans, boots and socks couldn't have been wetter there was no point in removing them. Here the rio was some ten yards wide, thigh-deep, very fast and not warm. Juana, who had gone spare yesterday about a six-inch rivulet, splashed merrily across as though dawn bathes in melted snow were her favourite hobby. As the sun rose above grey crags Rachel glanced back the way we came yesterday and gasped – "*Look!*" I looked, to see 'our' pass, and the peaks around, catching the first horizontal rays on a glittering tiara of new snow. We wouldn't have made it across today.

Briefly we walked through a world all sparkling – the frosted valley floor brilliant as though diamond-strewn, the icicles depending from nearly cliffs coruscating like Waterford chandeliers, the new-crowned peaks ahead flashing like silver beacons. But already the near-equatorial sun was warm and within minutes our feet were sloshing instead of crunching.

We passed one more hovel, where grazing cuys scuttled away from us and a turkey-cock angrily pursued us; Andean turkey-cocks should be listed as Animals Dangerous to Man. Before climbing out of that valley we had to ford the river seven times, for topographical reasons with which I won't detain myself. Then our path rose steeply along a precipitous mountain of bare earth through which jagged rocks protruded at the most awkward corners. Directly below, in a narrow canyon, the river roared and foamed between boulders. Here the load caught on a rock and slipped to the river side, giving me my worst fright of this whole trek; for an instant it seemed Juana *must* go into the canyon. I yelled to Rachel to drop the leading-rope and stand still. Then, talking reassuringly to Juana, I crept onto the slope above her, prepared if necessary to release the load and lose the lot. (My diary I always carry on me; everything else was, in the circumstances, expendable.) But then Juana took charge. Slowly she moved forward, and Rachel sensibly hurried ahead leaving her to work out her own salvation. I slid onto the path – deprived of Juana's support, there was nothing to hold me on that impossible slope – and watched in sickening suspense as the load slipped further beneath her belly. Calmly she continued for another ten or twelve yards, until she reached a lay-by of sorts with just enough room for me beside her. And there she stood still, waiting for the mess to be sorted out.

The fact that our near-disaster was entirely my own fault didn't help during the reaction phase. When loading this morning my hands were too numb for efficiency, and then I stupidly neglected to check the girth before beginning that climb. One can't afford ever to be stupid on these paths. As usual, I took it out on Rachel, who had in fact shown admirable coolness and common-sense.

It was now 9 a.m. and we decided on a drying session before re-loading, lest the sun might soon vanish. By the time everything had been spread out the mountainside looked like an unsavoury second-hand clothes stall. We then sat on the edge of the canyon (indecently exposed) and enjoyed our breakfast of sleet-soaked buns while Inti did his work. Happily this is not a popular thoroughfare; an innocent campesino suddenly coming upon two naked females poised on a cliff-edge amidst a patchwork of steam-

Farmstead on a ledge

ing garments might well have lost his balance and ended up in the rio.

Within an hour everything was dry, except our boots, and soon we were at the foot of this mountain where we had to ford the rio yet again. Not long after, a bewildering sound seemed to come from beneath our feet: a booming, crashing roar. And suddenly we realised that the river had disappeared – just like that. Its gravelly bed was still there, full of gigantic smooth boulders but bone dry. Some recent earthquake chasm (1970?) was doubtless responsible for this conjuring trick.

Now began a classic rock-stairs descent off the puna. All the way that freakish river-bed accompanied us and at intervals we heard the boom of the hidden water. About half-way down the rio reappeared, as abruptly as it had vanished – gushing from beneath the mountain to return to its bed. It then created a series of superb waterfalls, so close to the path that we were spray-drenched and so noisy that conversation became impossible. Where we turned onto the steep flank of a grassy mountain our rio also swung right and calmed down to wind through a broad, placid, fertile valley. These level paths are usually restful, but recent rainstorms had reduced this one to greasy red mud and provoked several mildly hazardous landslips.

In the next valley our rio joined a wider stream (not even suggested on the map). Gazing down at this confluence, we remembered the black lake below the pass and felt vaguely sentimental; one doesn't often accompany a river from birth to death. And nine fordings create a 'special relationship'. Our path descended to the valley floor about half-a-mile upstream from the confluence, but no bridge was visible. "It'll be fun fording *that*!" exclaimed Rachel gleefully. I looked at the swirling brown torrent, some forty yards wide, and had my doubts. There wasn't even an obvious ford and our path faded away on the valley floor. But then, as we were passing the only hovel in sight, barking dogs brought a young man (Quechua only) to the door and he indicated the shallowest stretch. I undressed before wading in, hanging onto the bridle with one hand and testing the way ahead with my palo. "This *is* terrific fun!" enthused Rachel, from the dryness and security of the saddle, when we were half-way across. By then the water was above Juana's belly and coping with the current wasn't easy. "Won't be such fun if we're all swept down to the Amazon", I retorted sourly. But Juana was at her best today and soon we were safely on a pseudo carretera, all grass-grown and traffic-free. This took us through a serpentine valley of green bogland, grey boulders blotched with red-gold lichen, and tall rustling eucalyptus trees grouped around a few red-tiled dwellings. Then we discovered the reason for this carretera's 'pseudoness'. A bridge had collapsed, leaving only four slim tree-trunks in situ with wide spaces between them through which the rio could be seen racing rowdily. Juana sensibly refused to have anything to do with this calamity and we found a ford where the river was very nearly a raging torrent. It was much wider than at the previous ford and only thigh-deep; but the current was so much stronger that I had to fight hard to remain upright and even Juana wavered in her course, possibly because I was hanging on so dependently to her neck.

In the next gorge it seemed that Nature had gone mad. On both sides colossal cliffs exhibited the most bizarre designs – so dramatically sculpted by erosion and ravaged by earthquakes that an outbreak of superlatives is certainly justified here. Except that I can't think which superlatives to apply to that geological fantasia.

Beyond another broken bridge we heard something repellent: the distant grinding and growling of an internal combustion engine. "A *real* motor-road!" diagnosed Rachel. And so it proved. Around the next corner our track joined a rough, stony earth-road and during the rest of the afternoon we were subjected to the noise of *three* trucks. We are now on an off-shoot of the Lima-Pucallpa highway (completed in 1945) which links the Tingo Maria region of the montaña with the Big Wide World. Tingo Maria began as an experimental agricultural station, set up on the Middle Huallaga in 1938 with American help. It has since grown to a colony of some 30,000 settlers of mixed origins and (we're told) few morals. The surrounding montaña produces bananas, sugar cane, tea, coffee, rubber, cocoa – and coca. Tingo Maria's existence, in a region previosly unpopulated and inaccessible, is frequently quoted by Belaúnde and his supporters to justify a policy of more coast-to-jungle roads, despite the unique problems and enormous costs associated with road-building in the Andes.

Our pukkah (relatively) carretera took us into a long cultivated valley where I began to worry about Juana's supper; no Alf or oats could be seen among the maize and potatoes. Nor was there any grazing, so we decided to seek a hotel and fodder in La Unión. By 4.50, when the rain began, we were overlooking this grotty little town where gringoes are *not* warmly welcomed . . .

At the Hotel Dos de Maio a dishevelled, weaselly proprietor watched me unloading Juana in the shelter of the patio eaves and then led us to the corral. Leaving Rachel in our cramped room (no window, no candle, damp sheets), I set off into the twilit downpour in search of fodder. A sly-looking hotel-servant volunteered to accompany me as guide and an hour later we returned with four kilos of green oats purchased from four vendors, none of whom will sell me more in the morning. Rachel remarked that I looked gloomy; I always get uptight when Juana is underfed. From her point of view the puna, where she can graze all night, is far preferable to these cultivated valleys.

Tingo Chico. 29 October

The direct route from La Unión to Huánuco is via Rondos, but a recent major landslide has blocked this track. So today was spent on the road, which adds twenty-five miles to the journey as it switchbacks through a vast tangle of arid mountains. We arrived in the scruffy but friendly hill-top pueblo of Pachas at 11, having covered exactly ten miles. (This carretera flaunts kilometre stones!) Here we unsuccessfully sought fodder and bought a waterproof poncho for Rachel. (Heavy black mackintosh, lined with thick cotton: 2,400 soles. Being an adult garment, this comes to just above her ankles.)

Juana-worry marred today's trek. During the afternoon we stopped for an hour's grazing on a rare roadside patch of grass. Then came a long descent into the hot, dusty profundity of the Marañon gorge; this evening we are at 6,100 feet, our lowest point since leaving the coast. Black clouds were assembling around the nearby desiccated mountains as we crossed this senior tributary of the Amazon (some claim that the Marañon *is* the young Amazon), which here is close to its source, yet wide, deep and swift. A with-it suspension bridge, built in 1956, took our road onto the main Lima-Pucallpa highway – and also onto the 'main street' of this sleazy newish settlement (pop. approx. 400). Once Tingo Chico hoped to become an important river port; now it has an air of irremediable failure and seems to be inhabited chiefly by drunks, prostitutes and thin dogs. However, our anxious eyes had discerned from afar an Alf field on the slope behind the houses. We asked two bedraggled mestizo women – sitting on a doorstep, half-heartedly combatting flies – if/how/where we could buy fodder; but they only stared at us blankly before retreating into their casa and banging the door.

Then a startling figure entered our lives, a slim young woman who against this background looked like a *Vogue* advertisement. She came tripping towards us and said in English, "I'm Katie – I work in Lima Airport as interpreter. You come from New York? Soon it is raining. You stay tonight in my house and tell me about New York!" I broke it gently to her that in fact we come from Lismore, which has more in common with Tingo Chico than with New York. But still she wanted us to stay – and here we are.

When Juana had been corralled and fed, a platoon of children helped us to carry our gear to a huge, windowless warehouse with a concrete floor. Three single beds stood against one end wall, obscured by a ceiling-high muddle of sacks, boxes, bales, crates and old clothes. All was dirt and disorder and squeaking cuys and unfragrant odours. The eldest girl assured us that by bed-time space would have been cleared on the floor for our flea-bags. Then she locked the room and handed me the key, a sad sign that on this highway we are within the ambience of urban 'civilisation'.

I now had but a single thought: cerveza. Hastening to the nearest shebeen, only yards from our apartment, we found that it belongs to Katie's sister, Isabel, the wife of a truck driver and at twenty nine the mother of nine children under twelve. Both sisters were sitting at the counter chain-smoking and intently playing cards with two policemen returning on leave from Tingo Maria. They look alike: small-boned and large-eyed, with elaborately made-up triangular faces framed in crudely-permed raven-black hair. Isabel, however, seems interested only in male customers: it was Katie who laid down her hand of cards for long enough to pour me a beer. She arrived here yesterday to visit her mother, one of two teachers at the local (unequipped) school which has 120 pupils, many of whom walk five hours a day in pursuit of learning.

By now the evening downpour had started but this didn't deter Rachel from joining in an energetic ball-game with Isabel's platoon. Watching her skidding around on the muddy 'highway', it was hard to believe that she had just completed an eighteen-mile walk in enervating heat. (We agreed before leaving Chavín that henceforth Juana will be ridden only in the most dire emergencies.)

Later, Katie and I talked with the policemen, who were posted to Tingo Maria because they speak rudimentary English – supposedly an advantage when dealing with drug traffickers. As Peru's cocaine trade is now worth over $500 million a year (rivalling copper and oil as a dollar-earner), I'm sceptical about the official will to check it. (Several high-ranking army officers, and a few high-ranking ecclesiastics, are widely believed to be among the more professional traffickers.) According to one policeman, an estimated 900,000 of Peru's seventeen million citizens are *directly* involved in this trade. Many coca-growing peasants now bring their crop to Tingo Maria (recently nick-named 'Snow City') and are paid $3.50 a pound for sound leaves, to be refined into pure cocaine which fetches $2,800 an ounce in the US. Apparently the renowned prosperity of Tingo Maria is chiefly based on coca money, rather than on all those other wholesome crops we hear so much about.

Katie invited me to cook supper in their kitchen. This was another windowless cavern, beside the bedroom – and in an even worse state of filthy disorder, with cuy droppings and puppy pools all over the floor, and two rusty bicycles and three rusty bed frames thrown in one corner, and crates of empty bottles stacked between piles of planks, and a large bitch and three pups begging for scraps, and a sleek much-loved coal-black cat sitting regally on the long 'dining-table' amidst antique food stains. By the dim light of a smoking kerosene lamp I added soup-cubes and noodles to a saucepan of Marañon water that already looked like soup. Katie contributed a plate of boiled potatoes and as we ate told us how much she hates Peru. Before getting her present job she worked and lived for six months with a Russian Folk Dance group, based (for some not too obscure reason) in Lima. "Russia is a very civilised country where I would like to live. There *all* are cultured and have enough. In Peru we are not cultured people. Our men have a complex and are ashamed to help their women with babies and housework. I prefer foreign men. In Lima I have a baby who is half Russian. He is much more beautiful than a Peruvian baby. He will be cultured because he is half Russian."

The platoon arrived then – a wretchedly undernourished brood – and Katie cooked for them. To a large saucepan of water she added a quarter kilo of sugar, a tin of condensed milk and a half-kilo bar of cooking chocolate. All but the two youngest had one cup of this concoction, and a hunk of bread, for supper.

Then a mud-encased Lima-Tingo Maria bus arrived: the first

bus we've seen since leaving Cajamarca. During the dry season this 350 mile journey takes eighteen hours; now that the rains have started it often takes a week. Several aggressively drunken passengers pushed their way into the kitchen and demanded food. At which point a grotesque fact dawned on us – this squalid cavern was Tingo Chico's *restaurant* . . . As Katie served the five men (cold potatoes, chilli sauce, bread), we retired to the 'bedroom' and unrolled our flea-bags, having first spread our ponchos and space-blankets on the unswept floor. Rachel was soon asleep, despite much drunken brawling next door and a spate of shrill bickering between children and adults that is still going on as I write.

Stable in Hamlet on Mountain. 30 October

I hadn't been long asleep last evening when someone stood on my head: a novel experience. We each swore, in divers tongues, as Isabel appeared with the smoking lamp – followed by three other jostling men, redolent of pisco and demanding bed-space. When Isabel had shooed them out into the downpour, as though they were so many contrary hens, two of the three beds were occupied by Katie and numerous children, the younger ones whining and snuffling. As I was drifting back to sleep three sober bus passengers entered, shook their wet ponchos over me, climbed fully clothed into the vacant bed and switched on Katie's Russian trannie. Frightful punkish noises then woke the platoon and contrapuntal wailing and sobbing ensued. All of which acted like a lullaby on the newcomers and when they began to snore Katie switched off. Some time later I had a most vivid dream. We were circus lion-tamers, rearing cubs in our Irish home, and the neighbours, who were all Peruvian, were charging us with some unspecified crime in the European Court of Human Rights. I woke (it was 2.15) to find that two large pups had curled up between our flea-bags (a nick-name that daily becomes more apposite) and one of them was making pre-vomiting noises in my ear. I hastily knelt and flung him towards the door with a sort of scrum-half move-ment. He achieved his vomit a moment later – and returned to base, his wagging tail tickling my nose. At 4.10 he repeated the performance. This time Katie woke too and having sympathised with my problem embarked on an animated discussion about the ideal age for marriage. The three passengers then joined in – they hadn't much alternative, poor devils, Katie's bed being less than a foot from their's – and in the uninhibiting darkness the conversation became quite frank. Very frank, in fact. One had the impression all four habitually study American sex-manuals. I was rivetted, being of a generation that only knows two ways of doing it. Travel is *so* educational!

I rose at 5, like everyone else in Tingo Chico, and went with Isabel's eldest to cut Alf. On hearing our approaching voices Juana greeted us cheerfully, as she always does, so we were unprepared for what we saw on entering the corral. Rachel gives a crisp description – 'In the morning when we went to give Juana her breakfast Alfalfa we got an awful shock. There was a nasty cut on her withers. We looked around and saw a sharp piece of flint stickying out of the wall with blood on it. She had bled a lot from the cut and it had dripped down onto her hoof'.

Sick with anxiety, I dashed off to fetch our Crown Wound Powder and a basin of salted water. Juana's continuing to munch contentedly while I washed, dried and sprayed reassured me. Despite the depth of the wound, and the amount of blood lost (there was a pool on the ground), she was obviously not feeling too bothered. But the site of the injury meant that we had to load far back; today it would have been impossible to take her up or down a steep redura. Since this had to happen, the timing was fortunate; we can stay with the carretera until she heals.

This morning the sky was grey as we followed the Marañon upstream through a green, humid, semi-tropical valley. Long stretches of the carretera were impassable to motor-vehicles and almost impassable to us; now we understand why journeys can take a week – vehicles must wait at various points for the mud to dry.

Several times today we walked in convoy. Rachel, being more gregarious than her Ma, prefers these populated areas to the puna wastes – 'Just a little way out of Tingo Chico we were joined by two young women and their donkey. They were a very nice cheerful couple who said that their house had been flooded during the night. The road was very, very muddy in some places. Juana and the donkey were right up to their knees. Sadly, it wasn't long before we parted, our friends going across a bridge the donkey made a fuss about, but they only roared with laughter. At about one, after we had been going up for a little, we came to a shamlet where there were quite a few drunk men who followed us and one sober one. Juana had been going slower and slower so in the end we stopped for about twenty minutes to let her eat. The men stopped too. One of them who had been the drunkest but sobered up a lot offered to swap watches but Mummy refused because his was the better. Then they offered coca. They walked on quite a while longer with us before we got to their house'.

As the road climbed the dusty, pale brown mountains became more barren. We stopped often to ask for Alf, or oats, or even barley or maize straw; but this is another drought area and the locals need every morsel for their own animals. So all day Juana had only two nibbles of tough dry grass which can't have done her much good. We were in quite a fodder panic when we arrived here and, after much persistent enquiring, found 100 soles worth of green oats.

This is a friendly hamlet. Seeing us unsuccessfully searching for a site – all the surrounding slopes are precipitous – our oat-vendor led us to an empty, doorless stable carpeted with barley-straw; and Juana is now safely corralled. As we unpacked, an enthralled crowd gathered around the non-door. Our host's small son brought (unasked) a pot of hot water for our coffee and when I went in search of pan other small boys followed, all polite and helpful. They guided me to the shack of a young woman who bakes at home and whose coarse brown bread is a treat after the insipid white shop buns we've been living on. While I was writing this by flickering-in-the-breeze candlelight, our host arrived to spread an enormous alpaca-wool blanket over our flea-bags; the campesinos have no faith in modern trekking-equipment.

Camp on sloping Ledge on Mountainside. 31 October

Another broken night because of squabbling dogs and merry-making humans; though that shamlet seemed so minute its night-life was hectic.

During the forenoon we said good-bye to the distant Marañon gorge and turned towards the Quichupunta Pass; now that we're on the carretera, things suddenly have names. Gradually climbing, we passed a few primitive hovels with vile tin roofs – in every country an inescapable consequence of motor traffic. (Not that we can reasonably complain about the volume of traffic today; two buses and three trucks in ten hours.) This pass was so easy that we were crossing it for half-an-hour, while the level road rounded the base of a remarkable solitary mountain – conspicuous all morning

– with a circular rock summit extending beyond its grassy support like a stone sombrero. On our left, beyond many minor ranges, a powder-blue line of smooth mountains, their crests apparently beneath us, lay along the northern horizon – more than 100 miles away.

At noon we came on an isolated shack displaying a roughly lettered sign – PAN VENDE. But not today . . . An elderly mestizo, with a week's beard and rheumatism-knotted hands, sat on a wooden crate in a dark empty room. He was drinking a home-made liquor of the poteen family while querulously chiding his son who lounged against the doorpost, chewing coca. In lieu of bread they offered me an Inca Cola bottle of liquor for 30 soles. Then a young woman called them to their lunch from a kitchen-hut some way up the opposite mountain. As there was meagre grazing nearby we sat outside the shack and Rachel sucked glucose tablets while I sampled the liquor, which was less deleterious than might have been expected. A moment later the young woman came bounding towards us with a plate of tiny boiled potatoes of varying colours: purple, white, pink, yellow, greenish, dark red. She was followed by the elderly man, carefully carrying a large enamel mug of delicious, herb-flavoured mutton soup, thickened with noodles – Rachel's treat, to balance my spiritual refreshment. Neither of them would accept payment, nor did they want to engage in conversation.

I am still being disconcerted by campesino aloofness. Although they so often do their duty by the passing travellers, offering what little hospitality they can, one is always aware of being kept at a distance – literally as well as metaphorically. Yet it would be misleading to use the term 'unfriendly'. In the little pueblo of Jacas Chico, which we reached after a few more downhill miles, we were warmly welcomed and a twelve-year-old girl was sent into the depths of a nearby valley to cut five kilos of oats, for which we were charged only 30 soles. Her mother produced hot water for coffee, to accompany the dozen musty-stale buns we found in a bare-shelved grocery.

Jaças Chico is the most impoverished town we've passed through – not counting shamlets. Its long, muddy main street is lined with attractive colonial dwellings and it must once have been prosperous. Now it's falling to bits and the near-impossibility of changing a 500 soles note proves its apartness from the money economy. I had to take my problem to the large but ramshackle home of a wool-merchant on the outskirts of the town. His tight-lipped little wife was deeply suspicious and disappeared with the note for five minutes, during which I could hear her discussing the situation in an inner patio. She then returned, unlocked an ancient, beautifully carved wooden chest in a corner of the living-room, took out an unexpected 'Jacobs Afternoon Tea Selection' biscuit tin and carefully counted out fifty ten soles notes. When I offered her 50 soles, as commission, she frowned angrily and thrust my hand away. Throughout the whole transaction she addressed not one word to me.

While Juana ate we sat on boulders talking with Lucia the oat-cutter and her family and friends. There was the standard debate about our sex; the majority were not convinced when we claimed to be female. Lucia's fourteen-year-old sister has recently had a baby which she nursed while talking to us. She was being much teased by a group of youths about her inability to identify the father, but neither she nor her kindly, chuckling mother was in the least put out by this. Jacas Chico is spectacularly sited on the edge of a plateau, high above the head of a long, narrow, fertile gorge. Lucia took me onto a nearby ledge and pointed down the gorge. "Huánuco!" she said. I stared, and after a moment could pick out a big town on a level plain forty miles away.

A redura reduced the distance to the next village by fourteen kilometres. There we had no alternative but to rejoin the road; on the surrounding slopes not even the campesinos have been able to devise a redura. By this stage I was, as Rachel observed, getting into one of my grazing tizzies. Then at last we saw a grassy site beyond a gorge so deep that its river is invisible though audible. Here Juana has a choice of grass, shrubs and herbs, but we are on a ludicrously sloping ledge with barely enough room for the tent. It's a cloudless evening, after much midday rain, and suffocatingly hot. We've run out of water (my fault) and there are swarms of insatiable winged predators – at least four different species. We've also seen, for the first time in Peru, a few giant bats.

Camp in Field near Huánuco. 1 November

This morning Juana was again dripping blood. We assumed that she must have rolled on her wound, which has been healing fast. But no . . . When I mentioned 'winged predators' last evening

I was being more accurate than I knew; the blood was coming from a vampire-bat bite on her neck. Fortunately an occasional bite doesn't bother equines, unless the bat happens to be carrying rabies.

By 6.15 we were moving through a magical misty silent world of soft silver clouds, filling the gorge below and piled above us on harsh massive peaks – but soon dissolved by an orange sun. This has been a glorious day, despite extreme heat. (For the first time we are below 6,000; Huánuco is at 5,400.) Down here, amidst a colourful riot of jungly trees, shrubs, flowers and creepers, one might be a thousand miles from the puna. All day we were descending a narrow valley beside the Rio Higueras, yet another of the countless sub-tributaries of the Amazon – via the great Rio Huallaga, which the Higueras joins at Huánuco.

At 9 a.m., in the shamlet of Higueras, we were greeted by a happy, barefooted, charming old man with a brown smile-wrinkled face. Yes, he could provide Alf . . . He darted nimbly down a slope to cut it and we sat on the steps of an almost-defunct shop, drinking its last bottles of cerveza and gaseoso. An odd (even depraved) breakfast, but we had already sweated gallons. The old lady behind the counter moved stiffly and had a pain-marked face. She gave Rachel six buns (*not* stale) and was reproachfully indignant when I tried to pay her.

Our Alf-provider took us into his closed-down shop to show us photographs of five soldier sons. One of the empty shelves has been converted to an altar on which fresh bouquets of jungle blossoms are lovingly arrayed (in old fish tins) before techni-colored pictures of Christ on the way to Emmaus, the Virgin Mary, the Little Flower, St Martín de Porrés and St Rose of Lima. Each picture was reverently taken down, shown to us and ex-plained. The oil-lamp and four candlesticks were empty, so when payment was refused for Alf I donated 100 soles – which couldn't be refused – for blessed candles.

Juana has had a good day. At noon we came to another shamlet where she enjoyed five kilos of Alf while we enjoyed an enormous meal of tripe and potato stew in a sleazy eating-house-cum-brothel (apparently). Two adolescents were blatantly fornicating in an alcove at the end of the dining-room while four children of about Rachel's age peered sniggeringly through the torn curtain. With so much open space around, I can't think why they had to do it there in broad daylight.

Down and down went the road, up and up went the temperature. Then we were into lush, profitable hacienda country, where the Spaniards lived in splendour; we passed the ruins of two Stately Homes. Now SAIS (Sociedad Agricola de Interés Social, which implements agrarian reform) controls all these miles of plantations and orchards – oranges, bananas, cane, maize, potatoes, a wide variety of vegetables, oats and Alf. Yet the locals look much more sullen and discontented than the Indians of the ascetic puna.

It was only 4, and we were within five miles of Huánuco, when this exceptional site appeared just below the road, concealed from it by tall eucalyptus trees. Nothing was grazing on all these grassy acres and there was no feeling of drought, penury, desperation . . . So here we are, helping ourselves. Nearby stand the graceful, melancholy ruins of another hacienda; and an elegant stone archway, engraved with a family coat-of-arms, spans the carretera – recalling the fact that it started life as a private road. The flies were intolerable until I had a brain-wave about exposing our faces, necks and arms to wood-smoke. Unlike most of my brain-waves, this one worked. (We are already so tanned and dirt-ingrained that an extra layer of brown won't be noticed.) While I've been writing this there has been a fabulous display of meteorites in the cloudless sky. Are we passing through the tail of a comet?

It's cruelly hot, even now, but I'm afraid to leave the tent open because of those dratted bats: they might actually *like* smoked skins . . . Today we passed two burros also bitten on the neck. According to their driver, the most effective deterrent is Milk of Magnesia, liberally smeared on the neck of the animal. But now, he said, it isn't sold any more in Huánuco Mercado because nobody can afford to buy it.

7

Paradise Lost and Regained

Camp in Field beyond Huánuco. 2 November

This evening we're camping beside a main road and suffering from culture shock. For two months we've been living in Paradise, taking for granted the absence of all those artificial materials, colours, shapes and sounds that form the background to modern life. When we saw two campesinos cycling to work this morning, not far from our site, their ancient machines seemed to me sinister heralds of High Technology. "Funny to have *you* going into a depression about *bicycles!*" said Rachel.

Huánuco (pop. 38,000) is described in the *South American Handbook* as 'an attractive Andean town' and one might find it so if one had just arrived from Lima or Trujillo. Arriving from nowhere (as it were), it seems a maelstrom of vulgar ugliness. Katie is now staying in Huánuco with an aunt and had invited us to call. We left Juana tethered to a papaya tree in the aunt's tiny suburban backyard, eating Alf, and Katie escorted us to the Mercado where (as in the shops) many ordinary goods are not available and prices are high. But we found a litre bottle of local honey (130 soles) – something Rachel has been craving for weeks. Katie then gave us a guided tour of the 16th-century church of San Francisco and informed us that it was a thousand years old, which horrified the pedantic Rachel.

In a café overlooking a treeful Plaza we had coffee and excellent cheese sandwiches. But there was no milk for our coffee and I couldn't buy any cheese, the food I miss most on trek. An elderly man at the next table, who looked as if he'd seen better days, blamed the present acute shortage of dairy produce on Agrarian Reform and was glared at by three young men at the table beyond who proved to be radical university students. Afterwards Katie told us that the elderly gentleman's family had once owned the hacienda beside which we camped last night.

Beyond Huánuco a dreary tarred road took us past an ostenta-
tious new university building. Although the tar had melted we
were sorry when the road reverted to Peru-normal; then each
passing vehicle left us dust-shrouded and choking. The traffic was
comparatively heavy and we passed a truck and a Dodge van
mashed together. Campesinos standing nearby told us that the
three in the van had been killed and flies were seething on the
freshly blooded ground. We must now present a Third World
appearance; a smart car coming from Lima stopped to investigate
us and the gracious lady in the front seat gave Rachel 100 soles
before driving on. All afternoon the humidity was – literally –
draining.

In this grassy corner of a steep maize field we are hidden from
the road by a cactus hedge. At dusk, as the daily downpour
started, a score of chanting, drunken men passed by on the road
carrying tall boards decorated with coloured baubles. This procession climbed to a casa above our site by another path, but two
old men broke away and came past us, singing their own duet.
Loaves of bread – baked in the shapes of men, animals, birds,
trees, mountains – were attached to their board, revealing that
they formed part of a wedding celebration. They warned us that if
the rain continued we would be inundated by the wide irrigation
channel nearby: a minor hazard I had already thought about.
Then they gave us a man-shaped loaf, at least half-a-kilo of plain
but delicious new-baked bread. I can still hear the Indian wedding
music – monotonous by our standards, but poignant and strong.

Camp on Ledge above Rio Huallaga. 3 November

On this 'highway' (which in fact is only an all-weather dirt-
track) the 20th century has not made its mark much beyond
Huánuco. I've now sufficiently recovered my equilibrium to
recognise that the traffic-flow, which yesterday seemed M4-ish, is
more reminiscent of a third-class road in County Leitrim around
midnight in January. Also, as Rachel shrewdly remarked this
morning, "If you want to find out what Peru is like you can't spend
all your time where there aren't any people". This was said as I
winced on the approach of the day's first truck.

We woke to feel surplus water from that irrigation channel
running under the tent floor and we were already sodden as we
waded onto the road through a calf-deep flood. Here we are out of

animal territory – the locals travel mostly by truck-bus – and little
Alf is grown. On the outskirts of Ambo we asked a young woman
where we could buy fodder; moments later she came hurrying
after us with a bundle from her own cuy-fodder garden crop and
would accept no payment.

Ambo is friendly, busy and undeveloped – the only town of any
size on the sixty-three mile stretch of carretera between Huánuco
and Cerro de Pasco. In the Mercado I bought hot-fresh buns, six
fat tangy bananas and ten enormous juicy oranges; a cash economy has undeniable dietary advantages. As we squelched on,
warm rain blurred our view of monotonous miles of cane-plant-
ations. Then suddenly the sky cleared and within an hour all was
dry beneath a savagely hot sun. Soon after we entered a sheer
rocky gorge, thinly scrub-covered, where the road ran high above
the excited young Huallaga and the sky ahead was filled with
sharp summits.

As evening approached I went into another of my grazing
tizzies. The climb from Huánuco to Cerro de Pasco is 7,450 feet,
most of that in the last twenty miles, and no mula can be expected
to keep climbing on an empty belly. When we came to this
road-side ledge, some twenty yards by fifty, it seemed wisest to
camp though Juana has only scattered low scrub to nibble; further
on she might have nothing at all. Luckily she likes whatever this
little bush may be, but the picket will have to be changed frequently. While I got the tent up Rachel climbed down a frightful
precipice above the Huallaga to collect the only available firewood. Here the roar of the Rio is so loud that, as I write, it is almost
drowning the sound of a passing truck.

Camp in Eating-House Backyard. 4 November

A depressing start when, close to our site, we passed the body of
a fine roan pony who had fallen over the precipice far above; we
could see the clump of grass that had tempted him and some was
still in his mouth. The road was littered with new rock-falls and we
kept to the rio edge. Not much further on was a patch of good
wasteland grazing which would have made an ideal site. Madden-
ing . . . One never knows where to stop for the best.

Rachel had squitters this morning (all that fruit!) and I insisted
on her riding for an hour or so. In the village of San Rafaél my
heart lightened as I bought an enormous armful of Alf for 100

soles. San Rafaél also has an eating-house and when I was tethering Juana to a verandah post I heard *English* voices, obviously associated with the Range Rover that not long before had overtaken us. It felt strange, after so long, to be able to speak 'normally' to someone other than Rachel. Carolyn and John Walton asked us to share their table, changed one of our American Express travellers cheques and invited us to spend Christmas with them at their tea-plantation in the montaña beyond Cuzco.

In the sprawling mining-settlement of Huariaca we saw three llamas (our first) standing outside somebody's hall-door, wearing brightly-coloured ear-ribbons to placate evil spirits and increase their fertility. For centuries this has been one of Peru's main mining areas and the mountains are hideously lined and pitted and scarred.

Since emerging from the Higueras valley, we've noticed a changed attitude towards gringoes. People are more communicative, despite our linguistic limitations which require them to make patient efforts to understand and be understood. These carretera-conditioned folk regard us as possibly interesting representatives of an outside world they *have* heard of, even if their picture of it is somewhat distorted. When we paused in this little village, near some open mines, the locals insisted on our camping for the night in a wire-fenced muddy yard beside the eating-house. And two families invited us to supper, though they knew we had already eaten an early meal in the 'restaurant'. (Both invitations were accepted, by Rachel and me separately.)

Tómas the Alf-vendor runs a tiny shop – almost bare-shelved, here as elsewhere – and while he was cutting Juana's supper his sixteen-year-old daughter (the eldest of five) produced a tattered *Geographical Encyclopaedia of the World* in English – the first book we've seen for months. This pre-dated the dissolution of the British Empire but showed our home pueblo; half the village crowded in to gaze at that unimaginable dot beside el Rio Agua Negra.

It was dark and sleeting as we stumbled along a rough path, ankle-deep in mud, to our first dinner engagement. Mencía, a youngish Indian woman, operates the petrol pump and lives nearby in a tin-roofed wooden shack. We sat at an unsteady table, covered with an oil-cloth and illuminated by a guttering candle in a Nescafé tin. Plates of rice and delicious vegetable stew were solemnly set before us and eight silent spectators occupied

First sight of a llama near Cerro de Pasco

Eating house near Jauja

Our saddle resembled this one

benches around the shadowy walls, watching us eat. Their grave faces, just touched by candlelight, looked like so many copper masks in some corner of a museum. Cuys scuttled and squealed underfoot, being benignly surveyed by a sentimental over-fat black-and-white bitch called Lassie. (Most Peruvian bitches seem to bear this name and most pet lambs and kids are 'Bambi'.) Noddle soup followed; the Indians, like the Tibetans, usually have soup after the main course. Then came cups of daisy tea made from bunches of dried flowers hanging above the wood-fuelled mud stove. This beverage is no doubt an acquired taste, which I feel no urge to acquire.

Back then to Tómas's house, where we were served, in the shop, with a piled plate of boiled potatoes and big bowls of noodle and goat-meat soup. Here the family ate at the same time, in the inner room, and we were attended only by a diminutive grey kitten of obsessive friendliness, and with a deafening purr, who eventually crawled down my shirt-front and curled up in padded comfort.

As I write this my stomach feels agonisingly bloated; it's not now used to one large meal in three days, never mind three large meals in one evening.

Camp on Puna beyond Cerro de Pasco. 5 November

Early this morning we passed through a dismal, stinking, litter-defaced mining settlement. Hundreds of horrid little grey huts, and dozens of even horrider blocks of flats, were crowded on the edge of a reeking red-brown river and overlooked by raped mountains. As usual in this region the walls were daubed with ¡APRA! and various other political slogans. Peru's mining settlements have always been centres of political unrest and would-be social reformers now try to use the powerful miners' unions as levers.

Leaving the highway, we took an old mining road to Cerro de Pasco. This climbed between bare mountains into a puna valley desecrated by telegraph poles, mining company jeeps and barbed wire fences – all of which made the scattering of thatched stone cabins look oddly anachronistic. But we were cheered by the sight of five llamas bounding along the mountain just above us and then crossing the road in front of an astonished Juana, who has never before seen the like. These comical creatures have an extra-ordinary action, like certain jointed toys with limbs and necks that move in different directions simultaneously. Near Cerro we saw many herds grazing. Llamas follow their leader so slavishly that the driver of a large pack-train need control only one animal.

We were approaching Cerro de Pasco by its brand-new satellite town of San Juan de Pampa, to which we took a redura up an escarpment used as an urban dump. Several happy hairy pigs were gorging themselves on decayed refuse and a drooling imbecile youth was poking through the latest deposit with a stick. Here we are again above 13,000 feet yet the noon sun was hot and I fear we'll always associate Cerro with the stench of that dump. From the top of the escarpment we could see the famous Junín pampa, one of the world's greatest high-altitude plains, bounded on the farthest horizon by a faint line of snow-tipped peaks and with Lake Junín (thirty-six miles long) just discernible as a glint in the distance.

San Juan is well laid-out, its houses brightly painted, its streets wide and airy. But already a super-abundance of litter, and a burgeoning graffiti culture, have tinged it with slummishness. Before descending to Cerro we enjoyed an excellent lunch in a neat, clean, good-value restaurant run by two friendly women who asked if there were many mad people in Ireland or was it only us . . .

Squalor takes over completely in the old settlement (pop. 29,000, altitude 12,990 feet) where an open pit of truly Andean proportions dominates the town centre. Gold, silver, copper, zinc and lead are found in and around Cerro. Its fate was sealed in 1569 when Aari Capcha was herding his llamas and lit a fire against a rock – part of which melted, to become a silver ingot. Between 1630 and 1898, $565,000,000 worth of silver ore was exported from Cerro. Recently, in old mining galleries eighty feet below a main street, workers found a hidden treasure trove of gold Spanish doubloons. The highest coal mine in the world is twenty-six miles away at Goyllarisquisga. (End of statistics.)

Cerro's attractions for the non-mineralogist seem limited. We escaped as quickly as we could – which wasn't very quickly because the whole place is a muddy maze of pits, holes, caverns and what look like sewage-works but I suppose are exposed galleries. Rachel reproved me for using unseemly language as I hauled Juana out of the umpteenth water-logged trench; she argued that it would be odd if three and a half centuries of intensive mining hadn't left a few marks on the place.

Not far beyond Cerro, Juana saw her first train; she's had a mind-broadening day. We camped early in a slight hollow, where she can enjoy an all-night ichu banquet, and while writing our diaries lay outside the tent in warm sunshine. Dozens of llamas were grazing on a low hill to the east. A spinning woman herded them away when the western sky, above a long cinnamon ridge, briefly became a glory of pink and gold and grey-blue cloudlets.

Camp on Junín Pampa. 6 November

Today began with an amber, green and crimson dawn which we watched from our flea-bags while eating bread and bananas.

On the crest of the next ridge we were directly overlooking the Junín pampas, here defaced by metal telegraph poles, tin-roofed mining settlements, railway lines and electricity pylons (my *bête noire* in any country: here offensive beyond words).

At a bar-restaurant in a soulless settlement we brunched off coffee and fried eggs. Five night-shift miners were footless drunk, inarticulately garrulous and vaguely amorous; when the proprietor apologised for their behaviour I assured him that if I were a Peruvian miner I too would get drunk as often as possible.

During the afternoon pylons and settlements were left behind and we could appreciate the snow-streaked mountains in the far, far distance; unreal peaks, like a five-year-old's drawing of 'mountains' – so needle-sharp and remote one couldn't quite believe in them. Behind us rain-clouds were massing over Cerro de Pasco. Soon they were also massing ahead of us – and to the west, where those silver peaks seemed even more fantastic when half-shrouded in blackness. Then came thunder and lightning: strange, flat cracks of thunder, for there was nothing to cause an echo on the weird flat immensity of this plain. And still the sun continued to shine on us, while the dark sky all around was dancing with livid zig-zags. Then suddenly a violent wind drove the clouds towards us and within moments the temperatures had dropped many degrees. Hastily we camped, fighting the gale for control of the tent; we had just secured it when the downpour started. Poor Juana! Here she has nothing but wretched clumps of coarse scrub, fit only for a camel. This is not puna, but a bleak, grey, stony wasteland such as one associates with the Gobi Desert.

Camp near Lake Junín. 7 November

After the deluge, last night became a thing of beauty, all star-bright silence and peace. A night when the endlessness of the universe – which seems so near, looking up – puts all human concerns in perspective and to worry about anything would be absurd. Nor was it any colder than a mid-winter frosty night at home. I should know, having been out three times to change the picket.

Today we covered only twelve miles because of Juana's malnutrition. By 8 we had reached good grazing near the lake, where she breakfasted while we watched a variety of unidentifiable birds feeding on the wide marsh between water and shore. The lake was still invisible and remained disappointingly so all day, hidden by high reeds.

In a non-mining red-tiled pueblo we met a kind young woman leading by the hand her all-dressed-up daughter whose fifth birthday this is. Taking pity on our fodder crisis she led us down long streets to a casa behind a high mud wall where, after much eloquent pleading, she persuaded an exceedingly grumpy old man to sell us 100 soles worth of dried oats – a colossal bundle. These were a novelty to Juana, who at first pushed them around the footpath disdainfully. "She doesn't *deserve* to be well fed!" exclaimed Rachel in exasperation. However, Her Faddiness eventually decided to make the best of it and while we brunched she munched.

We were on the edge of the pampa all afternoon, where it merges into vividly green mountains on which dry stone walls mark the fields and the isolated thatched stone dwellings have half-doors. Beside most village houses stretch long corral walls and on some, as in India, dung was drying. But nowadays, in this treeless area, the majority cook on kerosene stoves, or bottled gas stoves if they can afford them.

For Juana now it's either a feast or a famine: last night nothing, tonight both excellent grass and dried oats. And irregular feeding is *not* suited to the equine digestive system. We plan to have a rest-day tomorrow in the little pueblo of Junín, staying for two nights in a hotel if the fodder-supply is adequate.

Camp near edge of Junín Pampa. 8 November

We were distracted while striking camp by a flaming dawn – all orange and scarlet – a divine conflagration. One could only drop everything and look. Here the sky seems so close one feels almost translated to heaven at such moments.

By noon we were in Junín, a charming pueblo, both visually and humanly – fine colonial buildings, streets neat and clean, people warmly welcoming. But alas! nobody could produce fodder. Our first concern was to send an 'All Well' telegram to the British Embassy in Lima, as we had promised to do at the first opportunity. (We passed through Cerro de Pasco on a Sunday.) Junín's little used post-office was down a side street and the telegram cost 12 soles for twelve words, whereas a letter would have cost 16 soles. The post-master explained that as most campesinos can't write they use post-office clerks as scribes, dictating telegrams to relatives in the cities. This fascinated me. In the Middle East and India, where most people have always been illiterate, the village scribe is an immemorial institution. For millenia the Arabic and Hindu cultures have been highly literate and so letter-writing has been taken for granted by the peasantry. But pre-Conquest Peru had no written language and the notion of communicating through letters remains strange to this day.

We left Junín sadly, glancing over our shoulders at a menacing cloud build-up. We had been assured that we would soon reach good grazing but as we crossed the barren plain – not a sheep or a goat or a llama in sight – we wondered . . .

When the blizzard started at 2.30 Rachel agreed that we shouldn't complain because the wind was behind us. As she put on her waterproof poncho I covered the load with our cape and wrapped myself in a space-blanket. Then for two and a half hours we plodded on through swirling soft snow that restricted visibility to about fifty yards. It wasn't intolerably cold but soon our feet were numb. And poor Juana, with head down and ears back, was misery personified. At last Rachel began to crack up; for the first time she complained, of cold feet. I knew the agony she was enduring – you might say we were both in the same boot – but as the sky was lightening slightly I urged her to keep going in the hope that soon we could set up a *dry* camp. Then the snow became rain/sleet and soon there was a lull, though the clouds remained low and unbroken. We rushed the tent up and were just putting down the last peg when the sleet started again.

As I was writing this Rachel drifted back from the edge of sleep to say drowsily – "Do you know what *you're* like? You're like those Spartan mothers who left babies out all night on mountains to see if they were worth rearing!"

Camp amidst Cactus beside Stream. 9 November

The fodder crisis forced us to rise early, despite the intense cold. But our hands were so numb-clumsy that we didn't get off until 6.15, still wearing all our night-clothes and with the tent – an unpackable sheet of ice – draped over the load. A rough level track (in theory motorable, though we've seen no vehicle all day) took us around the snowy shoulder of a long mountain, with the edge of the Junín pampa on our left. As the sun rose, a herd of llamas was released from a Co-op corral on the gentle slope above and went bounding uncoordinatedly towards their grazing-ground. Soon we were off the mountain, following a llama-path redura across an apparently endless expanse of springy turf. The deep blue sky was cloudless, the silence profound, the air crystal: a line of sharp peaks to the north seemed quite close, yet according to the map was seventy miles away. Suddenly I wanted to turn somersaults – a recurring temptation, sometimes given in to, when the beauty of a landscape goes to my head. No doubt a psychiatrist would prescribe therapy for such behaviour on the part of a woman approaching her forty-seventh birthday. But here this temptation has to be resisted because so much vital equipment is carried in my bush-shirt pockets.

Eventually Juana found some breakfast – a patch of ichu grass not cropped by llamas – and a few miles further on we came, without any warning, to the edge of the plateau. Beneath us lay an immense circular valley, its newly-ploughed sides red-brown below grey rock escarpments, its floor holding a large, scattered, red-roofed pueblo with many green fields between the houses. Even from a distance, there was an air of tranquillity and prosperity about San Pedro de Cacas. The Andes contain so many separate, self-sufficient little worlds – from mountain to mountain and valley to valley and pueblo to pueblo there are dramatic contrasts in the atmospheres created by the locals: welcoming or indifferent, hostile or helpful, sullen or cheerful.

San Pedro is cheerful – and looks it. The sturdy two-storeyed houses around the main Plaza have humourously carved wooden balconies and are painted blue, green, white, yellow, pink. The unusual little church has two vaguely Norman towers: one shocking pink, the other lupin-blue. Although these grieviously offended Rachel's austere taste I thought they added to the pueblo's air of spontaneous gaiety. The further south we move, the better maintained are the churches.

Juana munched green oats while we relished stale bread and slightly 'off' bottled olives, washed down by several cups of café con leche – a rare treat, milk being so scarce in the sierra. We had found San Pedro's thatched, white-washed café by chance: no sign indicates its function and it contains only two small tables. The owner, Martin, is an engineering student on compulsory vacation from San Marcos University, now closed because of political unrest in Lima. Although a devout Catholic, he would support the Communist Party if they seemed likely to overthrow the army junta. But this, he feels, is impossible; the Party in Peru is so disunited that few take it seriously. Like too many of his generation, he is impatiently contemptuous of Peru and longs to emigrate. (Yet he would probably have taken massive umbrage had we gringoes criticised his country.) It upsets me to find, among the more intelligent young whose talents are desperately needed here, this compulsive longing to escape . . . Not that one can blame the individuals concerned; they are merely reacting to centuries of corrupt leadership. Inevitably they feel trapped in a country without a future – for them. And the more they are told about Peru's natural wealth and potential for 'greatness' – a favourite theme of political leaders – the more restive and resentful they become. Martin had quite a lot to say about the Monroe Doctrine. He concluded, "Latin America's riches have never been exploited for Latin America. So why should we stay at home and work harder to make the gringoes richer?"

Beyond San Pedro the rocky gorge of the infant Rio Palca led us to the head of a narrow green valley. This is an area of friable rock where the mountains' broken crests look like primitive weapons stacked against the sky. On our way down we passed dozens of mysterious-looking caves, grottoes and caverns. By noon this twisting valley had widened and become lavishly fertile. For the first time we were in market-garden country, surrounded by acres of beans, carrots, peas, turnips, spinach, lettuces, onions, carnations, gladioli and roses. These orderly humdrum plots seem incongruous at the feet of mountains whose sheer slopes are all smooth grey rock, allowing nothing to take root. Above the river we saw, for the second time since leaving Cajamarca, traces of ancient terracing; and some of the terraces had been inexpertly restored.

One of the Incas' main achievements was to increase the area of arable land throughout the sierra by terracing and irrigation, but post-Conquest their entire agricultural system collapsed. This was partly owing to that tragic depopulation which has been so feelingly described by John Hemming. 'Disease was important, but was not the main cause of the sharp decline during the first forty years of Spanish rule. That decline resulted more from profound cultural shock and chaotic administration. Since the death of Huayna-Capac the people of Peru had lived through a numbing series of catastrophes. Their calm, rigidly organised society was shattered in quick succession by a ferocious civil war, a bewildering conquest by foreigners totally alien in race and out-look, two mighty attempts at resistance, and a devastating series of civil wars among the invaders . . . In such turbulent times, many natives grew so deeply demoralised that they lost the will to live. This is still a serious threat to primitive peoples who witness the collapse of their way of life . . . A group of aged Inca officials interrogated in the 1570s described this pathetic condition. "The Indians, seeing themselves dispossessed and robbed . . . allow themselves to die, and do not apply themselves to anything as they did in Inca times." This same demoralisation led to a sharp decline in the birth-rate, a phenomenon accelerated by population movement and the disruption of the Inca marriage system.'

The unremitting communal work of clearance, terracing and irrigation requires considerable man-power, highly organised. And it was not to be expected that the traditional mit'a duties could be performed during those fatal decades of confusion, epidemics, fear and despair which followed the arrival of the Spaniards. Nor, over the past 400 years, has there been any motive, from the Indians' point of view, to pick up the pieces. The damage done by the Conquest to their way of life – and their psyche – was irrepar-able. The Catholic Church could not replace the relatively simple religions they had evolved to suit their own needs. Nor did the setting up of an independent Peruvian nation bring them any relief or hope. And the many humanitarian projects dreamed up by do-gooding foreigners to raise their standard of living and entice them into our cash economy have made little impact on people *who do not want to be as we are*. One is led to the heart-breaking conclusion that the Andean Indians have reached the end of the evolutionary road and are a race without a future, apart from a minority of exceptional individuals. In 16th-century Peru the Spaniards in effect (though not deliberately) committed genocide. In North America the English and French did the same thing deliberately, and so more obviously and efficiently. Some people are infuriated by historical 'ifs' but I have a weakness for them. *If* the British rather than the Spaniards had conquered Peru, would they have recognised the value – to themselves – of the Incas' extraordinary organisational abilities and contrived to exploit the country's wealth without wrecking its social structure? Or would they have been even more ruthless than the Spaniards, regarding the Andean Indians as vermin to be exterminated? Or was the Inca Empire so inflexible in its isolation, and so dependent on the unquestioning obedience of contented millions, that it would have disintegrated in the wake of any outside interference, however willing the invader might have been to compromise? That is probably the case.

Alf is also grown in this valley and as we waited for a bundle to be cut we watched fields being harrowed with the reluctant assistance of a donkey or small pony. One man dragged the animal along by the halter: another followed behind, bent double as he lent his outstretched hands on a flat board through which long nails had been hammered. I've seldom seen such an ineffectual improvisation. In Baltistan something similar is used, but there bullocks are trained to draw the harrow willingly and children sit on the board to provide the necessary weight. Other fields were being prepared for replanting by more traditional methods, the men working as a team to turn over the soil with digging-sticks that seem unchanged since Inca times, while their womenfolk followed behind breaking up the clods with stones bound by creepers to two-foot poles. One sees more modern implements on sale at most markets, so presumably some campesinos actually prefer their own familiar labour-increasing devices on which no cash need be spent.

When we passed through the attractive little pueblo of Acobamba, huddled between eucalyptus-covered slopes, it was gruellingly hot; we had been descending all day. Three friendly mestizo youths accompanied us for a few miles down the ever-widening valley and diagnosed that Juana badly needs carrots. Rachel was scandalised when they provided these by casually pulling a bunch from a field we happened to be passing. "We must pay the farmer!" she whispered frantically. But when I offered soles our friends laughingly rejected them. Alas! Juana equally emphatically rejected the carrots: life would be much simpler if she weren't so choosey. Happily this valley has fields of Alf around every other corner, so tonight she can eat her fill.

Because of intensive cultivation it was hard to find a site. But at dusk we came to this patch of wasteland, scattered with horse-dung, between the track and a swift stream. It is perilously cramped – only about fifteen yards by five, with giant, razor-sharp cacti growing all around the tent and barely enough room for Juana to lie down. As Rachel searched for firewood (surprisingly scarce here) she met a young campesino woman and her two schoolgirl sisters, who were weeding a bean-field. Then distant laughter indicated that Rachel was happily practising her Castilian. As she remarked yesterday, "Speaking bad Spanish is the best way to make friends. If you speak none or too much it's not so barrier-breaking". One little girl brought me an armful of dry leaves and twigs and within moments had our fire going. Her older sister soon followed, with a gift of broad beans which so delighted Rachel that against my advice she ate them raw. As I wrote that last sentence the girls reappeared by moonlight to present us with a skirt full of potatoes. Unfortunately the embers are now too low to bake them and we have no spare firewood.

Camp on very steep, very stony Mountain Ledge. 10 November

An hour after setting off we came to another little pueblo, Pomachaca; the map shows that this is among the more densely populated regions of the sierra. As we descended an empty cobbled street in the residential suburbs, one of the old heavy wooden double-doors swung open and we were observed by an elderly woman with fine-boned Spanish features, clad in 1920s widow's weeds. She watched our approach, standing beneath her handsome stone archway, then stepped forward and graciously invited us to desayuno.

Within the tidy patio-cum-corral, firewood was stacked high against one wall, sheaves of straw against another. Rabbits hopped and cuys scuttled within their separate runs and a small enthusiastic mongrel bestowed affection all over the place. When Juana had been given a sheaf of paja we were invited to sit on a wooden bench on the verandah, screened from the patio by grass lattice-work. Soon an Indian servant appeared, bearing on a tarnished silver tray very chipped enamel mugs of very weak coffee and a few brittle hunks of the stalest bread I have ever eaten anywhere. I could tell from Rachel's expression that good manners were costing her dear; unlike her Ma, she is easily nauseated by foods that are past their prime.

Meanwhile several neighbours had joined the party: all elderly ladies, grave of visage and soberly clad. Most Peruvians are vague about Ireland – though they regard it as an *important* country, because mainly Roman Catholic – and we were asked many questions. But there was no reference to the Northern Ireland tragedy, of which few people here are aware. (How many British or Irish people are aware of Peru's political violence problems?) Eventually our hostess's son Manuel, aged thirty-ish, came hurrying in with a few fresh biscuits wrapped in newspaper. Mercifully even Rachel realised that this was an occasion for restraint and did not swallow the lot on sight.

Manuel asked to be shown our route on the map and when his grandmother, aged eighty-six, heard that we had passed through Junín, she summoned her servant to fetch a rusty lawyer's deed-box containing family treasures. This was unlocked with a key taken from the recesses of her skirts and, after much rummaging through yellowed letters and newspaper clippings, she produced a blurred brown photograph of an Irish priest who in 1921 had worked in Junín. Fr McMahon was his name – it was written on the back – and perhaps we had heard of him? He was a famous man and had baptised Carmel, her daughter (our hostess) and three of her six sons. Everyone politely concealed their disappointment when I confessed that we had not heard of Fr McMahon.

This group also expressed a disquieting contempt (not too strong a word) for Peru and were full of admiration for Western Europe and North America. I felt quite embarrassed by what seemed to be an acute national inferiority complex. Then afterwards I wondered if it *was* that, or something more personal and complicated, to do with the humiliating decline of their own families in a Peru that since Independence has been governed – more often than not – by unscrupulous scoundrels. When our hostess took me into the house it seemed the very epitome of decayed gentility. The only touch of freshness and colour was provided by three vases of gladioli arranged in front of a large statue of the Virgin Mary in an alcove in the hallway. Manuel followed us around – a spiritless, lost-looking, pale creature who bore an uncanny resemblance to the mildewed portrait of his great-great-grandfather in the dining-room. This ancestor had owned a vast hacienda between Pomachaca and Acobamba – where we noticed all those unusually fertile fields, now in the control of a Co-op. But during his lifetime, according to Manuel, the family fortunes declined because he spent too much time in Lima and his mayordomo deceived him. A sadly commonplace story in Peru. As we were preparing to leave – bridling Juana and tightening the girth – Manuel said with sudden vehemence, "The Spaniards should have gone a hundred years sooner. When they left, Peru was already too rotten to rise as a nation". Then he heaved a sack of paja (a present for Juana) behind the load and expertly flicked and twisted our rope to hold it in place. The family retains a few hectares of land nearby, on which Manuel works himself, side by side with the descendants of those campesinos who once were virtually owned by his forefathers.

That interlude had a faint flavour of *The Bridge of San Luis Rey*; *timelessness* tinges the whole Peruvian ambience. In the pueblos, however, it is not the reassuring timelessness of remote places but rather a sense of stagnation, or of weariness with a present that somehow hasn't really arrived . . . I've put all that badly; writing conditions tonight are less than ideal and anyway it's not an easy atmosphere to convey.

From Pomachaca our track continued its gradual descent, passing countless fields of farm crops, vegetables and flowers. In every Mercado flower-sellers are conspicuous because the devout regularly buy fresh bouquets to honour their favourite saints in the parish church or to decorate domestic shrines.

In the busy, straggling town of Hualhuash women Alf-sellers were sitting on the pavement outside the Mercada and as I negotiated for 100 soles worth the hungry Juana escaped from Rachel and almost trampled a baby to death. This wasn't Juana's fault; campesino mothers have a habit of leaving their infants – looking exactly like rolled-up blankets – strewn about on the pavements.

The six level miles to Tarma, on a tarred road wreathed in petrol fumes under a savage noon sun, were more exhausting than a sixteen-mile climb on the puna. This is a built-up area; new casas abound, fast motor-traffic flashes by, and on the outskirts of Tarma – a town of some 30,000 inhabitants, at 9,100 feet – we even saw four advertisement hoardings. To avoid the main street, where Juana was bothered by melting tar, we turned into a side-street and walked parallel to a noisome canal full of litter, rotting vegetables and bloated animal corpses – rabbits, rats, dogs, cats. *Not* naice . . .

We were determined to avoid the Tarma-Jauja motor-road and by good luck appealed for guidance to a kind elderly man whose home shamlet is on the old route between the towns. He led us up a grassy track which he insisted was the Camino Real, pointing to its width, and to the smooth stone slabs beneath the turf, as proof of his claim. Soon after we had left him, our track joined a dusty-white dirt-road that could be seen for miles ahead, running level through a village before vanishing around the shoulder of the massive mountain on which we stood. Scrutinising the barren way ahead, through binoculars, we realised that Juana would have no grazing tonight. So we set about securing a load of the Alf that grew on terraced ledges below the road. Its owner proved to be a cheerful, handsome, middle-aged Indian woman who sent three small nephews leaping down the terraces with bill-hooks to cut the second-tallest crop: different ledges were at different stages of development. The tallest, which was flowering, would be unsuit-able mule-feed though it's said to be best for cattle.

It takes time to cut 100 soles worth so we loosened the girth, gave Juana a paja snack and sat on the edge of the precipice gazing down the valley to Tarma in its furnace-like hollow, now far below. The opposite slopes of smooth-crested mountains were a rich red, streaked and patched with the green of eucalyptus plantations and, below them, with the light green of Alf and the darker green of potatoes. Down the length of the valley, three large cemetaries were visible on the lower slopes – none near a village. These conspicuous rectangles had high mud walls, arches roofed with cacti over their gateways and rows of white-washed 'blocks of flats' for coffins.

Soon we were joined by the Alf-owner's son, a striking-looking young man with coppery skin, an aquiline nose, straight, shoulder-length hair, long narrow eyes and a melancholy ex-pression. The fluency of his English astonished us until he explained that he had lived for a year with a Canadian family in

Lima. Then he entered San Marcos University, to read modern languages and history, but after two terms found himself dangerously involved in politics with no prospect of achieving anything but threats to his own future – even to his life. "I don't want to be a revolutionary", he explained, "I only want to reform things quietly. And for that I could get no support. So I came home." He nodded towards 'home', a cluster of solid dwellings and stables on a wide ledge half-way down the mountain-side. He continued, "It is more important than going to demos in Lima if I can help to educate the local campesinos. I am pure Indian. I have no Spanish blood – I hope! And the Indians need education. Not only book-learning, but the sort of education that will give them the confidence to look other Peruvians straight in the eye and claim justice. Not any sort of special favours or concessions – only *justice*, which they have never had." He pointed down the valley at the remote flat roofs of Tarma. "See that town of Tarma? Do you know that exactly 440 years ago, in 1538, Captain Alonso Mercadillo and his Spanish troops spent seven months in Tarma, when they were supposed to be subduing the Inca's army at Huánuco, and they robbed and looted and raped and enslaved, and tortured the Inca chiefs to make them give up their silver and gold . . . And a few years later Pizarro *gave* all the Indians of Tarma and Junín to his treasurer, Riquelme! He *gave* them, as though they were llamas, and said their owner had only to convert them, quickly, to Christianity, and then he could use them on farms and down mines. Afterwards the Spaniards argued that anyway the Incas had owned those people, so they were never free. That is a dirty half-truth. They were never free like European people: they and the Incas knew nothing about that kind of freedom and didn't want it. But they were well housed and clothed and free from hunger and insecurity. They were content and not abused and they understood Inca law and religion: it made sense to them the way European laws and Christianity never could. You have heard talk of a united Peru, with all the citizens equal and working together for the good of the nation? That is nonsense. It can never happen. There is no room in Peru for two races whose minds have never met after 450 years of sharing the same country. Either the Indians take over or they go even further under as the others 'exploit' the land with new technology. I know in my brain we must go under. But still with my heart I want to bring the campesinos into the modern world and help them to survive there

– because they are my own people. My mother thinks I should
have stayed at university. I am clever, I speak good English and
French, if I don't bother about the campesinos I can get on. But
get on to where? In Peru if you get on you must ignore – forget
about – those who can't get on. Then I wouldn't be happy. Yet in a
way my mother is right and I'm wasting my time. Most campesinos aren't interested in being educated to live in the modern
world. They want only to live well in their own world. They don't
really want to be part of a cash economy – their minds and spirits
don't work that way. Perhaps they would only be happy if Peru
could go back to 1520 and remain undiscovered! My professor in
Lima said, 'History has left them stranded'. Probably he is right.
And this is very sad." Abruptly our eloquent companion stood up,
as his three little cousins scrambled onto the road with their loads
of Alf. I asked him then for his name and address, feeling that I
would like to keep in touch with him. He stared down at me
impassively for a moment, before shaking his head. "No – I'm
cutting off now from the outside world. I can only help my own by
going back into their world – not just *visiting* it, while half my mind
stays elsewhere. This you may think stupid. But it is the only way,
like going into a monastery to contemplate. So we will not keep in
touch, unless sometimes you think of me and wish me good luck."

Having written as I did last night, it felt strange to hear my own
feelings so exactly echoed this afternoon by that remarkable young
man. Although dressed like any other modestly prosperous campesino in this fertile valley, and living in a simple home, our friend
had what can only be described as 'an Inca aura' – partly owing to
his unusual appearance, but also because of a certain air of
authority that had nothing to do with his position in society. Put
on paper, his words may seem ambiguous; they might be no more
than the vapourings of an unbalanced young man who sees himself as the Messiah of the campesinos. But he didn't sound like
that. Something utterly genuine, and not unduly idealistic, came
through as he spoke. Rachel afterwards observed that it would be
nice to meet even one Peruvian who was full of hope for the future.
But then – could such a person be taken seriously? Why does one
feel that there is less hope for Peru as a whole (not just the Indians)
than for Pakistan and India, which have far greater material/
social problems? Is it because they have fewer *spiritual* problems?

This campsite is sensationally uncomfortable, yet so beautiful
one doesn't really mind. It is on a very steep slope which is also very

dusty, very stony and very thorny. At first sight it seemed quite impossible, if only because of the law of gravity. But *in extremis* most things are possible and we briskly set about clearing a tent-sized space of stones sharp enough to puncture the floor and thorny bits of dead cacti. Eventually I got the tent up (and rainproof, I hope) while Rachel was collecting a meagre supply of poor quality fuel. Many blunt stones remain beneath it, embedded in the hard soil, but these won't worry us because the floor is carpeted with 1) Juana's poncho, 2) Juana's two sacks, 3) Juana's waterproof cape, 4) our space-blankets, 5) Rachel's waterproof poncho, 6) Rachel's woollen poncho, 7) Rachel's saddle-blanket. We live in luxury. Because of the fuel-shortage – not even enough boiling water to melt soup-cubes – I recklessly opened our precious tin of milk: a shocking extravagance, at 65 soles, but it does make Nescafé that much less soul-destroying.

Our main frustration at present is that bottle of honey bought in Huánuco to console Rachel on the fireless puna. As soon as we came within shouting distance of the puna it congealed and has remained inaccessible ever since. (Why put honey in a narrow-necked bottle? *I* don't know – ask the campesinos!) We always sleep with it between us, optimistically telling each other it must one night thaw. Rachel somewhat incestuously – not to say perversely – refers to it as 'Our little son'. By now we have almost given up hoping for nourishment from it, but it is acquiring some of the solacing properties of a teddy-bear: a thing you cuddle while falling asleep.

It is a cloudless evening and as we set up camp the contrasting colours of our world were almost intolerably beautiful. Below, the soft green of a lush valley floor; above, the gentle blue of a late sky; on our side of the valley, vast pale grey precipices sweeping up and up; on the far side, barren slopes glowing a fiery red-gold as the sun set. Those opposite mountains have been dramatically split (by earthquakes?) and their deep ravines, oddly devoid of water or vegetation, are studded with weirdly-eroded, free-standing, high red rocks. And when I say high I mean cathedral high . . .

We ate our supper of raw potatoes, sardines and oranges as the moon rose – quenching all but the brightest stars – to create another sort of beauty. A scene of subdued brilliance, of mysterious radiance – the mountains all shimmering silver, velvet blackness in the valley. Why does moonlight seem to deepen the night silence? When Rachel had retired, I sat looking and listening: and there was nothing to hear. Even Juana had stopped munching.

I don't feel too sorry for our mula tonight, despite a total lack of grazing; she has vast amounts of both Alf and paja. We were interested to see how she moved from one pile to another; I'd have thought she'd far prefer the fresh Alf and finish it first, but not so. She spent about ten minutes on each pile and, before leaving it, marked the verge with droppings or a squirt of urine. Now my only worry on her behalf is the impossibility of her lying down on this gradient. Normally she relaxes frequently during the night, for brief periods – always as close to the tent as she can get, which we find rather touching.

My 'study' is being predictably mobile tonight. Juana's thick leather saddle-pad serves as a desk and I lean my left elbow on my rolled-up jeans and bush-shirt. (Before writing I always change into my 'pyjama' husky-suit.) Normally this is a comfortable arrangement but here my desk and I have been inexorably slipping towards the edge of the precipice so, between paragraphs, I have to wriggle back to square one, pausing en route to remove cacti spikes from my limbs. And the torch – equally sensitive to the law of gravity – often falls off its stand of a saucepan balanced on a water-bottle and is in any case made much less effective by the bright moonlight. There must be easier ways of writing books . . .

Rachel pointed out this evening that so far we have almost kept pace with Pizarro and his men on their historic march from Cajamarca to Cuzco; which of course is a coincidence – we're not 'racing' them. The conquistadores left Cajamarca on 11 August 1533 and reached Tarma on 10 October; we left Cajamarca on 9 September and have reached Tarma on 10 November. Like ourselves, the Spaniards paused in Tarma only long enough to feed their horses; the town is so closely encircled by mountains that they feared an ambush where horsemen would be at a disadvantage. Pizarro's secretary, Pedro Sancho, graphically described that night on an exposed mountainside near Tarma: 'The men remained continuously on the alert, with the horses saddled and the men themselves unfed. They had no meal whatsoever, for they had no firewood and no water. They had not brought their tents with them and could not shelter themselves, so they were all dying of cold – for it rained heavily early in the night and then snowed. The armour and clothing they were wearing were all soaked'. It's odd that in 1533 there was *snow* in early October in this area. And

odder still that they didn't carry water with them from the valley;
by then they must have known that it isn't always available on the
heights. We may think this not an ideal site, but at least we're
warm, dry and fed. And tomorrow morning we won't see the
corpses of over 4,000 Indians, killed in one of the battles of the Inca
civil war – which was the sight that awaited the conquistadores on
11 October. On which of these moonlit mountains did they camp?
Possibly on this one, if our guide out of Tarma was correct and we
are now on an Inca road.

Camp on Grassy Bank of Stream. 11 November

We slept well, in defiance of gravity, and were back on the
dirt-road by 6.15. For an hour and a half it hair-pinned up that
arid mountain, then suddenly fertility was restored as we arrived
on an immense ledge. We rejoiced to see fields of Alf around
Huanchal, an attractive and friendly village. The one-tabled 'café'
– also a bare-shelved shop – could offer only hot water, with which
we made our own coffee while Juana breakfasted. I was glad to see
the end of that tin of milk, which I had been gingerly carrying in
my shirt pocket.

Then we were climbing again, towards the puna. There was
much activity on the mountainsides: ploughing, harrowing, fertilising, potato planting. Teams of men wielded their digging-
sticks rhythmically, singing as they worked. Lines of burros
carried guano up narrow paths to high terraced fields. Groups of
women chanted sweetly and plaintively as they put down the seed
potatoes, their skirts tucked up to knee-level. Long after the track
had taken us abruptly onto the puna, we could still hear those
ancient incantations floating faintly through the thin pure air.

Today's pass was marked by a solitary stone farmhouse. Outside a young Indian woman sat spinning in the sun, surrounded by
a quiverful of tiny filthy children. She ignored our greeting. For
hours no other dwelling appeared, yet we passed many flocks of
puna-coloured sheep, visible only when moving, and a few small
herds of fine cattle. At noon we stopped for lunch where the grass
grew long and nourishing. As usual Juana rolled vigorously when
the load came off; then to our astonishment she remained lying
down while grazing, an eccentricity no doubt prompted by her
unrestful night. While eating we marvelled at an improbable
mile-long ridge, on the far side of the track, composed of sym-

metrical layers of silver rock and green turf, like an elaborate sandwich cake – perhaps one made for the New York Irish on St Patrick's Day. The Andes are full of surprises. Then we lay back on the soft warm grass and I gazed into the sky and went drifting away on an ocean of content. One remembers those moments, when just *being alive* seems a matter for the most profound gratitude to whomever or whatever is responsible.

Even now we are sometimes deceived by the scale of these landscapes. At 3.30, from the edge of the puna, we were looking directly down on the village of Tingo Paccha. To the east rose a convulsion of snow-crowned mountains. To the south, seen at the far end of a cleft in a massive rock-wall – as though through a kaleidoscope – eucalyptus plantations marked the pueblo of Acollo Marco. Those trees then seemed so close that we felt confident of reaching them by sunset and dining on baked potatoes. But that was not to be. It took us an hour to reach Tingo Paccha, using a precipitous redura through ploughland, and another hour to get off a wide grassy ledge swarming with donkeys, ponies, oxen, cows, sheep, pigs and poultry. From the many scattered hovels dogs of every shape, size, colour and texture came racing towards us barking hysterically – yet simultaneously wagging their tails. (Few Peruvian dogs are genuinely dangerous.) At 5.45 we were still in that narrow cleft, between rusty-red cliffs, walking not far above a frenziedly frothing tributary of the Rio Montaro. When we emerged into slanting sunlight, via a dicey tree-trunk bridge of which our mula was rightly suspicious, Acollo Marco was still several miles away and there was no accessible grazing to be seen. (At Tingo Paccha we had been able to buy only a poncho-full of chopped straw; no Alf is grown there.) But soon a semi-circle of soft green grass, some fifty yards long, appeared just below the track on the bank of the curving tributary.

We saw an inexplicable phenomenon as the sun set behind a towering cliff of sheer brown rock. No clouds were visible, yet broad colourless rays of light – in fan-formation – came streaming brilliantly up into the pale blue sky, almost to the meridian. This display lasted for over ten minutes and the effect was uncanny: very beautiful but also slightly frightening. My reaction helped me to understand the alarm felt by primitive peoples during eclipses, or the passage of comets.

As we ate buns and sardines a few clouds gathered and rain sprinkled. But now, as I write, the moon is free again and smooth rocks gleam silver in the bed of the swiftly singing river.

8

Jauja:
First Capital of the Conquistadores

Jauja. 12 November

Nobody could accuse me of being either conventional or tee-total, yet I'm slightly shocked by the campesinos' drinking hours. This is Sunday and when we reached Acollo Marco at 8 a.m. there were more men lowering beers in the cafés than there were women emerging from the pleasingly simple 17th-century church. A campesino who starts drinking at sunrise is unlikely to stop until he falls into the arms of his wife, usually to be found somewhere nearby awaiting this outcome. He will by then have spent enough to feed his children well for a week; at 70 soles a litre cerveza is expensive even for us. Chicha however costs only five or ten soles a litre, depending on its quality, and it would make sense for the government to encourage more home-brewing, if necessary by restricting the cerveza supply. But the fat-cat brewers would not approve of that; starving campesino children are no concern of theirs.

While Juana breakfasted off freshly-cut Alf, we each devoured a mound of fried potatoes mixed with onions, tomatoes, chopped goat-meat and peas, and topped with two fried eggs. As we ate, the standard debate about my gender took place among staff and customers. The longer this trek goes on, the more disinclined are the Peruvians (especially the women) to believe that I am Rachel's *mother* rather than her father. And this evening, when I confronted a mirror for the first time in months, I could see their point. By now I scarcely look human, never mind feminine, with hideously bloodshot eyes (dust and wind), a dirt- and sun-blackened face, thick cracked lips and hair like a gorilla's mane. Add to that my Peruvian army boots, bulging bush-shirt, ragged jeans, broad shoulders and deep voice – it's no wonder I'm addressed more often than not as 'Señor'.

A two-hour walk down a wide cultivated valley took us to the

mountain above Jauja, since pre-Inca days an important town
and now the scene of a famous Sunday market. We scrutinised the
surrounding fields through binoculars and, seeing acres of Alf,
decided on a four-day halt. This morning we were worried by a
small sore on Juana's backbone beneath the crupper leather; this
will require rest and care to prevent its turning nasty. Also, her left
hind shoe needs replacing.

Clearly Martín de Porrés – a 17th-century Lima boy and the
patron saint of animals – was on Juana's side today. Within
half-an-hour of arriving here we had found both a secure corral
and a reliable Alf-merchant who has promised to provide 300 soles
worth twice a day during our stay. She is an elderly, rosy-cheeked
Indian woman whose regular stand is on a corner only fifty yards
from the entrance to Teresa's corral.

Teresa was the first person we met in Jauja, when I entered a
grocer's shop in search of cerveza. She was standing at the counter
– a good-looking young mestizo woman, though over-weight.
(One sees few shapely Peruvian women, of any age or race.) In her
arms she carried a toddler and the shop-keeper was carefully
measuring three tablespoonsful of cooking oil into her little plastic
bag. On seeing the gringoes she at once invited us to lunch –
adding frankly, "I need much chance to practise English which I
study in Lima but now forget". Taking this ball of hospitality on
the hop, I asked if she knew of an *empty* corral for our mula. (I
didn't want to spend all my time in Jauja guarding Alf from
voracious pigs.) Teresa promptly offered her own corral, empty
but for one piglet too small to matter. She led us to her home in the
next street, where the usual double-door gave access to a large
patio with a water-tap and an ancient iron sink in the middle (the
family bathroom) and spacious but semi-derelict rooms opening
off on three sides. The weed-filled, padlocked corral is behind an
empty barn that occupies the fourth side. When I explained that
before turning Juana loose we must unload her, Teresa recommended the new Santa Rosa Hotel in the main Plaza. New hotels
are not really our scene, but the difficulties of guiding a laden mule
through Jauja's narrow streets on market day were extreme and
when we came to the Santa Rosa, before seeing any more appropriate hostelry, we cravenly booked in.

Actually the Santa Rosa is quite congenial. For 250 soles we
have a lofty third-floor single room with a wide window looking
across the valley to nearby snow-peaks and affording a grand-

stand view of the hub of the market in the Plaza below. The furniture – bed, table, chair, wardrobe – is of skilfully hand-carved wood. And the staff are friendly, welcoming and by temperament helpful though an endemic inefficiency often renders their helpfulness inoperative. There are of course snags; despite (or because of?) its newness, the Santa Rosa has no running water and the six lavatories near our room, which have glamorous sky-blue fittings, stink most horrifically.

When we had turned Juana into the corral, with a washed and dusted wound and a banquet of Alf, Teresa insisted on our staying to lunch which she was cooking on a tiny kerosene stove in a cramped, earth-floored, outhouse kitchen. We began with small plates of spaghetti, flavoured with an unfamiliar chopped herb and accompanied by half a hard-boiled egg each for Rachel and me. Then followed watery soup that had been made from one gristly bone, and a few small potatoes. As we ate we realised to our discomfiture that we were in fact eating Teresa's lunch . . . A matter we remedied immediately afterwards. Town poverty is a frightening thing. If we accept a plate of potatoes from a campesino we are not depriving anyone of food; but Teresa has to find *cash* to buy potatoes.

Teresa's small son is called Vladimir. Both his parents were leaders of Lima's left-wing student revolt, which prompted the government to close the universities. Like Katie in Tingo Chico, Teresa is unmarried. Surprisingly, in a country much influenced by Iberian Catholicism, unmarried motherhood seems to be no disgrace among what must I suppose be described as Peru's lower-middle-class. Yet Teresa's life is not easy. The government provides no social security and Vladimir's father, who has a reputation for recklessly propagating the species, contributes nothing to his Jauja son's upbringing. Teresa's brothers give what they can, which is very little. At twenty-four she is the youngest of a family of five. Her father, a primary school teacher, died of TB when she was seven and as the only daughter she has always been close to her mother. After Vladimir's birth Mamma moved to Lima to help look after him while Teresa continued her studies. When the university was closed a few months later eleven students were jailed for eighteen months and sixty more, including Teresa and Vladimir's father, were blacklisted by the police. At about the same time a sister-in-law died in Jauja, as a result of a backstreet abortion, and Teresa returned home to look after her widowed brother, Lonni (Alonso). Lonni is thirty-five but looks much younger; despite being one short of the shilling he has six sons (the eldest sixteen) – all intelligent and charming boys with whom Rachel quickly made friends. Mamma is still in Lima, where she works as night receptionist in a grotty hotel where younger women receptionists would not be safe. Teresa claims that at present she herself would find it hard to get a job in Lima, having been blacklisted – which argument surely assumes an improbable level of efficiency among the police. She is open about her Communist sympathies (Maoist: the Russians are despised for turning 'capitalist'). In her opinion the Church in Peru, as distinct from foreign nuns and clergy working here, is still supporting the junta dictatorship though many of its leaders have made courageous anti-government noises.

Back in the Santa Rosa, Rachel pointed out that my jeans are in a state of disrepair beyond the bounds of decency. I'd been vaguely aware of a draught around the crutch and on examining them I realised that she was absolutely right. So we set out on a serious shopping expedition.

'Colourful' is the excusable cliché adjective for Peru's open-air markets. Not only the campesinos' bright garments, but most of the goods on display – from flamboyant jungle fruits to gaudy plastic sandals – give the scene a peculiar visual hecticness. And in Jauja the atmosphere, too, is gay, despite obviously slack trading. Yet these markets are also uncomfortable reminders that the invasion of Peru by our capital-intensive industries has had a catastrophic effect. Because Third World governments encourage this disruptive investment thousands of Peruvians are unnecessarily destitute and demoralised, with no outlets for their talents and inherited skills. Here there is no reason for blankets and skirts and shoes and crockery to be made in factories. To argue that those investments add to the GNP, or bring in needed foreign currencies, is irrelevant. These effects may make Peru look more prosperous in the World Bank's next Table of Statistics, but in terms of benefits to human beings they merely ensure that the Haves get more.

Drapers' stalls abound and we soon found a promising collection of trousers and slacks: no jeans are sold here. A friendly crowd gathered to watch Señora measuring me and much amusement was caused by my rear being too large for most of the garments on display. But at last I was fitted out with a pair of navy-blue slacks which will be kept for best; while trekking I'll remain indecently exposed. As we were walking away with our purchase, for which I had gladly paid 2,400 soles – the correct price, according to a sticky label – Señora came rushing after us waving 400 soles. We'd been accidentally overcharged: that sticky label belonged to *another* pair of slacks . . . This sort of honesty partly explains the blessed absence of haggling in these markets. Most items have a fixed price and if you don't like it you can push off. This suits me as I'm not a bargainer by nature; to *have to* haggle, as is the custom in some countries, embarrasses me quite ridiculously.

To celebrate my augmented wardrobe we had café con leche in a large restaurant near the Mercado. At the next table six silent men were drinking hard and frequently peeing, with astonishing accuracy, into a circular hole in the floor which lacked even a token enclosing wall. I like people to be sensibly unhibited about their natural functions but this seemed to be going a little far.

At sunset the market was quickly packed up. All over the town, pathetic family groups had gathered around Pappa's insensible form. Coca-chewing wives sat blank-faced beside their prone husbands, often with a baby at the breast and a cluster of children nearby, supping off scraps scavenged from the Mercado garbage-heaps. Some men were standing leaning against a wall, their feet far apart, their heads on their chests. Others were sitting slumped in doorways, or on the steps of the church. Others lay stretched out anywhere, like so many corpses after a battle. Their degradation was painful. At times it is impossible to feel proud of being a European. We may belong to a great civilisation but other peoples have paid – and are still paying – the price.

The same. 13 November

Jauja is history-sodden, at least by the standards of a country without a native written language. This morning we descended to the banks of the rowdy Rio Mantaro to view the remains of an Inca suspension bridge once vital to the flow of traffic throughout the Empire. Hernando Pizarro wrote home: 'The mountain road really is something worth seeing. Such magnificent roads could be seen nowhere in Christendom in country as rough as this. Almost all of them are paved'. However, without fibre-rope suspension bridges across unfordable river barriers these roads would have been useless; and the conquistadores were quick to realise the importance of capturing as many bridges as possible.

We rambled on for two miles to a few mournful lakeside ruins which recalled the days when Jauja was one of the most crucial Inca bases for the control of newly-conquered populations. Before that, it was the tribal centre of the Huancas. Pedro de Cieza de León mentions these ruins: 'This valley of Jauja was all so thickly settled that when the Spaniards entered it, they say, and it is believed true, there were over 30,000 Indians. Now I doubt that there are ten thousand . . . In all these regions there were great lodgings of the Incas, although the most important ones were at the head of the valley, in the part known as Jauja, because there was a great wall there where there were strong, finely built lodgings of stone, and a house of the sun virgins, and a very rich temple, and many storehouses filled with everything to be found. Aside from this, there were many silversmiths who made goblets and vessels of silver and gold for the service of the Inca and the adorning of the temple. More than 8,000 Indians were on hand for the service of the temple and the palaces of the ruler. All the buildings were of stone. The roofs of the houses and lodgings were of thick beams, covered with long thatch. Before these Huancas were conquered by the Incas, fierce battles took place . . .',

The Inca nobleman, Huamán Poma, did not think much of the Huancas. In his *Letter to a King* (the king was Philip III) he wrote: 'The Huanca Indians are very cunning and deceitful. It is their habit to rob women whenever they can and to drive ignorant people out of their homes and farms, which these Indians then keep for themselves. They also succeed somehow in enlisting the support of the friars for their malpractices. The girls wear petticoats and cause a lot of trouble by becoming the mistresses of the priests. The married ones go so far as to give evidence against their husbands so that they can be free to sleep with the Spaniards'. *Letter to a King* was written between 1567 and 1615. By then the demoralisation of the Indians was far advanced and Poma suggested sensible proposals for cleaning up Peru; they haven't yet been implemented. *Letter to a King* is fascinating – I became absorbed in it last night – but also profoundly depressing.

As Francisco Pizarro and his men descended towards Jauja on 12 October 1533 they saw below them the Quitan army, commanded by Yucra-Hualpa. Then, as they advanced, their greatest ally – Indian disunity – became evident. The natives (Huancas) surged onto the road, rejoicing to see invaders who, they imagined, would deliver them from the Incas and restore their autonomy. It was not long since they had been absorbed into the Empire. And already their allegiance to their new rulers had been shaken by Pizarro's murder of Atahualpa, dynastic squabbles at Cuzco and the consequent weakening of Inca authority, both moral and practical. Also, as John Hemming has pointed out, the Spaniards were helped by 'the indifference of the native masses to the fate of the upper classes of Inca society'. Incidentally, Mr Hemming firmly discounts the tiresome, tinselly-romantic notion that the Indians were overawed by the Spaniards because they identified Pizarro with the returning creator god, Viracocha.

The conquistadores spent a fortnight here and, by the time they left, Jauja had been set up as the first Christian capital of Peru. This may strike us as a little premature, when the Spaniards were only half-way to Cuzco where a mighty Inca army awaited them. But the refusal even to think about defeat was what enabled a few hundred men to conquer an empire that stretched from Ecuador to Chile. So Pizarro chose suitable buildings to serve as a church and a Town Hall and left behind eighty Spaniards – forty with horses – as the first citizens of the municipality of Jauja. The stupendous loot already wrested from the Incas was also left here, much of it now regarded as the property of the King of Spain, the rest belonging to individual conquistadores. Therefore many wills had to be made, and other complicated legal documents drawn up, before the crack troops left for Cuzco.

Not long after, Jauja was for Francisco Pizarro the scene of a joyous personal celebration. This fifty-six-year-old bachelor had lost no time acquiring a royal Inca mistress, the fifteen-year-old Quispe Cusi (known to the Spaniards as Inés Huayllas Nusta), daughter of the deceased Inca ruler, Huayna-Capac. In December 1534 this princess presented Pizarro with a daughter, born at Jauja and christened 'Francesca' in the 'capital's' tiny church. Both Indians and Spaniards seem to have regarded this distinguished mestizo as a good omen for future racial co-operation and many tournaments and jollifications marked her birth. Pizarro doted on Francesca and promptly saw to it that she was legitimised by Royal Decree, which document is dated 27 May 1536. Inés gave her lover a son in 1535, but they never married. Instead, Pizarro arranged for her to marry another conquistador, Francisco de Ampuero, and their descendants are the powerful Ampuero family of modern Peru. But that was an unusual match.

Most of the Spanish leaders helped themselves to Inca princesses – who had been brought up to understand that they should cohabit only with the Inca himself, or with a prince of the blood royal. Yet the conquistadores rarely married Indians, preferring to choose a wife from among the Spanish women who were soon setting sail for Peru by the boatload.

Modern Jauja had a mini-crisis today when senior schoolboys organised an anti-government march (or someone else organised it for them) and policemen armed with machine-guns as well as 'normal' weapons were to be seen patrolling every street. Some slight tension was generated, chiefly by the sight of those machine-guns, but neither police nor boys looked seriously violence-prone. Here as elsewhere, the ordinary Peruvian policeman seems a decent type, if not very bright.

Teresa was depressed this morning. Last night Lonni went on one of his occasional binges, which do his 'condition' no good, and he had left the family without a single sole for today's meals. At least we were able to remedy that situation.

Teresa, too, longs to emigrate. She owns two hectares of land – her share of Pappa's legacy, now let – and would like to sell it and settle with Vladimir in Mexico. But at present only those rich enough to ignore the law are free to leave Peru. When I warned her that Mexico has a monumental unemployment problem she wasn't deterred. Like many young Peruvians, she is much given to escapist day-dreams. We were appalled to discover that she is employed two days a week to teach *English* in the local secondary school: Rachel is better qualified to teach Spanish. Teresa herself admits that she merely copies texts from books onto the black-board, and her pupils copy those into their exercise books, and neither she nor they understands more than ten per cent of the words used. English is compulsory in all Peruvian schools, though few teachers know the language. The mental dishonesty encouraged by this policy is most disquieting. How to breed a nation of hypocrites . . .

The same. 14 November

Yesterday Juana's sore seemed to be healing well so we were shattered this morning to find that it has developed into a vile abscess. (Shades of poor Hallam in Baltistan!) The only local veterinario, since Jauja became a motorised region, is a taxi-driver who animal-doctors in his spare time. With Teresa's invaluable help we tracked Domingo to his home and when he had seen Juana he gave me two 'prescriptions' for injections, one to be bought at the smart Agricultural Supplies shop, the other at the no less smart Veterinario Supplies shop. Both of these establishments have a First World aura and are full of the sort of glossy, sophisticated advertisements one never sees elsewhere in Peru. It's shocking that such shops, packed with expensive, high-powered drugs, can flourish in Jauja despite the lack of a qualified veterinario. Most people doctor their own animals – under the guidance, Domingo told me, of travelling salesmen representing multinational companies. Again we are lucky in our veterinario. Domingo is 'muy simpatico': a chunky little man with shrewd bright eyes, gentle hands and a pronounced limp – the result of a mule-kick twenty years ago. His unfailing punctuality boosts one's confidence in his professional abilities. Recently he declined a job as a drugs company rep. "It is not honest. I have seen fathers spending 1,000 soles on rubbish from these shops while their children go hungry. Now farmers are frightened not to spend. They've been told their animals will get new diseases and die if they don't use drugs regularly." When Domingo advised us that Juana urgently needs carrots I explained that she won't even sniff at them, however finely chopped or with whatever mixed. We then agreed that a drugs company vitamin injection would be justified in her case! Domingo says she won't be fit to travel before Friday.

Rachel spent most of the day playing football with Teresa's nephews while I wrote letters. At noon there came a knock on our door and in walked Huamán, a tall, lean, dark-skinned gentleman, elegantly dressed with close-cropped silver hair. We'd met him earlier, in the Mercado, where he denounced the conquistadores – and everyone and everything Spanish – in a voice crackling with rage, as though Pizarro & Co. had just arrived in Jauja. He's as odd as two left feet and became feverishly excited on discovering that I'm a writer; he wants me to write a book about his obsession. He claims to be a pure Huanca Indian whose family have been locally prominent since the 15th century and his message is that Peru's prosperity can only be restored by transferring the capital back to Jauja. Seizing one of our maps, he pointed out that Jauja is as near to the centre of Peru as anywhere could be in such an irregularly shaped country. Like many of his compatriots, he takes an almost mystical pride in his own region but feels no national pride. (To me an understandable sentiment, and one to be much encouraged, globally, for the sake of mankind's survival.) He claims that Futbol was invented in the Jauja valley, where his ancestors wrapped their enemies' skulls in their enemies' skins and kicked them around on cold evenings to keep warm. In pre-Inca times, he said, the peoples of Jauja and Huancayo were more often than not at war, but resentment of Inca domination united them and they have been allies ever since. In 1948 they co-operated to build an airport – men, women and children voluntarily working together, *without pay*, to improve the region's communications.

The same. 15 November

Early each morning, while Rachel is still asleep, I enjoy a large glass of herbal tea sold from a barrow that appears in the Plaza just before dawn. This beverage is made from the condensed juices of various plants. Several litre bottles stand on the barrow top and a large kettle boils beside them on a Primus. A finger of your chosen juice (red, yellow, brown or green, or a mixture) is poured into a glass, which is then topped up from the kettle. The result is warming, palatable and presumably nourishing. The green juice, for instance, is extracted from Alf, which Juana considers very nourishing.

Here Wednesday is another market-day and by sunrise scores of stalls were appearing – some carried by barefooted down-and-outs, some balanced on push-carts, some tied to bus roofs, some in taxis, a few in motor-vans which also contained the merchants' wares. Soon the stalls had been assembled in rows across the wide Plaza, and on the pavements of adjacent streets; and by 7.15, when Rachel and I went to the Mercado for breakfast, most goods were on display.

Mercado breakfasts suit the Murphys' camelesque life-style. Today we each had several fresh buns with two fried eggs, followed by large plates of pork and maize soup made interesting by arcane bits of entrails the existence of which one had never suspected. All around us cheerful family groups were eating dinner-like meals: rice with pork, chicken with chips, stew with boiled potatoes – or various combinations thereof. They had probably been walking half the night, carrying goods to market. Most 'restaurant' stall-holders are helped by their children who

prepare vegetables, chop meat, pluck chickens, gut fish. Usually
Mamma cooks and Pappa serves up. Nobody fusses too much
about hygiene but the end product is almost always delectable.

This is one of the most imposing Mercado buildings we've seen
and Rachel particularly enjoys the floral aisle: fifty yards of stalls
piled high on both sides with carnations, Easter lilies, roses, irises,
gladioli and many other unidentifiable blooms. Nowadays, however, not all the food stalls are occupied because of inflation; a sad
old man who was having trouble finding buyers for his excellent
cheese (we bought the lot) told me that this was the first year he
had seen an empty stall at Jauja Mercado – and he has been
coming here for sixty-five years!

Wandering across the Plaza, we marvelled at the variety of
goods available, despite inflation, but were depressed by the
dearth of those beautiful and useful objects for which Andean
craftsmen (and women) were once famous. The chicha stalls also
offered buckets full of salted pigs' trotters, and dishes of delicious
firm brown trotters' jelly which we were told is rich in protein;
some campesinos are unexpectedly nutrition-conscious. Down a
side-street several merchants were selling, for a few soles each,
what looked like fifth-hand sex-and-violence comics and soft-porn
magazines. These prompted negative thoughts about the value of
literacy in the sierra.

At a road junction, a tall, well-built young man, looking comically incongruous in a natty city suit, was standing behind a table
piled with new books and delivering an eloquent spiel about their
contents. The bright cover suggested a primary school text book; it
depicted a super-healthy campesino family of four (!) encircled by
fruits, vegetables, flowers and herbs. Examining a copy, we saw
that it was a well-produced volume (of mysterious provenance)
denigrating the indiscriminate use of modern drugs and urging a
return to traditional herbal medicines in cases where there is some
evidence that these really do have curative properties. So far so
good: but Natty-suit's sales patter was suspicion-raising. Yet his
audience of eleven unhealthy-looking campesino women, all with
babies on backs, was listening with touching attention, verging on
awe, to this odd mixture of quackery and common-sense. At
intervals he paused, frowningly studied the group, then suddenly
pointed to an individual and diagnosed – 'Anaemia!' or 'Nerves!'
or 'Rheumatism!' or 'Kidney trouble!' Then he turned to the
relevant page and read out a remedy which would cost the patient

nothing but the trouble of preparing it. His cure for alcoholism attracted a few extra listeners. He advocated a combination of herbs and fungi, prepared in liquid form and stealthily introduced into the husband's diet over a period of a week; this would make the patient feel so ghastly after his next binge that he'd go on the wagon forever. Any children attracted by Natty-suit's ringing tones were at once turned away because he had a lot to say about the Billings method of contraception, which he explained could be used either way – to increase or lessen one's chances of conception. The book has several rather clever coloured illustrations to help women determine their most fertile days. But as Billings has been proved disastrously unreliable, even in scientifically-minded societies, it seems unlikely to reduce the Andean population explosion. (Which amounts to a one hundred per cent increase in the last thirty-five years.) Natty-suit's preaching of the Billings Gospel may mean that he represents some religious sect. Eventually five women bought the book, though it costs 240 soles; I hope their husbands approve. When I tried to get into conversation with Natty-suit he brusquely dismissed the gringo; as Rachel noted, he was the only impolite person we've met in Jauja.

Animals are sold on the edge of the town where we saw four young mestizo women sitting by the roadside, looking festive in elaborately embroidered bodices, long multi-coloured and multi-layered skirts and brilliant, handwoven shawls. Each had a hairy brown piglet for sale and this porcine quartet was tethered together, happily rooting on a patch of grass. When Rachel stopped to scratch their backs one woman jokingly urged me to buy a cerdo for my hija. We sat beside them and the usual questions were asked; most women register bewildered sympathy on learning that I have only one child. These four already had several children each and thought the Pill a good idea, even if the padres are against it. But three out of the four said their husbands disapproved, many children being needed to make the most of one's land. Of course you need less if you have fewer children. Yet every good farmer's instinct is to make his land as productive as possible and hereabouts no couple can do that without several pairs of helping hands and feet. There is also a deep-rooted fear of children dying and aged parents being left uncared for and homeless. It ill-becomes us who are State-pampered to criticise the 'fecklessness' of those whose only security, now and for the future, lies in a sufficient number of able-bodied offspring.

We discussed the parlous state of the Peruvian economy, on which these young women had stronger views than might have been expected. Two of the four had gone through secondary school; it's odd to think that many of the schoolgirls we see swarming through Andean towns, wearing with-it grey school-uniforms and neat ties, will soon be sitting on pavements clad in traditional attire trying to sell piglets or chickens.

As we talked, we were watching two blue-uniformed market-police closely questioning a wretched-looking old man who had been pushing a hand-cart laden with three sacks of rice. He was suspected of collaboration with a racketeer who has been attempting to 'corner' the local rice supply. A small crowd of silent, expressionless men gathered to listen to the questioning; one couldn't guess whose side they were on. Then the alleged racketeer arrived, accompanied by a senior policeman; he was waving a sheaf of dockets in the air and protesting his innocence. He *looked* like a small-time racketeer: paunchy, greasy, shifty-eyed. After much further argument, he and his 'accomplice' were firmly conducted into the nearby high-walled municipal compound-plus-jail. "Do you think he's guilty?" I asked our friends. They shrugged. "If he is," said one, "he'll be rich enough to get out soon. If he isn't, he may still have to pay to get out. So it doesn't really matter." On which rather discouraging note we parted.

All morning Rachel had been seeking a suitable present for Vladimir, whose second birthday this is. The choice was limited. A few stalls were piled with pyramids of violently-coloured boiled sweets in plastic bags which one wouldn't give one's worst enemy. Other stalls displayed rows of fragile plastic toys which any normally energetic small child would convert within moments to potential weapons of self-destruction. A crockery stall offered a selection of crudely-painted pottery money-box animals of sur-passing ugliness; reluctantly, Rachel bought a llama – the least repellent creature on view. We'd been invited to the party the day we arrived, when Teresa was already in a pleasurable tizzy about it. Birthdays are Great Occasions in Peru and for her this was an excuse to break out and have a beano.

The party began at 6.30 – and so did a thunder storm of truly Andean proportions. Sheets of blue lightning pulsated above the patio and the echoes of the last crashing roar merged into the next. I hurried out to reassure Juana, but our mula was undismayed.

Not so however the lonely little piglet, who was having hysterics in a corner and had to be taken to the kitchen and cuddled back to calmness.

There were eleven guests: nine cousins, all wearing coloured paper hats made by Teresa this morning, and ourselves. Lonni, not yet recovered from his recent lapse, appeared once at the door, peered at us morosely for a moment, then vanished. The square, high-ceilinged room had rough, dirty, once-white-washed walls inexplicably decorated with faded framed photographs of long-since-dead members of the Swedish royal family. Two small candles, set on the long, wobbly table, provided the only illumination. (Jauja has an electricity supply of sorts but Teresa can't afford it.) A rickety iron bed, now being used as a trampoline by the younger children, occupied one end wall. A small dresser held Teresa's library, mainly Maoist; there was no other furniture. Torrential rain hammered on the tin roof, the earthen floor was uneven and the broken double-door blew open in the gale if not blocked by a large stone. All afternoon Ferdy (Lonni's eldest) had been tinkering with a primeval record-player which he at last induced to work. A plastic bag of 45 rpm Andean songs and dances was then taken from the dresser cupboard and the boys danced in the cramped space available while the little girls sat po-faced on the bed and Vladimir thoughtfully rubbed segments of an orange into his hair. When we had all toasted the birthday boy in non-alcoholic chicha, flavoured with cinnamon, the feast was solemnly carried through the storm from the kitchen on the far side of the patio. First, stewed cuy with potatoes in a mild curry sauce; then The Cake, mixed by Teresa and baked, not entirely successfully, by a cousin of hers who lives nearby and has an oven. Rachel surreptiously slipped her share to me: not hard in the gloom. Everyone's helpings were meagre and Teresa herself hardly ate anything. Vladimir's only presents were from the gringoes and his mother (a plastic train engine). I have grown very fond of Teresa and was saddened by her stricken face when she cut the soggy cake. So much love and thought and money had gone into it . . .

The night was still and starry as we walked back to the Santa Rosa through empty streets flowing with rain-water. "That was a *good* party!" said Rachel. "Much more *sensible* than we have at home."

The same. 16 November

This morning we found Teresa weeping tears of anger. She had discovered that the cake was a failure because of a major emotional crisis in her cousin's household while it was being baked. Four years ago Pilar's handsome, smooth-talking husband migrated to Lima, got himself another woman and left Pilar to provide as best she could for their six children, the eldest being then aged ten. A month ago he reappeared without warning and Pilar, for economic rather than emotional reasons, decided to forgive and forget. But he stayed only a fortnight before deserting again, this time with the beautiful seventeen-year-old daughter of Jauja neighbours – who have put the police on his trail, to no effect. And yesterday morning, while the cake was in the oven, Pilar discovered that she is pregnant again. In such circumstance the Peruvian poor have no redress. If family members did not so loyally support each other in adversity, the level of suffering – mental and physical – would in many cases be intolerable. Generally, marriage (or the lack of it) is taken lightly here. There is complete freedom for irresponsible men and no security for women and children.

Domingo has pronounced his patient cured but advises us not to leave until Saturday to give her time to recover from possible anti-biotic side-effects. He wouldn't accept any fee, saying that we have had to spend too much on injections. Today we hogged Juana's mane, and Rachel groomed her to brilliance. Viewing her after this beauty-treatment, Domingo remarked that if we sold her here we could buy a sturdy pony for half the price fetched by an elegant mula. His eyes twinkled when I reacted rather as though he'd suggested I should sell Rachel. Not only do we love Juana but she – God knows why! – loves us. Even when fodder is not an issue she follows me around Teresa's corral, rubbing her forehead on my shoulder, and when she hears our voices in the patio she greets us delightedly from beyond the high wall. One can't exchange animals as though they were mere motor-cars! And Domingo would, I suspect, have been quite shocked had we acted on his suggestion.

The same. 17 November

Tonight our bodies are clean, our hair is shining and even our

toenails have been pared: an abnormal state of affairs brought
about by immersion in a tributary of the Montaro, some ten miles
away. Would that we'd known of this pool's existence much
sooner! This morning Teresa invited us to join herself, Pilar,
another cousin (Milla) and all their fifteen children on a laundry
expedition. The town's feeble water supply forces many Jauja
families to do the weekly wash as their (and our) ancestors did – in
rivers and streams. We all assembled outside Pilar's house more or
less punctually, but then there was a financial crisis: nobody had
enough soles for the bus fares. (For adults 40 soles return, for
children 10 soles – quite a lot of money.) My offer was gratefully
but firmly declined and Pilar's eldest son went sprinting off to
borrow from his paternal grandfather who owns a licensed coca-
shop. (The coca-trading scene is at present very confusing; we are
sometimes told that under the junta government *all* coca-selling is
illegal.) Meanwhile, five bundles of laundry wrapped in blankets,
and an enormous battered tin tub, and the three smallest children
were all piled into a cycle-cart and we followed the barefooted
cyclist to the bus terminus on the edge of the town, near the
municipal cemetery. A funeral had just taken place and groups of
subdued campesinos in black petticoats and shawls, or dark
ponchos, were gathered outside the imposing fifty-foot gateway
through which could be seen much fanciful topiary. Women were
selling cerveza and roast pork snacks from handcarts and several
men were lying, already 'stocious', on mock-marble seats in the
shade of a double row of cypresses.

Our ultra-decrepit bus was so thickly covered with red-brown
mud that it looked like a prehistoric monster; one expected a long
neck and small head to appear at any moment. Its driver looked
like everybody's image of an escaped mass-murderer. A burly
man, he had long arms, a square squashed face, virtually no
forehead, tiny red-rimmed eyes and a mouthful of jaggedly broken
black teeth. In practice, however, he was a splendid character who
went to great trouble to secure the laundry and tub on an already
over-loaded roof, said the children could travel free because times
are so hard and drove with Vladimir on his knee to ease the
congestion.

The laundry pools are near a village, on the flat green floor of a
fertile valley all criss-crossed with lines of swaying eucalyptus and
surrounded by chunky grey-blue mountains. Here the tributary
flows clear and swift. But in three places, not far apart, it suddenly

quietens and spreads to form knee-deep pools with convenient boulders on which even the thickest blankets dry astonishingly quickly. "No wonder we get so thirsty in the Andes," commented Rachel.

Although washing clothes is not among my favourite occupations I wouldn't mind using this sort of 'launderette' once a week. All but the toddlers set to, rubbing and rinsing and stamping and wringing – hard work under the hot sun and I felt sorry for Milla, who is seven months pregnant. But her eldest son, an endearing boy of thirteen, quietly saw to it that she was spared the most strenuous tasks. We were much impressed by Pilar. Misfortune has not extinguished her sense of humour and she is a decisive disciplinarian – but also patient and loving – with her happy, affectionate brood on whom the family traumas have so far left no visible mark. Milla, Pilar's eldest sister, in fact leads an even grimmer life, coping with a loutishly alcoholic husband, eight children (one a mongol) and an almost defunct bakery-cum-grocery shop.

During mid-afternoon the sky abruptly clouded over, as has been the weather pattern throughout the past week. Theoretically this is the rainy season but it's getting off to an uncertain start. The cruel irregularity of the Andean rain-fall explains why the Indians' religion, from pre-Inca times to the present, has centred its main rituals on the weather. Too much rain can sweep away the precious top-soil, containing next year's food-supply, and wreck homes, barns, flocks, tracks. Too little rain can bring about the misery we saw further north and cause whole regions to be abandoned. When the Indians chant as they plant, they are not simply being light-hearted but are attempting to propitiate those divine agencies which control the weather.

Tomorrow we'll be back on the trail and this evening we consulted Domingo – an exceptional Peruvian, who can map-read – about our route to Cuzco. I was particularly anxious to find a redura by-passing Huancayo (pop. 260,000), which by Andean standards is a city. But Domingo said, "It is far from Cajamarca and your mula is getting tired. You must keep her on the easiest road. She is not fit now for difficult paths where you cannot get her good food."

9

Stresses and Strains

Camp beside Restaurant on Motor-Road. 18 November

It was 10.30 before we had extricated ourselves from the fare-well hospitality of a series of Jauja friends. Teresa made a signif-icant remark as we were leaving: "It's only an hour's bus ride to Huancayo so you'll be there early this afternoon". Huancayo is thirty miles from Jauja and we are on foot. This sums up what is wrong with the mental processes of many Peruvians.

Today's fifteen miles ran straight and level through densely populated (almost one hundred per cent Indian) countryside where the many villages are set back from the road amidst aro-matic pine-groves. This broad valley produces forty per cent of all Peru's wheat and we saw a few small tractors; but family groups still do most of the work. The fact that an all-Indian population produces so much of the national wheat crop in such a small area surely proves that given a chance the indigenous people are not lazy, whatever else. The larger fields were sheltered on four sides by tall eucalyptus trees, and amidst the cacti hedges broom flowered brilliantly. We may not care for tarred roads and tele-graph wires, but it lightens the heart to see so much simple – 'appropriate' – prosperity in the Andes.

We are camping on a wide, humpy patch of grass between the carretera and a new jerry-built restaurant. The Indian proprietor wouldn't allow us to pay for our supper though the bill came to over 200 soles. Rachel regards this as a Red-letter evening; for the first time in Peru we have been able to buy *fresh milk*, which she misses as much as I miss cheese.

Camp on verge of Ploughed Field. 19 November

An unquiet night. Three parties of drunks leaving the restaur-ant fell over the guy-ropes. The motor-traffic was heavy, fast and much given to horn-blowing. The local dogs fought apparently incessantly, only pausing to howl at the moon. And when torrential rain fell during the small hours the tent sagged and leaked.

Pedro de Cieza de León described this valley as 'one of the finest things in Peru'. He wouldn't if he could see it now. For miles, approaching Huancayo, urban squalor disfigures the landscape – rusty tins, broken bottles, filthy sheets of newspaper. And the walls of countless shoddy but pretentious new 'villas' are daubed with political graffiti. And wayside crosses commemorating the victims of bad driving are more numerous than kilometre stones, though this tarred road is smooth and straight.

For an hour we were walking through the hot, dusty, litter-strewn, fume-poisoned city. In the centre a large area had been cordoned off for a Communist Party demonstration; at least 3,000 enthusiastic student-types were hoping to hear impassioned speeches but it was rumoured that the speakers had been arrested on their way from Lima and Cuzco. Hundreds of police, wearing full riot gear and brandishing machine-guns, stood between the demonstrators and the surrounding spectators. Several senior officers were patrolling the nearby streets, idly toying with their revolvers and warning people not to join the demonstrators as there was going to be trouble. These hard-faced nasties were quite unlike the 'village bobbies' we've been meeting. Our arrival infuriated them and they curtly ordered us to leave Huancayo at once. For the first time, I was aware of being in a dictatorship – and not liking it. Some gene to do with the liberty of the individual took over, and for the next half-hour we dodged about on the edge of the demo., pretending not to understand the increasingly irate officers. They were urban types, and clearly afraid of Juana, so they never came too close. Amongst the crowd there was much sympathy for the demonstrators, not because they were communist but because they were brave enough to defy the junta. Yet the fact of such a demonstration being allowed to assemble – even if the speakers were arrested – and the other fact of gringoes being able to ignore police orders with impunity, indicate that this Peruvian dictatorship is not among the world's worst. Indeed, Peruvian governments, whether civilian or military, and however deplorable by our standards, have traditionally been among the more humane Latin American régimes.

Beyond Huancayo a quiet dirt-road took us onto a wide, windy plateau where every square foot of land was ploughed. Alas! no Alf grew amidst all these pale brown fields, some already green-tinged by sprouting wheat. So tonight our mula has only a sack of maize-straw (which she despises) bought in the nearby village of Huacrapuquio.

Hovel on High Pass. 20 November

A day of extraordinary contrasts, with an unfortunate ending. By 8.30 we had climbed into a high green valley and descended into a low green valley, very narrow between intensively culti- vated mountains. Here three girls, driving sheep to the puna, obligingly cut Juana a sheaf of grass on the valley floor. They would accept no payment: it was "a present from the local Co-op".

Easy reduras took us in and out of three more valleys, past several shamlets and through much cultivation onto the puna. There we passed a huge herd of half-wild ponies and foals: an unusual sight. We were back on the dirt-road, at 12,000 feet, when the sky suddenly darkened while continuous rumbles of distant thunder sounded like the rolling of ghostly battle-drums.

For two hours our road climbed along the desolate flanks of almost-sheer mountains, their rock-crests supporting charcoal clouds. Then another turn brought us to an area where less precipitous slopes were teeming with activity as families ploughed tiny stone-walled fields. From here our road was visible for miles ahead, climbing to a high pass marked by a few tiny hovels. That last stage was not enjoyable; a hail-laden gale opposed us. And when at last we reached the pass a solid-seeming wall of sleet was moving towards us across the stark barrenness that stretched ahead. We rejoiced to see that one of the hovels described itself as 'Bar-Restaurant'. Motor roads have their compensations.

We gratefully accepted Aurora's invitation to spend the night on the bar floor; the blizzard then shrieking across the pass was the most severe weather we've encountered in Peru. I corralled Juana behind the hovel where a lean-to provided some shelter; Aurora had assured us that after the blizzard we could buy fodder in the nearby village of Tongos. While I was clumsily unloading with numb fingers, several men and women taunted me – behaviour quite out of character with what we have hitherto seen of the campesinos. These mestizos were potato planters, huddling in the shelter of the corral wall, and when Aurora heard their jeering she rushed out to pour vials of Quechuan wrath upon them – which they ignored.

Aurora is a remarkable young woman, an Indian of what I think of as 'the Inca type'. Taller than the average campesino, she has a thin narrow face, an aquiline nose, ebony hair worn in a bun, bright quick eyes and a touch of haughtiness that could seem out of place – yet somehow doesn't – as she stands behind a homemade bar-counter against a backdrop of almost-empty shelves. This two-roomed shack is a family enterprise; Aurora's brothers built it five years ago, using stones gathered off the mountain. Not too many soles were needed to buy tin for the roof (thatch might put off the passing motor-traffic) and father made the shelving, counter, table and benches. For a time business was brisk and all the shelves were full; nowadays Aurora sells only a powerful home-distilled aguardiente (quite unlike anything else I've ever tasted) and meals based on home-grown ingredients. Listening to her story, that tired phrase 'and the poor are getting poorer' came suddenly to life. The room behind the bar is the family dwelling: a mere cubby-hole, but Aurora has only one son – Alfredo, aged six – and intends to have no more. The views of her meek husband, Victor, who works on his father's land, were not mentioned.

By 4.30 the blizzard was over and as the sky cleared Victor arrived home, his boots leaking, his poncho saturated, his teeth chattering. At once he had to adjust the roof; it had gone agley during the storm though held down by heavy stones. I then found a patch of coarse brown grass and while picketing Juana was approached by two youths who had been sitting in the doorway of the neighbouring hovel. I distrusted them on sight and their questions about our future movements got short answers. When I returned to the bar Aurora denounced them as "muy malo". Victor was at his evening meal, a plate piled with boiled potatoes. He is a diffident, kindly young man who worships his wife and son and seems somewhat in awe of the former.

I relished my solitary walk to Tongos, a two-mile descent along one wall of a steeply sloping ravine. As Tongos is too high for Alf I could find only poor quality oats which I humped in our sack. Carrying such a weight uphill made me aware of the altitude. By then it was dark and fiercely cold, yet the icy fires that burned overhead made clear my path.

Bewilderment was my first reaction when Juana, snuffling excitedly, came towards me. Then I realised that the picket had been stolen, almost certainly by our inquisitive neighbours. "It's such a *mean* thing to steal!" exclaimed Rachel. And indeed every campesino knows that on the puna, where an animal can't be tethered, a picket is the most essential of all pieces of equipment. Juana would never desert us now, but one remembers that dead pony near Huánuco . . . Aurora and Victor were humiliated and enraged, though not surprised. This means a forced march to-morrow, to the nearest pueblo.

The same. 21 November

I had just written the above, and was about to dislodge three pet hens from my flea-bag and go to bed, when loud voices approached and impatient fists battered on the tin door. Frowning, Aurora unlocked it and a dozen young men crowded in. Assuming that they were in search of refreshment, I hastily cleared the table of my literary impedimenta, placing everything on the bench beside me. The young men, however, had not come to imbibe but to investigate the gringoes. And their remarks were provoking Aurora and Victor to tense resentment. Yet clearly our friends were also a little fearful; they made no attempt to eject the intruders when they gathered round me shouting questions in an incomprehensible mixture of Quechua and Spanish. The small dark room – some sixteen feet by ten, its only lighting a flickering wick in a tiny coffee-tin of oil – now seemed even smaller. I kept half an eye on our gear, piled in a corner beside a barrel of kerosene. Some of the men were slightly drunk, but not their chief spokesman, Rodrigo, whom I'd briefly met in Tongos – a swarthy, smarmy character with broken teeth and curly tangled hair. When he sat opposite me two of his companions sat beside me, leaning forward and turning sideways to stare into my face. At first Rodrigo pretended to be welcoming and helpful, in a blatantly insincere way. Then abruptly he demanded our passports and documents. My immediate reaction was to ignore this impertin-ence, but tension was heightening in the room – for reasons I couldn't understand – and from the shadows Aurora vigorously signalled to me to be co-operative. Slowly, by the light of his own torch, Rodrigo thumbed through the two green booklets and the sheaf of Cajamarca documents. Then, rather disconcertingly, he produced one page of a school exercise book and a stub of pencil and began to make notes. Even more disconcertingly, he suddenly looked up, shone his torch in my eyes and asked accusingly why our visas had expired two months ago – a detail I had long since forgotten. Perhaps he was – however outlandish the notion – some sort of local official who would confiscate our passports. I leant forward and snatched them back and at once the atmosphere became so nasty that I felt glad Rachel was asleep. Several of the men who had been standing behind Rodrigo, leaning over his shoulder and advising him while he made his notes, produced their own torches and shone them in my eyes, shouting abusively at me. It was, I judged, time to switch off co-operation and try something else. Jumping up, I banged my fist on the table, pointed to the door and said – "Marcharse!" ("Go away!"). There was a sudden, complete silence. And then they went, just like that.

Victor was shaking with fright, Aurora taut with rage. I asked if Rodrigo held some minor post and learned that he has recently done time for attempting to smuggle cocaine into Miami, which explains his visa-spotting. Your average campesino has never heard of a visa.

I turned then to pick up my torch – and discovered that both our torches had been stolen from the bench beside me. This was infuriating; mine – a heavy waterproof specimen – will be impossible to replace in Peru. But my fury was as nothing to Aurora's. She exploded in volcanic Quechua, then thrust the key of the 'till' (a small wooden box) into my hand, told me to look after the bar and disappeared with a reluctant Victor into the icy black night – I then supposed in courageous pursuit of the thief.

Bemused, I found myself in a new role: *behind* a bar, carefully measuring out glasses of aguardiente for two gnarled campesinos who had appeared from God knows where and obviously didn't believe I was real. They seemed to speak no Spanish. The evening was becoming more unlikely by the minute.

At 10.50 Aurora and Victor returned, breathless, from Tongos. They had been organising a denuncia, which apparently is a legal device of some potency. By that stage I felt too exhausted to probe further. The hens protested with sleepy squawks when I moved them. Most hens *perch* on things but this lot like lying around and I'd no sooner wriggled into bed than they were roosting on my legs.

An hour or so later, Aurora shook me awake, with difficulty. I was to do my denuncia bit, prontitudo. Again the room was full of men; but these were the Goodies, loudly lamenting the misdeeds of the Baddies. The hens hardly bothered to squawk as I crawled out of my warm tunnel: they were adjusting to their rough night.

Rachel opened unseeing eyes, smiled seraphically, then turned over:

It was 12.30 a.m. Aurora handed me half a tumbler of aguardiente (equivalent to about half a pint of whiskey) and introduced me to Garcia, the Governor of Tongos – a rather grand title for a slightly obsequious old man in ragged trousers, a patched poncho and broken boots. He, assisted by his five henchmen, would write down my denuncia, and sign it, and seal it. Then very early tomorrow (i.e., today) Aurora and Victor, as witnesses of the crime (which of course they hadn't witnessed) would accompany me to Pampas's comisaría where we would present our denuncia to the police, make sworn statements and await appropriate action. By evening we and our torches would certainly be reunited. When I tried feebly to point out that I was far more concerned about the picket than the torches, Aurora brushed this irrelevance aside. She was gunning for Rodrigo & Co. – not for her unsavoury neighbours, much as she dislikes them. Her dedication to the recovery of stolen property is admirable, but it's plain that we've now become pawns in some complex local feud which I can't begin to understand – partly because all details are discussed in Quechua. We only know what we're told, which insufficiently explains a rumpus more suited to the theft of the Koh-i-noor than to the pilfering of two electric torches.

For lack of practice, it takes the average literate campesino a very, very long time to read anything, and even longer to write it. Moreover, Peruvians of every race and class have a strong weakness for bureaucracy. It was not clear to me why my denuncia had to contain a list of the contents of our pannier-bags and details of Juana's age, height, colour, brand, price, place of birth, previous owner, date of purchase . . . That, somehow, provided the evening's final touch of surrealism.

At 1.45 I thanked the Goodies, emptied my second half tumbler of aguardiente and tottered back to my roost. Some time later torches were shone on my face and the Goodies courteously wished me good-night. And not long after Aurora was briskly arousing me with the news that before leaving for Pampas we must go to Tongos to see another crucially important official who was not available last night.

It was 5.05 a.m. and I had an aguardiente hang-over, which is like none other. Icy air was knifing through gaps left by the cardboard that blocked the little window above our flea-bags.

Rachel – all bright-eyed and bushy-tailed – was longing to be brought up to the minute on recent events. The intrinsic lunacy of the whole enterprise, from our point of view, became even more apparent as I gave her a brief outline. "D'you really believe the *Peruvian police* will find *our torches?*" she asked. "No," I replied.

We took Juana with us, to spend the day in the greater safety of Aurora's parents' corral. By 6.30 we were in Diego's patio, where a baby girl, stark naked and filthy, was crawling around in the dust with two striped piglets and a starved-looking pregnant bitch. Diego's wife squatted in the sunny corner spinning and humming quietly; she looked several pence short of the shilling. I never did discover who Diego is or why we were there; at that stage I was wholly preoccupied by the novel sensations within my head. Aurora, occasionally backed by Victor, treated our host (or inquisitor, or whatever he was) to a Quechua monologue of considerable ferocity and eloquence. At the end she turned to me, pleading for corroboration. I recklessly nodded – and then winced. Diego stretched out a hand, requesting our passports and documents. Expressionlessly he pondered them, before asking – this was the ultimate *non sequitur* – how many languages my books have been translated into. "Not many, and I can't remember which," I said inadequately. "Japanese, Hungarian and Czech", said Rachel. Diego stared at her disbelievingly. Aurora seized my arm and said, "Write that down!" Diego handed me a scrap of paper and a biro. I began to suspect that I was still asleep and this was the sort of dream you have after too much aguardiente. *"Write it down!"* repeated Aurora. I wrote down 'Japanese' and 'Hungarian', then wondered despairingly how to spell 'Czech' – but realised after a moment it didn't terribly matter. Diego ordered me to sign the scrap of paper and he laboriously witnessed it before tucking it away under his poncho. I decided that undoubtedly I was dreaming. Diego stood up (the rest of us had been standing all the time: nobody asked us to sit down) and assured me that when I had brought him the necessary documents from the police and the attorney's office the local community court would retrieve our torches. Disguising my total disbelief, I made mumbling noises of gratitude and admiration and we departed.

On the packed bus to Pampas the landscape was invisible. As we hurtled around dozens of hair-pin bends I tried not to think about the only too imaginable ravines to left or right. At a police checkpoint on the edge of the town two young men passengers were arrested, charged with cocaine-running and taken away literally in chains. Aurora watched, thin-lipped. "They are friends of Rodrigo," she said.

Resigned to my pawn status, I made no effort to follow the proceedings as Aurora led us in and out of three cramped, twilit attorneys' offices full of litigious campesinos brooding over grievances and desiccated clerks filling out forms in triplicate. (One could write a tome about the grotesque functions of the attorney in Peruvian society – but I won't.) I obediently signed when and where I was told; for all I knew, I might have been signing my own death-warrant. At the newish and surprisingly large police station Aurora's tactics suddenly changed. Thrusting the denuncia and a sheaf of attorneys' documents into my hand, she instructed me to become very angry and insist on immediate and drastic police action. Then she and Victor effaced themselves, squatting against the wall outside while I entered the first of a series of offices and confronted the first of a series of uninterested and slow-witted police officers. Here bureaucracy reached a crescendo: a detailed description of the next three hours would sound like exaggeration – to anyone unfamiliar with Peru. Finally Aurora and Victor were summoned and closely questioned; in the presence of the police Aurora became unexpectedly deferential. But she achieved her aims. The senior officer signed and stamped my denuncia, and our attorneys' papers, and gave us an impressive seal-strewn document for Garcia, and another for Diego, delegating to them the responsibility for retrieving stolen property. After all that effort, Aurora was deeply wounded to see me trying to buy replacement torches in the Mercado. She seems genuinely to believe in the ultimate efficacy of her crusade against Rodrigo.

I had crassly assumed that Aurora and Victor would avail of their free bus trip to do some shopping in the metropolis, but when I suggested this Aurora said simply – "We have no money to buy things in a town." And it was obvious that neither she nor Victor knew their way around Pampas, their nearest pueblo. Eventually however we found a blacksmith who made a picket by thrusting an eighteen-inch iron bar into his furnace, bending the top and sharpening the end – ten minutes work which cost 300 soles. And the result was neither as convenient nor as secure as our stolen Mexican picket.

We waited on the edge of the town, opposite the police station, for whatever transport might materialise to take us home. Soon two young soldiers joined us, going to Tongos on leave, and then an aged and infirm campesino couple, leaning on sticks. The first vehicle to appear was a smart new Dodge van; it stopped and we all climbed into the open empty back. The driver was a plump, sleek mestizo with gold teeth and a gold tie-pin and a fur-lined coat; when there was a slight delay, because of the old couple being stiff in the joints, he shouted at us as though we were cattle. Then suddenly he realised that he had two gringoes on board. Jumping out, he switched on the charm, swept off his fur-lined cap, bowed and beamed and invited us to sit in front with him. He spoke fluent English and went rigid with horror when I suggested that the old couple should have the seats: this was *not on* . . . So I informed him that we would stay with our friends in the back. That grim journey took only thirty-five minutes because our driver never slackened speed, even on the most perilous stretches of a narrow, boulder-strewn, uneven track with thousand foot drops beyond the verge. The bumping was so violent that we avoided broken bones only by bracing ourselves against each other as we cowered in a miserable heap on the metal floor. The cold was intense, yet had we been walking it would have seemed a warm sunny afternoon. Why do so many gringoes *choose* to travel through the Andes by bus or truck? Our own thick cloud of dust obscured the landscape and almost suffocated us; this evening I'm still dust-encased, hoarse and sore-eyed, and my brown Husky jacket is silver. (Here no washing water is available: from this pass it's a forty-minute walk to the nearest stream.) Outside the bar, our driver insolently demanded 100 soles from each passenger though 25 soles is the standard charge for the journey. He was a not uncommon mestizo type, too contemptuous of Indians to sit beside them yet quick to profit from their needs. I gave him 200 soles for the eight fares and told him to get lost.

We paused only to collect Alfredo – Aurora's father was behind the bar today – then hastened down to Tongos where Rachel, Alfredo and I stayed with Juana while Aurora and Victor distributed the documents. I was beginning to feel rather bored by the whole charade. The aguardiente had shifted its scene of activity from my head to my guts and my stomach was throbbing in the oddest way; I've never before had a hang-over in that area.

We sat leaning against a colossal boulder in a sunny corner of the open yard – today has been cloudless – and Aurora's mother and two sisters prepared wads of coca for themselves, and a smaller wad for the six-year-old Alfredo; they urged Rachel and me to try a chew but we declined with thanks. I was worrying about Juana, tethered nearby on a useless llama-cropped patch of grass. The local fodder is poor and during these cold nights she is losing the flesh she put on in Jauja.

When Aurora and Victor reappeared it was plain that something had gone seriously wrong. Aurora erupted in Quechua to her family; she was spitting with rage. Victor smiled sheepishly at me, then bent down and whispered that Diego and Garcia were demanding a 'legal fee' of 500 soles each before acting on the denuncia. You could buy ten torches for 1,000 soles. I stood up and said that I must get back to the bar and do some writing. Aurora turned to me then, her fine eyes flashing, and ordered me to go to the government in Lima and have Garcia and Diego sacked. They are, it seems, Baddies in Goodies' clothing. They have no respect for the government, for the police, for famous foreign writers, for Aurora, for Peru's reputation abroad. I shrugged, said "Adios!" to everybody and stumped away up the mountain followed by Rachel – and Alfredo, who hero-worships the gringita. He *looks* like a frail three-year-old but is extremely bright. On the way home he volunteered the names of every shrub, flower, grass and herb en route. Pretty impressive. Sadly, this brightness will soon have been dimmed forever by coca-chewing.

Aurora and Victor returned only ten minutes ago, looking mollified. Apparently Diego and Garcia, on hearing of my attitude to 'legal fees', and my threats to complain about them to the government (!), decided to act on the denuncia for free. So Aurora is confident that by tomorrow evening we'll have our torches back. At first she was crest-fallen when I explained that we can wait here no longer because Juana urgently needs Alf. Then she solved that problem: on our way through Pampas the day after tomorrow we can pick up our property from the police station. She *seems* certain that the torches can be retrieved; and of course she knows more than we do about the methods of the community court.

Camp on Mountain-ledge by small Lake. 22 November

I hadn't realised, so distorting is motor transport, that another, still higher pass lies between Aurora's Pass (as we have understandably named it) and Pampas. As we were climbing towards it, soon after sun-rise, we saw several wriggling heaps of thousands of black and orange caterpillars. Other thousands were processing over the short grass and herbs in single file, their lines extending both ways as far as we could see – a remarkable spectacle and all happening above 13,500 feet. Here too grew an enchanting blue and white minuscule flower – its tiny perfection most wondrous – and also a glorious rose-pink flowering cactus. Approaching the pass, we saw two small, distant herds of sheep and llamas.

Then we were overlooking the still-remote Pampas valley – and beyond it our next obstacle, a contorted grey-brown mountain massif, filled the whole southern sky. We were almost level with its multiple summits and Rachel remarked that it would be convenient if Juana were a Pegasus-type. I agreed – not for reasons of transport, since I enjoy downing and upping in the Andes, but because we had run out of water and a hoof-conjured fountain would have been most welcome on our Mount Helicon.

At 2.30 we saw an expanse of best quality puna grass on a ledge some fifty feet above the track. With the rains imminent (probably), we are now anxious to keep up a daily average of 20–25 miles: but you can't do that with a starving mule. So we set up camp here, beside a still black lake at the foot of a long, golden-grassed ridge with battlements of silver rock. Today too was cloudless and the afternoon sun permitted us to lie out on the soft level turf. For an hour we wood-gathered, climbing down the almost vertical slope beyond the track in search of suitable dead scrub. (Some species won't burn.) We were drinking hot soup as the sun set, leaving a delicate glow of merging pastel shades above royal-blue mountains. (There should be some stronger word than 'mountains' for the Andes; after all, even in Ireland we have things called 'mountains' . . .) The stars came out – here so lustrous, alive, close – while the fire was settling to a shimmering crimson hillock. Then Rachel played her fideog, which is hardly distinguishable from the Indian pipe, and the mountains seemed to listen. On all the immensity of their slopes, no light twinkles; even the campesinos are defeated by such precipices.

Pampas Police Station. 23 November

Last night's heavy rain became a Celtic drizzle towards dawn, then stopped. We were away by 6.30, our road overlooking wide gorges where, far below, silver masses of shifting cloud were gently coiling and drifting, dissolving and reshaping, in a soundless unearthly ballet – one of the loveliest visions I have ever seen.

Pampas police station, overlooking a level grassy common, happens to be the first building one comes to. I dreaded being caught up once more in the inscrutable movements of its bureaucratic machine and was disposed to march briskly past. But then we saw familiar figures sitting hunched dejectedly on the wide steps that lead up to incongruous glass double doors. *"Baddies!"* hissed Rachel. And so they were: three of Rodrigo's friends, including the two who sat beside me in the bar when our torches were stolen. They ignored us as we walked up the steps.

We were courteously greeted by a tallish, handsome young officer, impeccably uniformed – not one of those we'd already met. Pedro spoke reasonably good English and assured us that investigations were proceeding satisfactorily. Soon our antorchas would arrive from Tongos, escorted by Aurora and Victor. I stared at him disbelievingly. "You mean you've *found* them?" "No, no!" said Pedro. *"We* haven't – but the village people are in charge. You will see how it is. The village people have their own ways." It was only 10.45 but clearly we couldn't walk off stage at this point. We unloaded Juana, stacked our gear in the hallway and went in search of fodder.

At noon Aurora, Victor, Aurora's father and three more Baddies, looking sullen and angry, arrived in the back of a truck-bus. But no one was bearing antorchas. A verbally violent Quechuan confrontation then took place on the common by the steps; the five Goodies, the six Baddies and five policemen all spoke together, apparently ignoring each other's statements, accusations, arguments. Finally two policemen and three Baddies were despatched to Tongos by whatever transport they could find and Pedro informed me that it was only a matter of time . . . Antorchas would come because the remaining Baddies were being kept as hostages. And indeed the three had to spend the rest of the day carrying loads of heavy builders' rubble from the police corral to the nearest ravine, at least a mile away. In these parts there's no hifalutin nonsense about first proving your man guilty.

The hours passed slowly. We treated our friends to lunch in the Mercado, took Juana to the blacksmith, fodder-hunted and explored Pampas in depth – not a richly rewarding experience. At sunset I asked permission to camp behind the police station and Pedro invited us to spend the night in what is quaintly known as the 'Casino', a large room at the back of the station containing only a never-used table-tennis table and two rusty, punctured bicycles leaning against one wall under a coloured photograph of the junta. And still no antorchas . . . I organised a doss-house for Aurora and Victor – now both in a panic about Alfredo, who has never before been left all night without either parent. Then I smuggled two bottles of cerveza into the casino, where Rachel was already asleep on the concrete floor, and entertained Pedro. When he joined the police force three years ago, after graduating from San Marcos University, he had ambitions – now withering – to improve its efficiency and reduce corruption. He said the police are at present being pushed into the background by the army, which development is creating much resentment within the force and much unease among the general public. "If revolution comes," he said, "there's no doubt whose side the police will be on!" But he thinks revolution unlikely – "Peru is still stable enough to change governments without widespread disorder. We are not Bolivians!"

As I was changing the picket, at 8.30, what looked like a satellite appeared high up in the sky, moving slowly through the blackness. It was in fact a vehicle crawling down from 'Aurora's Pass'. Half an hour later the truck stopped outside. In the hallway, Pedro and I met the two policemen, Rodrigo and another Baddie who was carrying a large bundle of dirty blankets. This he carefully unrolled on the desk in the front room, to reveal – how wrong we'd been! – antorchas, in perfect working order. Pedro nodded casually and said something dismissive. The two policemen saluted and went off to their sleeping quarters. Rodrigo and his aide, eyes to the ground, turned and slouched away into the night. Pedro handed me a document to sign acknowledging receipt of recovered property. "But *how* were they found?" I asked, signing with a flourish. Pedro smiled. "They weren't *found*: the thief was persuaded to give them up." "But how?" I persisted.

Pedro sighed. "It is hard for me to explain and for you to understand. These people are very superstitious. They believe still in all kinds of spells and omens and bad luck. They understand very little about the rest of the world. They are easy to frighten. So – they are told you are a famous powerful person. All over the world people are reading what you write." (Here a penny dropped!) "And now because of them you are going to write about how wicked Tongos is. Then many people think badly about Tongos. And that makes bad luck. The village has drought, landslides, floods, maybe even an earthquake. Animals die and children have diseases. And for this the bad men will be blamed. For days the village council puts this pressure on the people who are guilty – and the council itself believes what it is saying, or at least half believes it. All these documents are not just bureaucracy. They are like the llama foetuses and parrots' hearts and so on which witch-doctors use. They help to build up the pressure. Then usually the thief's nerve goes and he gives up what he stole. For you this is not how the law works and maybe you think when we know who is guilty he should be arrested and go to jail. But if *we* punish when the *village people* recover, then we upset the whole system. And it is a good system in the sierra where communities are small enough to use these pressures. The punishment for such men is disgrace for themselves and their families. Most village Indians are honest and hate thieves. For Rodrigo this sort of punishment doesn't matter. He is already a known criminal and despised. He is a cousin of Aurora and has cheated her father out of many soles and made much family trouble." (Another penny dropped.) "But he was not the thief. He has bigger ideas. He wanted to blackmail you for having no visa and get a lot of money. But Aurora says you frightened him – I don't know how. And then afterwards he got more frightened because Aurora said you are so powerful with many government friends in Lima." Pedro paused and smiled. "Maybe now I should arrest you! But how can you renew a visa in the sierra? You cannot tie your mula to the top of a bus and go to the Immigration Office in Lima!"

On which civilised note we bade each other good-night. I'm looking forward to the morning, when Aurora and Victor join us for a farewell celebratory breakfast. They too will have to sign documents – for reasons unclear – before returning to Tongos.

Camp on Ledge of steep Mountain. 24 November

A few miles beyond Pampas our rough dirt-road left the fertile valley floor and turned left to force its tortuous way through this mighty massif. Today has been one of the most spectacular of the entire trip. A steady 22-mile climb – we now have kilometre stones! – ever round and up, and round again and up again, with new combinations of melodramatic vistas appearing at every corner. "Seeing's believing", commented Rachel sagely at one point. She added, "You know, you won't be able to write *properly* about all this – it's not the sort of thing you can *describe*." Too true!

We were then overlooking a canyon in which the Empire State Building would seem like a garden shed. Later, as we stood above a panorama of heart-lifting splendour we counted eight distinct shades of mountain blue, ranging from navy-blue to the palest powder-blue – depending on the remoteness of the range, its geological nature and botanical garb (if any), the relative position of the sun and the shadows of occasional high white clouds. One never becomes used to the Andes; a sense of wonder suffuses every hour.

This region's only defect is Alflessness.

Camp on High Puna. 25 November

Today began with one of those brief, perfect experiences which seem detached from the rest of life: flawless memory-jewels, to be cherished forever. Leaving Rachel asleep, I crawled out to dress at 5.15. The dawn world was profoundly still. In a sky of the most delicate blue-green, a pale gold crescent moon shone – brilliant alone but for the morning star, poised steadily luminous above a slim silver cloud that lay along the darkness of the eastern mountains. I sat entranced, motionless. Then the green tinge faded and the blue deepened. Moments later, Venus was extinguished as the cloud glowed rose-pink while violet shadows filled the valley far below. At which point Rachel pulled back the flap and asked, "What are you doing sitting there on the frost looking like a zombie?"

This morning's olive-green puna was broken by many gullies of raw red earth and stark outcrops of black and silver rock. Our road climbed to within a hundred feet of a dramatic two-pronged peak first seen yesterday, when it seemed a remote, inaccessible summit. Soon after, the sun began to draw dense vapour from the apparently bottomless abyss on our left. The effect of that swift, sinuous upward movement was quite eerie, as though we were being privileged to witness some secret elemental rite. "Imagine," said Rachel, "we're seeing clouds *being born!*" The natural result of seeing clouds being born promptly followed: they enveloped us. Then a gusty wind got up, and through the hesitantly dispersing mist we glimpsed vast nearby chasms and distant snow-streaked ranges.

For two sunny midday hours we sweated hard as the road switchbacked just below a series of rock-peaks. Then it sloped

to an abandoned mine where a solitary campesino woman was
herding llamas; and from there we could see it soaring ever higher
to cross a pass on which a few hovels stood out against the skyline.
We are camped on a narrow ledge below that pass, the only
possible site for miles around. As the condor flies the pass is
scarcely half-a-mile away, as the road winds it is an hour's walk.
Now rain is hammering on the tent so that we can hardly hear
ourselves think and water is audibly running below the floor.

Camp by Rio. 26 November

A pewter-grey morning, the stillness broken only by post-deluge
water rushing down every slope. When we reached the wretched
shamlet on the pass its entire population – about thirty coca-
chewing people, ragged and filthy – turned out to view us incredulously. Maize straw was provided as a gift for Juana who
embarrassed us by ungraciously refusing it; she approved of the
brand of puna grass on offer last night.

For the rest of the day we were only rarely on the carretera. This
was a region of contrasting mountains: some smooth and grassy
green to their summits, some angular, rocky and barren. Many
llamas grazed in long, broad, velvet-turfed valleys and their
astonished herds stared at us mutely as we passed.

We walked for eleven hours today and are now camped beside a
turbulent young rio only vaguely suggested, and left nameless, on
our maps. There is barely room for the tent on a grassy ledge just
above the water and surrounded by low scrub and acres of stony
riverbed. In theory such sites are verboten, especially at the
beginning of a rainy season; but we could find no other level patch
for many miles around and it was already dusk when we stopped
here.

This long, narrow, twisting valley is Alfless and oatless; only
potatoes and Inca vegetables are grown on the precipices above
and below the scattered hovels. Juana is again losing condition
and we plan to give her a few days rest in Ayacucho if the local Alf
supply is adequate.

Mayor Police Station. 27 November

By 7 we were climbing onto the first of a series of bulging
mountains overhanging the valley floor. Tremendous greenery-

filled chasms separated these mountains and to gain half-a-mile our mud-slippy track had to curve around each chasm for three or four miles. In the keen morning air our bellies felt very empty; last night we ate the last of our Jauja supplies – a small tin of beans and four stale buns between us. After three hours the track dropped again to river-level, before climbing to a shamlet just below a high pass. Here we eagerly sought food, but there was none; most of the campesinos were away in their fields. Then a brief precipitous redura took us down to Churcampa – an enchanting pueblo of helpful people, steep cobbled streets, an unexpectedly imposing Plaza, an eating-house serving chips and omelettes and an ancient woman with only one ear who reluctantly agreed to provide Alf.

From Churcampa's wide green shelf one overlooks an uncanny landscape, far below. This immensity of arid red earth is criss-crossed with convoluted dry river-beds, and long ridges that would seem mountains almost anywhere else, and what look from a height like mere heat-cracks but are in fact deep fissures littered with jagged hunks of rosy-hued rock. An appropriately melo-dramatic redura took us down so fast that we could *feel* the air thickening as though the extra oxygen were a tangible substance. Then for miles our level path wound between clumps of young spear-cactus, their cool blue-green refreshing amidst this desic-cated wilderness. The only other vegetation was a low, nasty-smelling dark green bush that not even goats will eat. Soon we were sweat-soaked and we paused often to gulp pints of sun-warmed water. The hot silence created a curiously tense atmos-phere. No breeze stirred; no bird or insect flew or called; there was no movement but our own. Occasionally we glanced back in awe at the cordillera from which we had just descended, a blue, flat-topped mountain wall filling the northern sky and rising sheer from this barren ledge. For it was no more than a ledge, as we realised when without warning we were *overlooking* a turmoil of lesser mountains. Through a gap, we glimpsed the Mantaro canyon far below; seen from such a height, the broad brown river seemed unnaturally immobile and noiseless. Hereabouts it has carved a horseshoe loop through a phalanx of mountain massifs; from where we then stood, it was both in front of us and (though invisible to the east) behind us. To reach the little pueblo of Mayor, on its left bank, we had to descend another two thousand feet on a ladder-steep and perilously narrow path.

Approaching Mayor, today's weirdness reached its climax as

STRESSES AND STRAINS 203

we plunged into a world where Nature has gone mad. For a time we lost the path and went wandering bemusedly through a labyrinth of ravines. All around us the soft cliffs – red, grey, yellow – had been transformed into battlements and turrets and squat towers and soaring spires; a lunatic extravaganza of erosion made to seem even more improbable by many small clumps of a translucent flesh-pink cactus we've never seen before, and giant candelbra cacti like green echoes of the rock spires, and thickets of prickly pear, and threatening sword cacti with misshapen stems fantastically contorted into attitudes of pain and protest. Here a powerful feeling of unreality overcame me, as though I were having hallucinations. And Rachel's reaction was similar. She said: "This can't be *real*! I've always imagined the moon would look like this!"

Mayor is almost as weird as its hinterland; most of the few inhabitants look a trifle crazed, which is not surprising. At first it seemed a deserted village; we saw nobody while walking down a long street of single-storey adobe houses – all padlocked, though it was then 6.10. Later we learned that there has been mass-migration to Lima. The main Plaza was also lifeless, apart from a haggard, spinning campesino woman squatting at the half-closed door of an empty shop. She scowled at us and said there is no food available because Mayor is too far from everywhere. This however was an exaggeration. Little can be grown in the pueblo's desert-like surroundings, but a carretera of sorts runs on the far side of the Mantaro and basic supplies come in by truck. Unfortunately these do not include fodder and as Juana had had nothing to eat since 11 a.m. we were frantically worried. Coming to a second, smaller Plaza, we saw an unexpectedly large police station and went to beg for aid and advice. The police, not being native to Mayor, are the most normal people around. A fat, cheerful senior officer invited us to spend the night as guests of the force and despatched a junior officer to requisition Alf from the only local who grows it – on a minute strip of irrigated land near the Mantaro. So I'm writing this sitting on the concrete floor of an empty room with Rachel asleep beside me *on* her flea-bag because it's too hot to be *in* it. Juana is audibly munching in a nearby patio where a life-sized statue of St Rose of Lima, patron saint of the Peruvian police, stands in one corner with a few dusty plastic flowers at its feet. In another corner are two barrels which a small boy fills twice daily with murky Mantaro water for police ablutions and cooking. The

Mayor restaurant, where Rachel ate an inferior lomo saltado while I (too heat-exhausted to eat) drank six litres of cerveza, is the filthiest we've seen. Even the celebrated Murphy immunities may not preserve us from its after-effects.

Camp in muddy Stubble-field. 28 November

Below Mayor the young but mighty Mantaro swirls loud and swift around the base of a gigantic black cliff jutting out from the opposite mountain. At 6.30 we crossed a new suspension bridge and for the next two hours were in a barren gorge which even at this hour was heat-tormented. Here the erosion mood was pure Gothic; we might have been walking between the ruins of a thousand cathedrals. The fluted pillars were pale grey or brown, boldly streaked with red or pink; and occasionally, at the foot of these cliffs, great oblong symmetrical chunks of rock or clay stood isolated like giants' altars.

At the confluence of the Mantaro and the Huarpa we turned due south, to ascend the Huarpa valley on a track that takes a trickle of motor traffic from Huancayo via Pampas to Ayacucho. The hills on our left were an astonishing bright pink and orange, a few cane-fields grew by the river, and for miles the track ran between blossoming shrubs and low trees on which lines of berries, like coral necklaces, hung below long, serrated leaves.

At noon we came to an isolated hovel and rejoiced to see CERVEZA scrawled in huge white letters across the gable wall. An emaciated young man with a withered left arm runs this shebeen; he was not quite sober when we arrived – and I wasn't quite sober when we left. The cerveza supply had run out, but on being informed by Rachel that this is my birthday he provided instead several glasses (I can't remember exactly how many) of home-distilled cane spirits: not the most energising potation at noon on a very hot day. And Juana was given a large pile of chopped cane stalks which, mercifully, she condescended to eat. This mestizo couple have six small children and we've seen no more wretched campesinos in Peru. They grow a little cane and maize, and fish in the river, and sell a few drinks to the occasional passing truck-driver. The twenty-four-year-old wife sounds tubercular when she coughs. Before leaving we distributed our precious half-dozen oranges, bought in Mayor, amongst the children – one of those futile gestures of guilty generosity that afterwards engender a vague shame because of a suspicion that the main motive was to ease *one's own* discomfort . . .

Climbing away from the Huarpa, our track ran between heat-radiating cliffs of soft grey clay and porous rock. When a little van appeared we had had fifteen minutes warning: its noise in that valley seemed an aural crime. It drew up beside us in a cloud of fine dust; the young driver had witnessed our departure from Pampas and was full of sympathy, assuming we couldn't afford motor-transport. He gave us a kilo of pickled olives, ladled out of a huge wooden cask.

An hour later, from the crest of a high ridge, we saw Huanta – a biggish pueblo – looking deceptively close on the floor of a round fertile valley where Alf grew tall. On our way down we tried hard to buy some but nobody would sell, at any price, and we both sensed anti-gringo vibes. In Huanta – an attractive pueblo, architecturally if not humanly – we paused for rice and mutton stew. But I can never enjoy a meal when Juana has nothing. Soon we were climbing out of the valley between *acres* of Alf, yet here too nobody would sell. As the light faded we left all crops behind, and all hopes for Juana's supper. Briefly we considered theft, but couldn't quite overcome our inhibitions. This site, on the edge of a stony, crudely ploughed stubble-field of sticky clay, offers our mula only sparse grass, growing along a damp ditch between tent and road. Rachel, ever optimistic, gathered fuel by torchlight and I attempted the fire ceremony. But everything wetly resisted a whole box of matches so we've had no celebratory hot drink.

Camp on lush Pasture. *29 November*

This morning a memorable insect crawled onto my hand off one of the Diana-bags that had been out under the flap all night. Its fat grey-green body was about an inch and a half long, its hairy legs at least three inches long and its slowly waving antennae still longer. Even Rachel, who is abnormally well-disposed towards all God's creatures, had to admit that it looked exceedingly disagreeable. Many Peruvian insects are of Andean proportions and peculiar aspect; my experience of them is wide as I often uncover specimens on lifting a big stone to hammer the picket.

After a night of non-stop rain, heavy sticky mud clung irritatingly to boots and hoofs as we struck camp. Poor Juana was in an understandably anti-load mood and today has been marred by fodder-worry. For long hot hours we marched around a succession of dusty grey mountains with not a hovel or an animal to be seen. By noon we were on a naked rock-ridge overlooking an immense pallid semi-desert dominated by La Quinua's monument – a conspicuous pillar commemorating the Battle of Ayacucho. (On 9 December 1824 a mestizo force under Marshal Sucre thrashed the Spanish army and decisively ended Spanish rule in Peru.) Our road could be seen wriggling frenziedly around countless impenetrable ravines on its way across this sun-scourged landscape. And nowhere was there a mouthful of vegetation for our mula.

Beyond the semi-desert we abruptly rejoined the tarred costa-to-selva highway, which gradually descended to river-level (the Huarpa again). Here we were diverted by dense swarms of two-inch crickets enjoying their mating season – hopping and copulating all over the road like an animated carpet. Luckily for them there was little traffic. For three hours we followed the rio through a heavily populated valley where many crops are grown, but no Alf. However, on this site – a little-used soccer pitch on the outskirts of a village – the grass is long and lush.

Camp on steep rocky mountain. 30 November

A day of disappointments. We had planned to spend some time in Ayacucho, exploring the town and its surroundings (both of exceptional interest) while Juana put on flesh. But alas! even with the assistance of a kind university lecturer we could find neither corral nor Alf-merchant. The bigger the town the less easy it is to cater for a mula's needs.

Ayacucho prides itself on its record of political activity, usually organised by the university students. The university is one of the oldest in the New World, dating from 1677. The town was founded on 9 January 1539, as a military post to protect travellers from the guerrilla bands of Manco Inca, a grandson of Huayna-Capac. And this morning the military were still much in evidence as numerous army jeeps drove through the narrow old streets with arrogant recklessness, their youthful crews brandishing revolvers, rifles and machine-guns.

At 8 a.m. the atmosphere was enjoyably tense in the central Parque Sucre, as though the crowd was awaiting not a student rally but some daring display like parachuting or motor-cycle racing. Citizens of all ages huddled in groups excitedly exchanging conspiratorial whispers. It was rumoured that a bomb had been placed *somewhere* in the town centre . . . Then hundreds of jubilant-looking grey-uniformed children swarmed into the Plaza: all the schools had closed for the day. Many small boys produced balloons from their satchels and inflated them; they had evidently been hoping for a Protest Fiesta.

We tethered Juana outside a restaurant down a side-street with a small sheaf of oats, the only fodder available. As we breakfasted, four tall blonde gringoes came in – the first foreigners we've seen since leaving Chavín. They looked like albino giants, so accustomed have we become to the tiny dark campesinos.

By 10 the post office had decided to close for the day; and outside the bank, where we went to cash a cheque, striking clerks were occupying the pavement. They explained that their action had nothing to do with the student rally and apologised profusely for inconveniencing the gringo. I in turn explained that Irish gringoes are used to their own banks going on strike for six or eight months. That fascinated them – as well it might! But we do need cash, so we tried the hotels; all were firmly closed and refused to open. The owners were viewing the scene from first floor balconies and, in reply to my pleas, shouted that to open would be peligroso. At which point I began to wonder if intimidation also happens in Ayacucho.

By noon a Communist Party student leader was fervently addressing a large appreciative crowd in the Parque Sucre and army jeeps were blocking all the adjacent streets. Our university friend then advised us to leave because if shots were fired Juana might bolt. I thought it unlikely that shots would be fired but if we wanted to find grazing it was time to go – most reluctantly, for Ayacucho is the loveliest town we've seen since Cajamarca.

At 3.15 disaster struck. Without warning, Juana lay down on the track – carefully, not disturbing the load – and made it plain that she *could not* go on. Obviously her collapse was genuine; she is not a mulish mule. Rachel promptly burst into tears and I felt likewise but restrained myself. "She's going to die!" wailed Rachel. "Nonsense!" I snapped. "She's just got the knocks – you've only to look at her to see she's not *ill*." Which was true.

But what next? We were on a narrow path, midway across an almost sheer mountain, with 300-foot cliffs above us and grey slopes below, falling for a few thousand feet to a scrub-filled gorge. About a thousand feet down we could see a curved protuberance, like a beer-drinker's paunch, on which the gradient eases and a bushy herb, favoured by Juana, grows sparsely. Normally, one would have described that bulge as inaccessible. But necessity is the mother of recklessness. We unloaded Juana, which wasn't easy as she lay there looking puzzled by her own misfortune. Then patiently – it took some time – we coaxed her to her feet and I led her over the edge. Very gradually we zig-zagged down, toing and froing across that sun-baked skiddy vastness of loose earth over rock. Juana didn't slip nearly as often as I did; indeed she supported me, and my four subsequent journeys down, carrying instalments of the load, were much more exhausting and nerve-wracking.

From every practical point of view this site is a masochist's paradise, yet aesthetically it ranks among our Top Ten. The northern horizon is still dominated by that flat-topped cordillera between Pampas and Churcampa – now a hazy blue majesty of mountain, reigning over all those lesser peaks and grey ridges and green valleys that stretch chaotically from its base to our present site high above Ayacucho. Looking back over such a region, to a barrier as mighty as that cordillera, provokes an absurd incredulity at the realisation that one's own two feet (not to mention one's daughter's nine-year-old feet) have carried one up, across, down and over *The Lot* . . . While in action this feeling never comes: then one is getting on with the job. But sites like this, which allow a panoramic view, make it impossible to repress a frisson of triumph.

Setting up this camp has been my most gruelling Andean experience, for a variety of reasons – the severe gradient and shifting topsoil, the cruel afternoon heat on a barren rock-mountain, an empty belly (Ayacucho's bank strike has left us with a major problem) and suppressed anxiety about Juana. I *think* it's only the knocks; just now she has been rolling and kicking very happily (if not very prudently) near the edge of our bulge. And she is enjoying the green oats which I spent the late afternoon prising out of a reluctant campesino in a distant valley at the end of the gorge. Yet I'm more worried than I've admitted to Rachel. Cuzco is still over 350 tough miles away. Everything will depend on the fodder supply and the omens are hard to read at this season.

10

Thrills and Spills

Camp on High Puna. 1 December

An uneasy night. I changed the picket thrice and each time I woke had the impression of being suspended from the mountain-side by a bit of rock inserted between two ribs – an illusion, of course, but one with an uncomfortable basis in reality.

Finding a small scorpion under the tent made Rachel's morning; her only complaint about the Andes is the lack of wildlife. She and I (wo)manhandled the load up the brutal gradient to make life easier for Juana. As we struggled with the last instalment Rachel glanced back and saw her staring anxiously after us, straining hard at her picket – unprecedented behaviour. We were deeply touched: as Rachel said, "You'd expect her to *want* to see the back of us at this stage!" Surprisingly, she was in excellent form this morning.

We ourselves are now on a spartan diet because of the bank strike. It will take us at least a week to reach Andahuayalas, the next town with a bank, and we cannot change travellers' cheques elsewhere as no one in these parts has ever heard of such things. We are down to 935 soles, of which 600 must be kept for fodder leaving 335 to feed two people for a week; and a simple meal for one in a wayside eating-house costs at least 100 soles. Our emergency rations are but a lovely memory and our food-box contains only a kilo of ship's biscuits (nothing else was available in Ayacucho where most of the shops had closed), a small tin of instant coffee, a small tin of sardines and a dozen soup cubes. "That's a co-incidence!" exclaimed Rachel cheerfully. "We can each have one mug of soup every evening." There's no denying she has a positive approach to life's little drawbacks. Let's hope she feels equally cheerful the day we drag our emaciated bodies into Andahu-ayalas.

Twice this morning the road dropped into deep glens, glossy with long grass, and we stopped for Juana to graze while we

washed in swift brown streams, clear and cold. Towards midday a
solitary shack appeared by the edge of an oatfield far below the
track and I slithered down to buy a gigantic bundle of oats from a
young man who spoke only Quechua. I could scarcely heave the
awkward load onto my back but the young man made no attempt
to help; then he stood staring as I struggled back to the track. This
brand of unchivalrousness seems odd to us but is quite natural
here: *and* quite logical. Women tough enough to walk from
Cajamarca to Cuzco should be able to carry loads up hills . . . Yet I
still get my cultural lines crossed occasionally and find myself
inwardly reproaching the campesinos for their lack of gallantry. So
it was today, perhaps because hunger is making me peevish. I
found it much harder than it would normally be to carry a heavy
weight up a steep slope of sticky soil at an altitude of over 12,000.
No wonder the permanently under-nourished Indians have to
chew coca every day to keep going.

While Juana guzzled we sat on a flat rock savouring our meagre
noon ration of ship's biscuits and watching the sky cloud over.
As the downpour started a young woman hurried down from a
nearby potato field and warned us, rather superfluously, that we
would soon be very cold and wet. Although she could see that
Juana was just beginning a large meal she offered us no shelter.
It's remarkable that we have never once been invited into an
Indian home; in my experience of peasant communities, this
degree of aloofness is unique.

The sun was shining again as we roped the surplus oats behind
the load and continued towards the high puna. By 3.30 we were at
13,500 feet and still climbing with a strong wind at our backs. That
shack was today's last trace of humanity. Here are no dwellings,
no people, no animals, no traffic: just us and a desolate immensity
of pale brown and olive-green undulations, sweeping away to an
encircling rim of distant mountains. All afternoon the great and
healing silence was broken only by rumbles of remote thunder and
the small shrill alarm calls of black and white lapwings. Towards
sunset we could see storm clouds piled high in the northern sky,
their dark mass repeatedly riven by golden zigzags.

This superb site is on a long ledge of soft turf with acres of
top-quality puna grass nearby. The western mountains are flat-
topped and, as I began to write, a broad orange band of after-light
was glowing most strangely between their royal blue bulk and the
inky clouds above.

Another Camp on High Puna. 2 December

We allowed Juana her freedom last night so that she could make the most of the exceptionally good grazing. Predictably, she moved closer and closer to us and was almost *in* the tent by morning. Today it was our turn to march on near-empty tummies. We had no breakfast, having finished the ship's biscuits last evening, and at noon we shared the last tin of sardines. Rachel never once complained, but perhaps she was mentally composing a letter to the NSPCC about being expected to walk twenty-two miles on half a tin of sardines at 13,700 feet a week short of her tenth birthday.

Five vehicles passed us during our twelve hours on the road: two buses and three trucks. Otherwise the landscape was unmarked by humanity. This was Andean grandeur at its most sublime: an overwhelming, exalting combination of surreal rock summits, lake-strewn moors, vast circular grassy valleys, apparently bottomless rocky gorges and ever-changing, wondrously tinted skyscapes. I got so 'high' on this mix that Juana suffered an alarming misadventure during the afternoon. Rachel was leading us across a green valley floor when she misjudged the nature of the ground and Juana suddenly sank to her belly in a bog-hole. That was a nasty moment. I felt the sort of extreme fear that gives one unnatural strength. Mercifully the ground all about was fairly firm; Rachel didn't sink at all and I only sank to my ankles. We had the load off within moments, though not the saddle as the girth was inaccessible. Juana had panicked briefly – nostrils flaring, eyes rolling, breathing short and fast. But we talked soothingly to her as we unloaded and saw the panic ebb. There was nothing more we could do to help, apart from continuing to give loving verbal encouragement in steadying tones. She struggled hard, throwing her head high as she strained to free her forequarters. At the third attempt she made it, getting her forefeet onto comparatively firm ground. Then Rachel and I heaved with her to free her hindquarters. We were all trembling in reaction as we cautiously picked our way towards the nearest dry slope. When I had retrieved our gear we rested for half an hour before re-loading. This unfortunate incident was entirely my fault. We have learned from experience that these grassy valley floors can be treacherous and I should have had my eyes on the ground instead of feeling poetical about the clouds.

This is another superb site, near the edge of the puna and again with good grazing. But as usual at such altitudes there is no fuel so our coffee and soup cubes are merely tantalising. For supper we each drank several mugs of cold water. "At least we're not *thirsty*," said my philosophical companion. "And tomorrow we'll get to Ocros. And yesterday we only spent 50 soles on fodder, and today we didn't spend anything, so we'll have 150 soles extra for our own food tomorrow."

Camp in stony field. 3 December

What a day! Physically and emotionally it was by far the most demanding of the entire trek – and now I'm facing a sleepless night.

Last night we both slept deeply for an unbroken eleven hours; this may be nature's way of making up for lack of food. At dawn our world was piercingly cold and completely cloud-enveloped; as we began the long descent visibility was down to about ten yards. Both aesthetically and practically this was frustrating. We were being cheated of the view – always spectacular as one leaves the puna – and if any redura existed we couldn't see it. Then for a moment the shifting clouds allowed us to glimpse an unimaginable abyss just below the road and we realised that this was *not* redura terrain. Neither of us admitted to acute hunger pangs but we tended to snap at each other uncharacteristically.

Half an hour later the strengthening sun abruptly drew the vapour upwards, as though some gigantic stage curtain were being raised. Accustomed as we are by now to the magnitude and violence of the Andes, I felt my heart thudding faster as we stopped to stare. Below us, filling the whole visible world, lay a bewildering complex of serrated crags, unfathomable gorges, crazily interlocking spurs and sheer rock walls 2,000 feet high. But soon my elation and awe gave way to apprehension. How long would it take the carretera to find a way through? It suddenly seemed dreadfully possible that we might *not* get to Ocros before dark. And could Rachel keep going for another twenty-four hours without food?

Shortly afterwards I rejoiced, for the first time in my life, to hear the sound of a distant engine. The vehicle was approaching from Ocros and I decided to stop it and try to buy any food that might be on board. Twenty-five minutes later an over-crowded bus

Camp-site
on puna

Coca-chewing campesinos

appeared; when I tried to wave it down the driver scowled angrily, hooted loudly and kept going.

On the next mountain we saw what seemed a possible redura, though had we not been *in extremis* we wouldn't have contemplated such a descent for one instant. Thousands of feet below, my binoculars revealed a carretera bridge crossing a narrow river. From where we stood we could descend the puna-grassy mountainside if we tacked carefully and this open slope eventually merged into green pasture. We couldn't see what happened after that but if we then reached the river it might be possible – I reckoned – to follow it (perhaps walking *in* it) to the bridge and the road. Ominously, however, there was no trace of even the most rudimentary path. Rachel was keen to experiment but I argued, "If a redura is possible, the campesinos make a path". Quickly Rachel pointed out that hereabouts there aren't any campesinos, so the lack of a path was no evidence. Next we studied what we could see of the carretera; it was visible for many miles ahead, snaking around mountain after mountain and *still* at the level we were on. There was no clue as to where it began its descent into the chaos beneath. I decided then to gamble on the redura, though I was horribly aware that in our debilitated condition we might not be able to climb back to the carretera if the gamble went wrong.

Our descent of the grassy slope left us nerve-wracked and exhausted; and then our way was blocked by a sheer hundred foot drop extending right across the mountain. Leaving Juana to graze and Rachel to rest, I went on a recce. To the right there was no hope; an impassable densely wooded gorge, containing the river, separated our mountain from its neighbour. But to the left it merged with its other neighbour, which was fearsomely steep and covered with scrub. Here a faint goat-trail raised my hopes, but it petered out on the edge of a hidden chasm. Retreating, I found another pathlet which took me high above Rachel and Juana – only to end at the base of a semi-circular precipice pitted with caves where goat-herds shelter and light fires. By this stage I was bounding up the steepest gradients, operating entirely on fast-flowing adrenalin stimulated by fear on Rachel's behalf. Almost certainly she couldn't make it back to the carretera, nor could Juana carry her. We were all at the point of no return.

Scrambling down through the scrub, I heard a pony neighing. I paused and listened. When he neighed again I turned towards the sound and forced my way through a pathless copse of low trees linked by tough creepers. Then suddenly I was on the edge of a rocky ravine, of modest proportions by local standards. Beyond rose a gentle grassy slope on which stood three ponies. If they could reach that slope, Juana could get *off* it . . . I studied the ravine. On the far side an easy path led onto the ponies' pasture. But on my side there was only a rock stairs of such grisly instability that even Rachel and I would find it difficult. In normal circumstances no sane person would even consider bringing a mule down that 300 foot precipice. But the circumstances were not normal and I felt even less sane than usual. We could but try . . .

Turning back, I realised with a flicker of panic that I was lost. I blew my whistle long and hard and soon Rachel's whistle answered. Carefully I descended, noting landmarks. Twice more I whistled and the replies guided me. "You're a most *useless* traveller!" exclaimed Rachel when we were reunited. "What would your fans say if they knew how often you get lost?"

We spent forty minutes struggling through the copse; I had to clear a way for Juana by tearing down creepers that oozed a sticky and noisome fluid when assaulted. At the edge of the ravine we unloaded and commended our collective soul to whatever deity looks after lunatics in the Andes. I descended first and called Juana as one calls a dog. There could be no question of leading her or driving her on such a precipice; she had to feel free to make her own judgements. For long moments she stood gazing down at me with a comical expression of incredulity. I then abandoned every last shred of rationality and talked to her as though she were Rachel. "Come on!" I said. "You *have to* make it! You know we can't get back to the carretera. And we don't want to die of starvation on this goddam mountain. So get shifting!" Juana pricked her ears forward, moved towards the edge – then paused and glanced back over her shoulder at Rachel. At once I realised where we were going wrong and asked Rachel to join me. She was only half way down when Juana began to follow her.

"She should be in a circus!" said Rachel admiringly as we watched Juana recovering from her third skid on a long smooth rock slab. When at last she was safely down I imagined that our troubles were as good as over and my adrenalin inconveniently ceased to flow. Three leg-torturing climbs up the rock stairs to fetch the load and tack left me feeling dizzy and nauseated. And the ritual of re-loading – normally a routine chore – seemed like one of the labours of Hercules.

From the ponies' slope both road and river were alarmingly invisible and we could see that their homeward path led very steeply *up*, away from the carretera. Five minutes later we were enmeshed again in dense scrub – but not for long. Suddenly open ploughland lay ahead and the carretera was directly below us, scarcely 500 yards away. "We've made it!" I shouted, almost weeping with relief. Again we tacked, stumbling to and fro across the sticky new-turned earth. And from the edge of that field we were indeed overlooking the road – but it was thirty feet below us and the drop was sheer.

Speechlessly we surveyed the scene, noting with horror that two well-trodden paths led *upwards* from the ploughland to join the ponies' track high on the neighbouring mountain. We could also see far up the carretera and nowhere, in that direction, was it accessible from our slope. Another solo recce was indicated. I left Rachel and Juana sitting and standing in attitudes of dejection and went towards the river; but its mini-ravine held an impenetrable thicket of gnarled thorny trees. Fortunately my adrenalin had been re-stimulated by this new crisis. Returning to Rachel and Juana, I continued past them around the shoulder of the mountain. And there at last was a point where the embankment was not quite sheer and the drop no more than eight feet. I whistled and sat down. A long time later the rest of the expedition joined me. Again we unloaded, and this time Juana didn't hesitate. If she were an Irish mule I'd say she had a hunter somewhere up the family tree; she always gives the impression of *enjoying* even the most formidable jumps. Here she slithered down the first few feet, then bounded onto the carretera like a kangaroo. I hugged her neck and she rubbed her forehead hard on my shoulder: our usual celebration, post-crisis.

We were now in a sparsely inhabited area where potato patches appeared at intervals in the deep green valley on our left. The few locals we met spoke only Quechua and seemed half-afraid of us. Soon we turned a corner and saw Ocros on its eucalyptus-greened spur apparently fifteen minutes walk away, with the blue-hazed Rio Pampas gorge another few thousand feet below it. But so tortuous was the road that we didn't reach food (ship's biscuits again: there was no eating-house) for another hour and a half. One of the local policemen told us that our short-cut had saved us thirty kilometres – almost twenty miles. So that three-hour nightmare had after all been worthwhile.

In Ocros's one shop even Peru's ubiquitous tinned sardines were not available. It would in any case have been unwise to eat a big meal and we were happy to sit on the shop steps, surrounded by a riot of geraniums, slowly chewing ship's biscuits. Each hard, dry mouthful seemed a divine experience. We miss a lot, in the pampered West, by never knowing *real* hunger. This may sound sadistic, but I'm glad that Rachel is occasionally having to endure extreme hunger, thirst, cold, heat and exhaustion. She will never again take First World comforts and conveniences for granted. And as she herself remarked last evening, she now knows how a large percentage of the world's population feels *all* the time.

When we left Ocros at 2.30 the heat was enervating; it seemed incredible that only seven hours earlier we'd been suffering the agony of thawing hands and feet. Poor Juana was moving very sluggishly; Ocros lacked both fodder and grazing, but the policeman had assured us that Alf could be bought at the next village. Two and a half downhill hours later we proved him wrong. Although Alf is grown around Chumbes the inhabitants refused to sell any. Beyond the village we met a wordlessly friendly Indian woman driving two bony cows, five haggard sheep and a coughing lame pony; all the local animals are in poor condition so a reluctance to sell Alf is understandable.

We hurried down a steep redura through a brief downpour – refreshing at this altitude. Beside the track fields of potatoes and maize were protected by compact prickly pear hedges; otherwise the brown rocky slopes supported only desiccated scrub of no interest to Juana. At dusk we reluctantly entered this level stubble field through a gap in its cactus hedge. As we were rushing the tent up in the last of the twilight four inquisitive ragged children arrived from nowhere and were rivetted by our activities. It is unusual for campesino children to be so outgoing and we encouraged their sociability. The boy was aged ten, the three girls ranged from nine to thirteen. Despairingly I asked if they could provide some form of fodder – even paja would be better than nothing – and then we realised that only the eldest spoke Spanish. (There is no school at Chumbes and the Ocros school closed six months ago when the two teachers left because they hadn't been paid for a year.) After some discussion among the children, Rachel and the older girls disappeared into the darkness to fetch paja – I assumed from the children's home – and the others helped me to collect firewood, of which there is an abundance nearby. Half an hour later the girls returned, each carrying a load of maize straw. When Rachel told me they had stolen it I didn't listen; recently Juana's need has been blunting my moral sensibilities. The girls hesitated when I asked how much I owed them, then said "ten soles": a fair price. The fascinated quartet hung around for another ten minutes, closely examining our equipment and watching our culinary activities (soup cubes and coffee!). But all the time they were being summoned by a clear though far-away female voice to which the eldest girl occasionally yelled a reassuring reply. Like most mountain peoples the campesinos can communicate by shouting over distances for which we would use a telephone. When the children left, Rachel and I were crouching by the fire, intent on our coffee-water saucepan, and twenty minutes elapsed before I discovered that Rachel's Diana-bag was missing.

"You should've shone the torch on them as they were going," said Rachel. Then she added shrewdly, "But you don't like suspecting people, do you?"

I blame myself far more than the thieves. To have left a so-easily-snatched bag lying around in the dark was an act of true imbecility, especially as these children had obviously been mes-merised by our few possessions. This is an extremely serious loss. The bag contains our space-blankets, all our high-altitude cloth-ing apart from husky-suits – which go with the flea-bags in my larger Diana-bag – and Rachel's jodhpurs and my new slacks. How are we to survive on the puna without these garments? There hypothermia is a real danger, as the Bradts have noted – 'this simple and efficient killer is often in the news under the name of Exposure'. We need almost everything in that bag; perhaps I should make an effort to recover it in the morning, however remote my chance of success.

When Rachel had gone to bed I built up the fire and went on drinking coffee to console myself; as a result I can't sleep. Just now I listed the stolen items, with their prices, because for insurance purposes I must report the theft in detail to the local police. (Wherever they may be!) Incredibly, that tiny bag contained over £90 worth of clothing – at a conservative estimate, forgetting inflation. The irony is that these garments can be of no use to anyone living at this altitude, though if the children had enough initiative they might sell them to campesinos who herd flocks on the puna.

Camp on Spur of Forested Mountain. 4 December

Rachel was still asleep when I slid out of the tent at 5.30. The dawn air felt like cool silk and the sky was pastel-clouded. A narrow but distinct pathlet led me through six bare brown fields towards the source of last evening's shouted commands. Soon I could see in the distance a wretched stone hovel isolated on a high ledge; no other dwelling was visible. As I climbed towards it there came a dramatic surge of colour in the eastern sky beyond the Rio Pampas. Suddenly the long cloud banks above a line of smoky-blue peaks were gold and crimson and the vast contorted land-scape all around me was drenched in rose-pink brilliance. I stood still, forgetting everything – our lost bag, my vile coffee hang-over, my exhaustion after an almost sleepless night. During such Andean moments – and they are frequent – one's own state of mind or body doesn't matter.

Continuing upwards, I wondered about the composition of the thieves' household: on that would depend my plan of action. In remote areas gringoes are occasionally murdered for no apparent reason so the presence of openly aggressive males would prompt a prudent retreat. Most Indians are too docile and gentle for their own good but the exceptions can erupt into ferocity under the combined influence of drink and drugs.

As I reached the ledge a bent, wrinkled old woman came hobbling out into the sun, half-closing her eyes against the light. Behind the hovel the two older girls were releasing four goats from a decrepit corral. They and their granny looked equally alarmed when I called a greeting. After a moment's silence Huarmi, the Spanish speaker, replied in tones of forced jollity. Meanwhile the goats were scampering away unheeded down the mountainside. Suddenly I was inspired to take notebook and pencil from my pocket and wage psychological warfare – an entirely unpre-meditated ploy. Standing about ten yards away from the hovel I wrote quickly, scowling at the page and glancing up between every few lines to scrutinise the girls, their granny and our immediate surroundings. I ignored Huarmi's ingratiating attempts to con-verse and granny's hoarse, frightened Quechuan questions. Silence fell. Tension built up. For ten minutes I pretended to write: and ten minutes can seem a very long time. Then abruptly I closed my notebook, stepped forward and informed Huarmi that I would soon be returning with the police to take her away to prison because she was a thief and people who stole from gringoes always went to prison. Her indignant denial of guilt was unconvincing but I did admire her for standing up to me, though her shifting eyes were full of fear. She urged me to search the hovel, to 'prove' her innocence. As I stood in the centre of the one small dark room granny pawed at my arm, croaking agitatedly in Quechua and peering up at me with half-blind, bloodshot eyes. The two younger children crawled out of a pile of filthy torn ponchos on the mud floor and stared at me in scared bewilderment. There was no furniture; a few threadbare garments hung from the low ceiling; a few goatskins were stacked in one corner. This was more like an animals' cave than a human habitation and my reaction was a strong spasm of self-disgust. Vividly I could see myself from outside: a hectoring, bullying Privileged Person ruthlessly taking advantage of the stupidity, ignorance and superstition of a half-crippled crone and a bunch of starving children – simply to retrieve possessions which I could well afford to replace. I faltered for a moment, longing to be able to turn away and leave these misfortunate people to enjoy their loot. Yet I dared not relent. Here and now those stolen goods were irreplaceable and without them we could not complete our trek.

Again I took out notebook and pencil, stared grimly around that pathetically naked shack and silently made pretend notes. After a few moments Huarmi, who had been standing by the door, turned and fled across the ledge. With surprising agility granny hobbled after her, screeching abuse. I followed and saw Huarmi hesitate, then turn back. She stared sullenly at me while granny continued to abuse her. Then slowly she raised a hand and beckoned me.

In silence we crossed three stubble fields beyond the hovel, then came to several acres of maize securely cactus-fenced; the only way in was via a difficult 'stepladder' of two interlocking dead trees. And there among the high maize stalks lay our bag, wide open. Each garment had been shaken out, no doubt in the hope of finding hidden cash, then hastily stuffed back; but nothing was missing. I felt weak with relief and found myself thanking Huarmi profusely: a rather inappropriate reaction. Only our financial crisis prevented me from giving granny a few hundred soles to compensate for the trouble we'd caused; amidst such poverty one gets one's ethical knickers into the most frightful twist. Now, having had all day to reflect on the incident, I can see that I was over-reacting. But I shall never look back on this morning as my

Finest Hour. And the whole episode revealed that my waffling on last evening about Rachel sampling the reality of Third World suffering was based on fatuous self-delusion. We may seem (indeed we *are*) fairly spartan in comparison with your average modern tourist. Yet we need some £90 worth of special clothing to enable us to survive on the puna and we know nothing whatever about *real* privation. Our treks are just playing with hardship. When we go hungry for a few days, or endure extremes of heat or cold or exhaustion, these are no more than Interesting Experiences. The certainty of plenty and comfort lies before us and we cannot even begin to imagine what it feels like to go hungry and cold for a lifetime.

Back at base Rachel rejoiced chiefly about the recovery of *her* Diana-bag, a most precious possession with RACHEL in gold lettering on its leather tag. To celebrate we had a morning fire for the first time and a full-scale meal of soup and ship's biscuits and coffee – which non-spartan behaviour meant that we didn't get the show on the road until 8.30, when it was already uncomfortably hot.

Today's was the most dramatic – and debilitating – of all our Andean 'downs'. When we crossed the Rio Pampas at 1.15 p.m. we had descended 11,000 feet from yesterday morning's starting point on the puna. In four and a half hours we had experienced a bewildering variety of terrain and vegetation. Every moment the heat had become more intolerable as our track leaped down from ledge to ledge, each spectacular 'step' so wide that it had its own character.

Soon after starting we passed many ancient trees with grotesque roots spreading fifty yards or more and thick grey-green beards of rubbery creeper depending from each leafless branch. The next shelf was laden with low trees on which tiny spherical yellow blossoms dangled amidst delicate spring-green foliage. Then came an ex-hacienda covering thousands of acres – now a Co-op. In a lush paddock a dozen sleek ponies were grazing and their adjacent field of Alf tantalised us because we could find no one with whom to trade. Here we were back on the carretera and soon we came upon one of this region's few dwellings, an adobe road-side shack with a shaggy cactus thatch. Outside it stood three young women – two of them looked half-witted – and a small boy with open sores all over his face and a minute skinny pup in his arms. As we approached everyone bolted into the casa and the door was slammed. I knocked and pleaded desperately for Alf, but the only response was a scuffling movement just inside the un-glazed iron-barred window.

In a narrow, semi-tropical ravine we were tortured by clouds of the locally notorious Pampas fruit-fly – a misnomer, we thought, as this vicious creature is obviously carnivorous. Soon every exposed inch of skin was covered with bleeding bites; as the minuscule brown devils escaped our frantic swattings we could see their transparent abdomens distended and red-tinted with Murphy blood. Mercifully they ignored Juana who all morning had been persecuted by larger flies.

Where the road ran beside a noisy small river we refilled our container; within the previous three hours we had drunk between us five litres of water. Both sides of this humid ravine were hidden by an exuberance of exotic shrubs, creepers and mosses; and between road and river sugar cane grew eight feet tall, tempting us . . . We offered some to Juana, but she spurned it in her exasper-ating way.

The exit from the ravine was marked by an unnatural cliff, so *perfectly* square that at first we mistook it for the ruins of some gigantic fortress. Here we expected to see the Rio Pampas – but no. The road turned sharply north and gradually descended, between flourishing maize fields, along a sloping ledge. By then we were being maddened – almost reduced to tears – by the itchiness and painfulness of the fruit-flies' bites. We were covered in a paste of dust, sweat and blood when at last we saw the Pampas and realised why the road had been forced to meander so. Here is no gorge, as we had imagined, but a broad valley; and at only one point do the mountains come close enough to support the bases of a ramshackle suspension bridge. This swift and powerful river now fills scarcely one-fifth of its bed; I wish we could see it during the winter rains.

Having crossed the bridge – Juana now accepts such horrible-nesses as inevitable – we turned south to follow the carretera through a barren desert. The temperature would have been at least 110° F in the shade if there were any shade. I have ex-perienced nothing comparable since I was foolish enough to cycle across the Punjab in early June, on which occasion I ended up with heat-stroke in Delhi. We considered resting until sunset and walking through the night, then decided it would be too risky to leave Juana without fodder for another five hours. So we drank deeply and struggled on. I wore Rachel's riding hat turned back-to-front, Rachel wore a sweater with the sleeves tied under her chin and the back draped over her neck and shoulders.

Soon we passed a few circular bamboo huts with conical straw roofs – the dwellings of a work-gang for bridge maintenance. A friendly young couple clad in cotton rags, with sun-blackened skins, invited us to lunch and we could smell potatoes boiling. But in that heat the very thought of food made even Rachel feel queasy.

Our map might have been produced by one of those medieval cartographers who enjoyed letting their imaginations off the leash. It asserts that the carretera rises within two miles of the bridge though in fact the road runs level for many miles, curving around the bases of pale grey rock mountains from which heat radiated in perceptible waves. The thick air seemed suffocating and our only consolation was the disappearance of the fruit flies, which had stayed on the fertile side of the river. But their bites continued to goad us to demented scratching. The next three hours were hell. There was one ghastly stage when Rachel's breathing became difficult and I thought she was about to collapse with heat-stroke. But after a fifteen-minute rest she struggled gamely on, knowing that we couldn't camp fodderless.

At last we saw in the distance a river-level oasis of green trees enfolding red-tiled and tin-roofed houses. (This village is un-marked on our map.) Soon we were walking between banana plantations and orange and papaya orchards; outside a roadside shack we bought twenty oranges for 40 soles and their tangy juiciness revived us. But we never reached the village because a kindly old man directed us to a grassy redura that leaped out of the valley onto this blessedly cool mountain. At once we stopped to drink – we had been conserving our water supply – and emptied the container. I shall never forget the ecstasy of swallowing that hot, chemically-flavoured water. There is a *frantic* quality about extreme thirst that distinguishes it from extreme hunger.

This site is ample compensation for the afternoon's inferno. We are on a grassy flat-topped spur, high above the valley and over-looking forested side-valleys noisy with waterfalls. All around grow giant prickly pear and wild geraniums. Far below the Rio Pampas looks like a thin brown ribbon thrown on the pale immensity of its sun-bleached bed. To the north-west stretches the whole awesome expanse we covered today, backed by the long, level line of the puna from which we descended yesterday.

Camp by Stream on Grassland. 5 December

Today we look hideously disfigured because of our inflamed and swollen bites; but after a night of torment the itch abated.

We rose at 4.50, to gain more height while it was cool, and climbed steadily and steeply for two and a half hours to the top of a forested mountain. Our path was a rock-stairs with deep steps – hard on Rachel's short legs and also trying for Juana. We met a young couple having difficulty driving an overladen pony down the stairs; no doubt they live in the only dwelling we passed, a stone hovel amidst a few hard-won potato patches.

We remained at about 10,000 feet while crossing sunny expanses of grassland scattered with sheep, cattle and ponies. Here our few fellow-travellers were riding and looked surly and/or coca-bemused. Near the amiable, dopey little town of Chinceros we joined the carretera for a few miles, to food-hunt, and had a monumental meal of chips, steak and onions in a tiny eating-house. During the afternoon our redura dropped slightly to wind through a densely populated valley – where we found ship's biscuits in a solitary shoplet – before climbing to this long ridge of open grassland which restricts our view ahead; as far as we can see, to east and west, it sweeps up to the horizon in great green waves.

We decided to camp early in this sheltered hollow (between waves, as it were) when a cold gale began to blow against us. Rachel has been enjoying a stream full of giant tadpoles and beyond the stream fuel was provided by the only patch of scrub for miles around. As we drank our coffee sheets of rain obscured Chinceros, on the far side of the valley, and at sunset the sky was a mass of hurrying storm clouds, all copper and purple and riven by lightning. Then our evening was marred by Rachel's falling over a mini-cliff while peeing Niagara-wise in the dusk. Luckily it was only a ten-foot drop; in these parts it could have been 2,000 feet. But her right knee struck a rock and she returned to the tent pale with pain though resolutely tearless. Now when she moves in her sleep she whimpers slightly. Let's hope this doesn't impede her walking tomorrow.

The wind has dropped and I'm writing this outside the tent, lying on soft turf under a glitter of stars. Juana is loose – tonight will be a banquet for her – and has come to graze beside me. Her munching, and the thin quick song of the stream, only accentuate the silence all around us.

Camp on Balcony of Chicmo Municipal Offices. 6 December

We covered twenty four miles today, from which it may be
deduced that Rachel's injury – though the bruise is lurid – did not
affect her performance. Soon after 9 we reached the puna, just as
an enormous cloud came to squat on the landscape. We emerged
from the mist at noon, during a two hour descent above a canyon
so deep that on its grassy floor we couldn't distinguish sheep from
goats.

The next stage of that descent took us into a broad, well-watered
valley where everything looked *Irish*. Huge sleek cattle grazed in
emerald fields with dry stone walls or hedges that from a distance
resembled hawthorn; the scattered stone cottages were straw-
thatched; stands of tall hardwood trees made the lush, rolling
sheep pastures look like parkland; clover flourished by the roadside beside sparkling irrigation channels and acres of flowering
potatoes covered the lower slopes of the mountains. Nowhere else
in Peru have we seen such farming and this evening we were told
that the local Co-op is famous for its efficiency.

Towards sunset our road dropped abruptly into a rocky,
wooded glen where it was impossible to find a camp-site; we had
made a major mistake by leaving that fertile valley. But a friendly
mestizo woman told us that we were near a pueblo and at dusk we
reached this straggling village which seems to have been of more
consequence in colonial times than now.

Immediately we were surrounded by scores of men, women and
children, all pushing, shoving and giggling as they tried to
examine the inexplicable arrivals and their oddly-loaded mule.
When I asked for 100 soles worth of Alf there was a long silence,
though we'd just passed several Alf-fields. At the back of the crowd
a youth was now holding aloft a blazing brand (street lighting,
Chicmo style) and the twisting flame revealed people shuffling
their feet and whispering and looking doubtful. I don't much like
Chicmo's atmosphere, though I can't precisely define what puts
me off. At last a youngish man volunteered to provide oats; he
looked more alert than the average campesino but had one of those
nasty cunning faces to be found all over the world – narrow and
ratty. (It's odd how the universal virtues and vices can mould the
features of dissimilar races into identical expressions.) He added
that he'd expect 200 soles for oats because all gringoes are very
rich. (At the moment it would be hard to picture anything less

rich-looking than the Murphys.) A policeman then forced his way through the crowd and reprimanded Ratty for being rude to Chicmo's guests. The police – he said – would provide *free* Alf. Our self-appointed guardian angel invited us to camp on this spacious first-floor balcony, at the back of the decrepit colonial Municipal Offices. We are overlooking a rectangular common, surrounded by two-storey adobe houses, and Juana is securely corralled behind one of these, knee-deep in police-Alf. Apparently there are many livestock thieves in this area and the police so distrust the locals that once we'd carried our gear to the balcony one of us had to stay with it. Rachel then went off down the ebony-dark street between two policemen, to sup with them behind a shop where they have all their meals. She came back with 40 soles change out of a 100 soles note, yet she'd been given ample rice, fried potatoes and braised cuy, followed by two mugs of coffee; obviously she got the benefit of the police rate. Meanwhile I'd been eating ship's biscuits as we can't afford two suppers.

Here we've had five separate offers for Juana, two of them quite reasonable at 30,000 soles. Each man implored us to sell and assured us that the weekly bus from Chicmo to Cuzco would be more 'reposeful' than walking there. From what little we've seen of Peruvian buses on mountain roads, I doubt that. But the realisation that we're now within a 24-hour bus journey of Cuzco makes the end of the trek seem horribly near.

Andahuayalas. 7 December

A short day's trek, with an exhausting centrepiece and an astonishing end. Throughout the Andes we've had uncanny good luck. This morning Juana lost her off fore shoe on a precipitous redura leading down to a wide fertile plateau; and half an hour later we were in the biggish town of Talavera which includes among its amenities a *blacksmith*.

Antonio is the tiniest Indian we've met – a couple of inches shorter than Rachel – and he approached Juana with a judicious mixture of kindness and firmness. His son – the same height as Rachel – was equally likable though less cool in a crisis. And Juana made sure that this *was* a crisis. Antonio and son didn't use the Chavín device of tying legs to tail and my function was to hold the head-collar and administer comfort and admonition, as appropriate. Unfortunately neither had any effect. Juana tolerated the

removal of the old shoes with only a few token kicks. But whe
knives and nails came into the picture she grew more and mor
resentful, rearing up and pawing the air every other moment
which caused the crowd *and* the smiths to scatter rapidly, leavin
me as heroine, centre-stage. Rachel hugely enjoyed the whol
circus, squealing with laugher every time Juana stood on he
hind-legs. A fascinated crowd had followed us from the Plaza an
was now augmented by – apparently – all the residents of th
nearby street, some of whom brought placatory Alf offering
(purloined no doubt from their cuys) which Juana rudely spurne
When Antonio decided to bandage her eyes and ears I assure
him that this would only aggravate her ill-temper, and it did. Sh
raged around in circles, almost jerking my arms from their socket
until the bandages were removed. I then insisted on hobbling an
tail-tying and at last progress was made – though slowly an
hazardously, with many sudden lunges despite the inhibitin
ropes. When we left Talavera at noon I knew how people felt afte
a day on the rack.

Most of the terrain we've crossed on the way from Ayacucho
unsung in the history books (for Juana's sake we regretfully by
passed Vilcashuaman), but not so this province of Andahuayala
Long before the Spaniards arrived it was famous as the base of th
only enemies feared by the Incas, the ferociously brave Chanca
who claimed descent from a puma and wore puma-skins o
ceremonial occasions. Between 1350 and 1400 this tribe move
south from somewhere north of Vilcas and eventually subdued th
Quechuas, an ancient tribe then ruling Andahuayalas, whos
language was adopted for general use throughout the Inca Er
pire. In 1437 the Chancas invaded the sacred city of Cuzco bt
were repulsed by the Inca army under Pachacuti. Although
Chanca contingent later helped this Inca to conquer Tarma, th
tribe was never absorbed into the Empire. After the Cuzco defea
8,000 Chanca men and women retreated into the forests of Cha
chapoyas on the Upper Marañon and the Incas became obsesse
about the threat these formidable fugitives posed to the unity
the Empire. Now the Chancas as a distinct tribe are only
memory; the post-Conquest wars and epidemics wiped them out.

When the conquistadores had taken Cuzco, Diego Maldonad
el Rico (the Rich) secured Andahuayalas for himself and soon
became known as the richest of all Peru's 480 encomiendas. (A
encomienda was an estate from which a Spanish settler wa

entitled to receive produce though the Indians continued to own the land.) Maldonado was born in Salamanca and achieved fame as the luckiest of the conquistadores. For helping to capture Atahualpa he was given a cavalryman's reward (7,760 gold doubloons and 362 marcos of silver). As a gambler with dice he had soon won twice that amount in his spare time. After the murder of Atahualpa, when one of the Inca's despairing and beautiful sister/wives wanted to be buried alive with her brother/ husband, as was the custom, Pizarro instead gave her to Maldonado with the intention of cheering her up. Maldonado also won a major share of the loot taken from Topa Inca's palace. And soon after being awarded the fief of Andahuayalas he chanced upon several bars of silver, which had apparently strayed from a nearby Inca centre for smelting silver, gold and copper ore in wind-ovens.

When Maldonado died in 1565 he was widely regarded as a saint – though not by the Indians of Andahuayalas, on whom he had inflicted every abuse possible under the encomienda system. As an encomendero, he was not allowed to live on his estate and the Indians had to carry his 'tribute' to his town house in Cuzco. Pizarro kept his followers together in European communities where they formed an effective militia; and this suited the conquistadores, who had no wish to be isolated in such places as Andahuayalas. It was, however, part of the deal that encomenderos subsidised priests who did live among the Indians, busily converting them to Christianity – if necessary by intimidation. The greedy clerics sent to Andahuayalas by Maldonado have bequeathed to this area a tradition of implacable anti-clericism.

The two miles from Talavera to Andahuayalas are *tarred* and made hideous by what seemed to us a constant stream of fast motor traffic. Beneath the tar lie the firm foundations of the Incas' Royal Road to Cuzco; Andahuayalas was an important tambo with enormous lodging-houses and storehouses of which, alas! nothing remains. By Andean standards this is a built-up area where many newish casas look brash between tree-bounded fields of Alf, oats, maize and cane. It is also brutally hot, despite being at 9,700 feet. But we cheered up when we came to the outskirts of the town on its high ridges, surrounded by smooth-crested, forested mountains.

Like Talavera, Andahuayalas has a friendly aura. While I looked for a hotel with a corral Rachel sat beside a munching

Juana on the pavement of a narrow street off the Plaza de Armas. When I returned to report failure I could see from a distance that Rachel was jumping up and down with excitement and grinning all over her face. She had discovered, from a chatty passer-by, that two *Irish* priests minister to the spiritual needs of Andahuayalas and live in a house overlooking the Plaza. Not having talked to a gringo for six weeks – since leaving Chavín – she was delirious at the prospect of meeting compatriots. And when we introduced ourselves to Fathers Des and Bernie, five minutes later, the small-ness of the world was demonstrated yet again. Bernie – almost incredibly – is first cousin to our butcher in the tiny Irish town of Lismore.

Des has been here ten years and speaks fluent Spanish and Quechua; Bernie arrived only a week ago and is still suffering slightly from culture shock. At once Des set about organising a corral: not an easy task, but eventually Juana came to rest in the back yard of a new casa belonging to a young clerk in the Munici-pality. Moreover, permission was given for her to graze all day on the long, lush churchyard grass – and it's a big churchyard. We had eyed this grazing coveteously on our arrival in the Plaza: by now we tend to view all vegetation through the eyes of a mule.

While we were wolfing cakes and coffee in the Presbytery dining-room – neat, bright and spotless – I suddenly became conscious of our quite indescribable filthiness and smelliness. No doubt our hosts did too: they soon suggested that we might like to use their hot showers. There was a Jekyll and Hyde touch about the Murphys Before and After that visit to the baño . . . (My new slacks, which fitted perfectly when bought in Jauja, now need a belt.) We then booked into the Gran Hotel, almost next door to the Presbytery and snootily described by *The South American Handbook* as 'basic'. We reckon it's pretty luxurious for fifty pence a night. Rachel has the bed and I'm happy with the floor. Most important of all, there's a table and chair; a table to write on is the one home-comfort I do miss.

While Rachel cavorted around the town with Bernie – she is blatantly exultant about getting away from Mamma – I spent the afternoon engaged in deadly combat with the local bank. I have deliberately omitted my previous encounters with Peruvian banks. These institutions carry inefficiency, irrationality, xeno-phobia and sheer stupidity to the furthest extremes – and then some way beyond. No one who has not dealt with them would

Mountains above Ayacucho where Juana got 'the knocks'

A main street in Ayachucho

Ayacucho Cathedral

believe me if I described the simplest transaction within their portals. Suffice it to say that changing one cheque took three hours and forty-seven minutes. I emerged feeling that it couldn't be true, that I must have been playing a part in some ham production of a poorly-scripted skit on Latin America.

As we supped with our new friends Rachel and I caught ourselves gabbling incoherently and repeatedly interrupting each other – not characteristic behaviour, but this escape from our own company has quite unbalanced us. We have decided to spend four nights here; Juana badly needs a fattening rest. Also, 10 December is Rachel's tenth birthday and she has earned a real birthday party, complete with cake and *Irish* guests, instead of a tin of sardines and a mug of cold water on some mountain ledge.

Andahuayalas. 8 December

This is the Feast of the Immaculate Conception and therefore a Peruvian public holiday. (The Blessed Virgin Mary is Commander-in-Chief of the Peruvian Armed Forces.) At 6.15 a.m. an enthusiastic brass band lured us onto the Plaza where a group of dancers, wearing scarlet 18th-century military uniforms, was performing by the church gate. Accompanying them were two men, one dressed as a campesino woman, the other carrying a long pole with which he repeatedly tried to lift the 'woman's' skirts – *not* how we celebrate the Virgin's feasts in Ireland . . . But that primitive comedy – there were howls of laughter from the crowd as the 'woman' indignantly leaped away from the pole – perfectly sums up popular religion in the Andes. Outside the church door one of the parish's most precious treasures, a two-foot statue of the Virgin wearing a brocade, jewel-encrusted gown and standing on a globe covered in gilt paper, had been placed on a table to welcome worshippers to her Fiesta Mass. Then another, less bejewelled statue was borne across the Plaza on a gilded stand by a sallow, shrivelled elderly woman wearing a sodality badge and a solemn expression of concentrated piety. I couldn't help feeling that the Virgin would much prefer the skirt-lifting campesinos. As the town's middle-class mestizo citizens approached the church the dancers and their followers indulged in much teasing horseplay – running away with ladies' mantillas and trying to trip up sedate gentlemen. A few people were tolerantly amused and tossed soles to the campesinos but the majority made plain their contempt for these uncouth gambols. Christianity is not a unifying factor in the Andes. Yet one is aware of its importance on certain occasions and of the sincerity of the participants, however they may choose to express their fervour.

The Indians who live within reach of Church influence are usually very pious, and very superstitious, and the whole 'saint cult' – especially the Marian cult – is to them of the utmost importance. Yet the church here was recently redecorated, out of his own pocket, by a rich American priest who insisted on reducing the numbers of statues displayed by way of stamping out 'saint cults'. One is appalled by such crassness. The notions fostered by Vatican II have no relevance here. To the campesinos Christianity is of value only as a comfort. It is not a system of sanctions that raises their moral tone, or a system of philosophy that shapes their intellectual life, or a social service that looks after their educational and medical needs. If you deprive them of their saint cults, what have they left? They cherish their garish statues as *friends*. A favourite is a sitting statue of Christ, Lord of Justice. When Peru's corrupt legal system reduces campesinos to despair they kneel or lie – sometimes for hours on end – before this statue, confiding to it every detail of the inequities inflicted upon their race. I have watched them praying thus and it is a most moving experience. As the statue cannot take action on their behalf they are behaving superstitiously, according to with-it theologians. But who can measure the solace – the psychological benefit – to them? One can see on their faces a relaxation of strain and a smoothing away of grief as they explain everything to the Lord of Justice. OK – so their religion is an opiate. But how can it help them if outsiders try to prune it of 'idolatry'? It's cruel nonsense to think in terms of 'purifying' their faith, to bring it into line with modern Catholicism, when all their traditions, and their present stage of mental development, are so unlike ours.

Des admits that Indian mental and emotional processes are totally alien to even the most sympathetic outsiders, of whom he himself is obviously one. This comment consoled me. I've sometimes wondered if our failure to make personal (heart-to-heart) contact with the Indians is our fault, but I don't honestly think we can be blamed for it.

Andahuayalas. 9 December

Today when we lunched with Des and Bernie our fellow-guest was an elderly 'professor' who has lived for twenty years in Europe and now tries to teach English in the local schools. Her own English is flawless but she is passionately opposed to English being a compulsory subject in Peru. In her own case she says it's impossible to teach – without adequate materials – classes of 55 or 65, more than half of whom are simultaneously learning Spanish. She remarked (confirming our own observations along the way) that many youngsters now long to go to China, Russia, Eastern Europe or Cuba, rather than to North America. Yet English is still seen as the magic key to escape from Peru. She agreed with me that the national inferiority complex (often hidden behind a screen of chauvinism) is a psychological disorder which, together with a lack of genuine patriotism, or sense of nationhood, makes a chicken and egg puzzle. In her view an allied problem, common to all the Andean countries, is an obsessional mutual mistrust which prevents communities (not to mention the various regions and races) from working together and makes it almost impossible to run the Co-ops efficiently. Des interpreted the lack of hospitality as an extension of this mistrust: campesinos won't admit unknown gringoes to their homes lest we might steal. A shattering thought; I would never have arrived at that explanation.

This morning Bernie paid his first visit to the local jail, where remand prisoners are held, and was pleasantly surprised. Six men share a small clean cell, no more crowded than many campesino hovels, and each has a comfortable bunk. Some of these men have been waiting three or four years to be tried, usually for theft. A minority are wife-beaters who have been denounced by their victim. Often the wives regret, when it's too late, having complained about husbands who must then be fed by their families for an indefinite period – which may involve frequent difficult journeys from distant villages. The prisoners cook for themselves and those few who are neglected by their families are looked after by the rest. Tools and looms are allowed and the men do much wood-work, leather-work and weaving and may sell their products and keep the profits. It all sounds unexpectedly humane, apart from the fundamental snag that someone not yet proved guilty of a comparatively trivial crime can spend up to five years in jail awaiting trial.

We watched a pathetic campesino funeral this afternoon. The rough plank coffin held the body of a 13-year-old girl, the fifth TB victim in her family. Even in death there is no equality for Peruvian Christians. Poor corpses are buried in graves marked only by simple wooden crosses. Rich corpses reside above ground in their individual apartments in what we call 'Death Villages'. A macabre form of protection racketeering is associated with this distinction. Families must regularly pay rent for coffin-space in a Death Village and, should the payments lapse, their relative is buried: a threat calculated to unnerve the most tight-fisted as it is believed that moved bones provoke a spirit to chronic restlessness.

Andahuayalas. 10 December

Rachel should remember her tenth birthday. This is Sunday and Des advised us to attend a Quechuan sung Mass. Musically this was a most moving experience which in an odd way – quite inexplicable – made me feel closer to the Indians than I ever have before.

The church was less than quarter full; its interior looks bare and un-Peruvian as a result of the restorations and reforms of that insensitive American priest. Like most large Peruvian churches it has a Treasury in which are locked precious statues, crucifixes, relics and other objects of silver and gold, often heavily bejewelled, and also trashy plaster ornaments which are equally valued by the pious for their religious significance. Recently there have been many robberies from Peruvian church treasuries, but it's a point of honour (or superstition) that no one robs from his own parish church.

Last Sunday Des organised for the first time a collection during Mass. But the locals see no reason why they should contribute to the support of the clergy or the upkeep of the church building, while apparently receiving nothing in return. So the total number of soles donated came to less than £1.50. Yet Peruvians of all classes willingly pay cash for services rendered: a special Mass, a baptism, wedding or funeral. Indeed, they insist on paying, apparently feeling that without a financial sacrifice on their part the magic won't work. This shocks Des and Bernie, which is to their credit – though surprising, because Irish clergy have always expected payment, even from the poor, for performing their priestly duties.

John Hemming has noted, 'There were many fine, conscientious priests in Peru, and the monastic orders produced the humanitarians who agitated so tirelessly for the welfare of the natives . . . In the sixteenth century, as now, the only outsider who cared for the natives and devoted his life to them was often the priest'. Yet the encomienda system meant that men like Diego Maldonado could choose priests of their own ilk to serve their own purposes. The priest was the only Spaniard of any consequence legally permitted to live among the Indians and too often he became a third oppressor, emulating the encomendero and the curaca. In addition to all their other extortions, many clergy requisitioned Indian women as concubines. Felipe Guaman Poma de Ayala complained, 'the curates and parish priests, from the concubines at their disposal, produce dozens of children, increasing the number of mestizos. There are priests who have up to twenty children'. The pattern established then continues to influence Indian attitudes four centuries later. It was generally accepted that Peruvians became priests so that they could own land, use cheap labour and abuse their religious powers to acquire considerable wealth. So the average Peruvian boy, whether Indian or mestizo, still instinctively identifies the Church with a bullying, exclusive Establishment which he couldn't join even if he wished to.

We'd been looking forward to a mild shopping spree here but the local shops are poorly stocked for such a big town in such a rich farming district. Merchants are afraid to order goods that their customers may no longer be able to afford and today it took us over an hour to find a cake – *any* kind of cake – for the birthday party. And our food-box has been replenished only with the too-familiar buns, noodles and tinned sardines; no honey, cheese or even soup-cubes. Yet excellent meals are served at the friendly Mercado 'restaurant' where we always have breakfast.

Everyone seemed to enjoy this evening's party in a large, grotty, ill-lit restaurant where there was only one other customer. The service was appalling, probably because the restaurant owners are anti-clerical. But our meal of steak, onions and chips, though not a novelty, was appetisingly cooked. The bottle of Peruvian wine I discovered yesterday in a dusty shop was quite disgusting, and it also required courage to swallow Rachel's hard-won sponge-cake. But the symbolism of a birthday cake obviously mattered more to her than the taste. When she had retired we washed that taste away with rum and coke, an unlikely mixture to which I have become mildly addicted for lack of anything better.

11

'The Great Speaker'

Camp in Alf Stubble-Field. 11 December

Between Andahuayalas and Abancay the *carretera* wriggles wildly, taking 100 miles to find a way across territory covered by our *redura* in 50 miles or less. Here one fancies the Andes are making a last mighty effort to bar all outsiders from the sacred city of Cuzco. Pedro Sancho, Pizarro's secretary, wrote of this area: 'We had to climb another stupendous mountainside. Looking up at it from below, it seemed impossible for birds to scale it by flying through the air, let alone men on horseback climbing by land. But the road was made less exhausting by climbing in zigzags rather than in a straight line. Most of it consisted of large stone steps that greatly wearied the horses and wore down their hooves even though they were being led by their bridles'.

The conquistadores worried as much about their horses as we do about Juana, and for the same reason. On these irreplaceable animals depended the whole success of their expedition. It was the Spaniards' mobility as cavalrymen, rather than their superior weapons, that defeated the Incas. Only their horses enabled this tiny group to cross terrain such as no European had ever dreamed of, wearing sixty pounds (minimum) of armour at energy-draining altitudes, and to conquer a vast and well-organised empire. Whatever humanitarian liberals of the late 20th century may think of these ruthless adventurers of the early 16th century, no one can dispute the courage needed for their first penetration of these mountains. And by now, after months of following in their hoof-prints, sampling some of the same deprivations and anxieties, we cannot help having a warm fellow-feeling for them. When Juana's condition forced us to by-pass Vilcashuaman, we remembered how in much the same area Pizarro's cavalry had to turn back from an attempt to secure an all-important bridge because of their horses' exaustion owing to lack of fodder. And this afternoon, during a two-hour descent of an almost vertical *redura*, when our thigh muscles were burning with the strain of keeping the brakes on, we remarked how lucky we were not to be wearing armour . . .

The flavour of today's trek was quite unlike the flavour of a puna or river gorge trek. Although we were all the time on a redura, and passed few dwellings and no village, this seemed a region with a complex and active past. Such an aura of decline is not of course uncommon in the Andes; but hereabouts it's particularly marked and lays a patina of melancholy over the whole area.

By 8.30 a tough climb had taken us over a low(-ish) mountain onto sunny miles of smooth pastureland being over-grazed by too many flocks and herds. Below us lay an irregular bottle-green lake, some two miles by one, reflecting a semi-circle of round brown mountains. Our track passed close to a Co-op (ex-hacienda) stretching along the shore, its main buildings decaying, as usual, but with a newish adobe church and school nearby. At present the school is closed: another unpaid teacher. Innumerable farm animals of every species were being tended by elderly-seeming Indian women with blank worn faces: younger women were standing waist-deep in the lake cutting reeds for fodder. The incidence of gringoes using this redura must be low, yet nobody even glanced at us; we might have been invisible. Staring into various sections of the farmyard – an untidy, dirty shambles – we remembered the lady Professor's troubled comments on Agrarian Reform, which in theory she supports. "How *can* the campesinos be expected to run large estates? Nothing in their tradition helps them to think for themselves – they don't even have a living oral literature. Yes, it would be nice to see them managing their land and all having fair shares. But in fact rural Peru is now much worse off than it was before Agrarian Reform. You've found you can't often buy milk, cheese, eggs – even in the middle of naturally rich farmland. Ten years ago this was not so. And *look* at the state of the fields and animals and implements!"

As we walked on between rows of young eucalyptus (at least trees are planted) I again saw the Andean Indians as a doomed race, a people past being rescued by 'Outside Aid' because their death-knell rang 450 years ago and all their subsequent miseries have been part of an inexorable process of dissolution. This sounds negative, pessimistic, defeatist – even horribly patronising. But it seems to me a harsh truth, decipherable between the lines of the history books. Granted, the Indians are breeding fast – from less than a million 150 years ago to several millions now (well over half the population of Peru). And many of their customs and their main language have survived Christianity and the Conquest. An estimated million and three-quarter Indians speak only Quechua, which has recently been granted official status. But their literacy rate is the lowest of any comparable group in Latin America; and their diet is forty per cent below the minimum nutrition level acceptable in the First World. Virtually the entire rural population and sixty per cent of Indian town-dwellers have no drainage or running water. And the vast majority are, as we have seen, outside the money economy and despised by their mestizo compatriots. (Being outside a money economy could be an excellent thing if Peru were still ruled by the Incas: but it isn't.) Of course there are, and have been and will be, thousands of Indian migrants who can flourish in the modern world as 'adopted' citizens. My sad contention is that these are the exceptions and that the Andean Indians' way of life, as a thriving culture, was doomed the day the first Spanish horse set hoof on Inca soil.

The unexpectedness and violence of the Conquest – especially the Spaniards' treacherous and blasphemous (in Indian eyes) treatment of Atahualpa, and the sacrilegious sacking of the sacred city of Cuzco – administered a shock to the Indian psyche from which it has never recovered. This seems to be one of those historical tragedies painful to contemplate yet preordained. Nature insists upon the survival of the fittest; and the Spaniards represented a race that was mentally, though not morally, fitter than the Andean Indians. Blame and sympathy are equally out of place when one looks at it all from this perspective. Also, 'Never the twain shall meet' applies even more to the Europeans and the Andean Indians than to the Europeans and any Asian race – including the Chinese. So there was no possibility that the conquerors might try to heal the psychic wound they had inflicted on their subjects. Miguel Agia, a perceptive and eloquent chronicler, made a comparison as valid – and poignant – now as it was in the 16th century. 'The Spaniard and the Indian are diametrically opposed. The Indian is by nature without greed and the Spaniard is extremely greedy, the Indian phlegmatic and the Spaniard excitable, the Indian humble and the Spaniard arrogant, the Indian deliberate in all he does and the Spaniard quick in all he wants, the one liking to order and the other hating to serve.'

This basic incompatability, added to the usual political motives for denigrating the culture of the conquered, deterred even the most pro-Indian Spaniards from attempting to understand and appreciate the society they had shattered. It was of course a primitive society, for all its ingenuity. Yet like every social framework it had a unique value for its creators, fulfilling *their* needs as no imported culture, however 'superior', could even begin to do. It was a symptom of the 'instant-demoralisation' of the Indians that the Spaniards were at once able to recruit native curacas to collect tribute from the encomiendas, the curacas themselves being exempt from payment. Many Spanish commentators were repelled by the cruelties these men practised against their own race and quoted them to 'prove' that the Indians had been no better off under the Incas. They missed the point that such behaviour was a result of the Spanish demolition of the Inca Empire's built-in ethical and legal restraints.

When thinking back a few centuries, one has to guard against 'transposed values'. Many of the early encomenderos behaved barbarously by the standards of any age and their excesses deeply shocked the King and the Council of the Indies. Yet John Hemming reminds us that the Spanish authorities showed 'a genuine concern for native welfare throughout the colonial church and government. However much they exploited or abused the Peruvian natives, they left the Indians on their lands and stopped short of the slavery or extreme racial prejudice that has occurred in other European colonies'. Many chroniclers, including Alfonso Messia, were scandalised by conditions in the mines where the mitayos endured 'four months working twelve hours a day, descending 350–600 feet to perpetual darkness where it is always necessary to work with candles, with the air thick and evil-smelling, trapped in the bowels of the earth'. But all 16th-century European mines were worked under similar conditions; and the 'civilised' governments of present-day America, Britain and France are indifferent to the fatal diseases slowly developed by hundreds of African and Amerindian uranium miners.

By early afternoon we were approaching the crest of what seemed to be a long grassy ridge; many Andean mountains don't feel like mountains as one climbs gradually towards the summit over a series of lesser heights. On that summit we received another of those shocks of joy that no familiarity can lessen. Below us the mountainside dropped away for 4,000 feet into a narrow gorge from which came the rushing of an invisible river – uncannily loud in the thin air. (Our map shows the gorge but no river.) On the opposite mountain – much higher and some four miles wide – naked grey-blue precipices were scored by dark red vertical gashes, thousands of feet long. We could just discern a zigzag scratch, extending from base to summit like a pencil doodle – tomorrow's path. "Seeing it from here, you wouldn't think we *could* get up it!" exclaimed Rachel, unconsciously echoing Pedro Sancho. But first we had to get down, frequently a more tiring operation.

Below the bare escarpment our path plunged into a green twilight where for an hour and a half we were scrambling through exotic shrubs and flowers and ferns, and ancient low twisted trees wreathed in mosses and creepers. Then all was harsh hot brightness, on the stony summit of what would be a considerable mountain in Ireland. The next stage was complicated by a landslide. We were now directly above the river and a few months ago that landslide would have seemed to me an insuperable obstacle. But I've become Andes-hardened; and so has Juana, who as a beginner created major scenes about far less challenging perils. She calmly followed Rachel diagonally across and down that 500-yard expanse of loose grey slates and shale. Rachel has a monkey-like flair for coping with such slopes but I myself couldn't keep upright on this mixture. As I fatalistically slid on my bottom across the shifting débris, overlooking what can only be described as a raging torrent, it occurred to me that I may have a suppressed death-wish . . .

During the descent, we'd glimpsed hacienda-buildings in a ravine at the foot of the opposite mountain. As we climbed from river level towards the rim of the ravine, between straggling cane plantations, we could smell the Co-op's antique sugar refinery. This is the biggest hacienda we've seen: once a completely self-sufficient community but now run-down and populated (we fancied) by uneasy ghosts as well as moronic and/or sullen Indians who either can't or won't speak Spanish. They refused to sell us any fodder – even paja, of which there was an abundance in view. I longed to explore but we both sensed hostile vibes and suddenly that evening-shadowed ravine seemed a place of dark and heavy memories. So we hastened away.

Now the air was raucous with flocks of screeching, swooping green parrots, who always become semi-hysterical as bedtime approaches. Again we climbed steeply between cane-fields to this gigantic ledge overlooking the hacienda. Here we have a splendid view of the stately home, a magnificent colonial mansion, dignified and elegant and externally in perfect condition. Two zigzagging flights of steps lead down to acres of walled garden where clumps of giant bamboo mingle with tropical fruit-trees, and poinsettia, bougainvillea and climbing roses send fountains of colour cascading over grey walls. At home such a garden would be Open to the Public. Here it seems a pathetic, improbable footnote to the archaic splendours of the Creole centuries.

This field offers Alf after-shoots, an irrigation channel of clear water and ample eucalyptus firewood. There is however one snag: swarms of tiny vicious ants. As I was blowing the fire they swiftly attacked in their thousands – up my arms, into my socks, through the split in my jeans. (I've had pubic lice in Ethiopia but never before pubic ants.) Taken individually ants are not exactly scary, yet the pain of such an all-out attack can be almost unendurable. Luckily there were no passers-by to see me rolling naked in the irrigation channel.

Now Rachel is asleep and beneath an almost-full moon our black-and-silver world is held in a stillness that seems holy. On this ledge we are completely and closely surrounded by peaks and ridges, towering far, far above us – some sharp against the sky, some shrouded in moon-luminous cloud masses. I'll have all my life the memory of the beauty of these nights on the mountains – each so different, though it's hard to convey that difference in words.

Camp on grassy high Plateau. 12 December

We were on our 'pencil-doodle' path by 5.50, a heat-dodging device that didn't work. By 7 I was sweat-sodden. At 8.10 we reached a vast, turfy bowl-ledge suspended, as it were, between three peaks and holding a straggling village of shy but friendly Quechua-speakers. Two strenuous hours later we were on the pass overlooking a network of vividly green, shallow valleys beyond which, on three sides, stretched new ranges. One mighty nearby summit was composed entirely of colossal overlapping rock-slabs all sloping gently in the same direction. To the south-east a solitary snow-peak – Jayuri – flared whitely against the cloudless dark blue sky. That intense *blueness* is one of the simple daily pleasures I'll miss most when we leave the Andes.

By 2 p.m. we could see the ancient little town of Huancarama, far below us. Here Pizarro spent the night of 8 November 1533 and on entering the town was alarmed to find two dead horses belonging to his advance force. But a note from his brother Hernando reassured him. The horses had not been killed by attacking Indians but 'had died from the extremes of heat and cold'. Or so the Spaniards thought. It's more likely that these European animals died of over-exertion at high altitudes, despite the fact that the conquistadores rarely rode up steep paths.

We had a late lunch (noodles and sardines!) in Huancarama's one-table mud-floored 'restaurant'. There was no tethering-post so Juana followed us inside, as is her wont when left loose, and while we ate she contemplated a selection of garish commercial calendars with apparent enjoyment.

For the next three hours a traffic-less jeep-track took us along the edges of profound forested chasms, each with a spectacular waterfall leaping and glinting through the trees at its head. We rounded four mountains before coming to a high green plateau where our camp-site – a roadside strip of lush grass – is the answer to a hungry mule's prayer.

Camp in neglected Hacienda Field. 13 December

Depending on whether you see a whiskey bottle as half-full or half-empty, this has been our lucky or unlucky 13th.

When we set off at dawn the sky was clear after a night of heavy rain. An hour later we were descending from the plateau into rising clouds that half-hid a maze of cultivated valleys and spurs. An old man riding a rotund dun pony showed us a redura – rocky, narrow and very steep between high hedges armed with two-inch 'darning needle' thorns. Neat little dwellings stood on ledges and as we lost height the temperature rose like a rocket. By 8.30 I was dripping sweat. Then my left ear became impaled on a 'darning needle' and I fell some way behind the others. When I overtook them I saw Juana wedged in an odd stretch of track between two six-foot banks of red-brown earth. She was resisting all Rachel's efforts to back her out but from where I stood, slightly above them, an alternative animal-path was visible running along the top of the outside bank of this 'tunnel'. Numerous hoof-prints proved its function, though the bank was less than two feet wide. Intending to coax Juana back to the point where this top path branched off at the entrance to the 'tunnel', I hurried along the bank and took the leading-rope from Rachel. Seeing me up there, holding the rope,

Juana at once realised that this was the 'recommended route'. Obliging as always, she quickly backed a couple of yards, to where the tunnel was broader and the bank lower, and then jumped to join me. But of course she couldn't know this was *only* a bank and Rachel screamed with terror as she crashed over into a dense tangle of thorny scrub some eight feet below me. As I stood staring at her struggling in the scrub I felt that time-suspending mixture of disbelief and heart-sick horror produced by imminent disasters which one cannot avert. Below the scrub safety-net a precipitous maize-field sloped down to the edge of an unfenced cliff. Rachel joined me on the wall - tears streaming down her face – just as the scrub support gave. We watched Juana falling into the maizefield and rolling over and over and over – faster and faster – with no hope of being able to check herself on such a gradient. Then, miraculously, she came up against the only obstacle on that whole vast slope – a young eucalyptus tree, planted in mid-field. It seemed impossible that she could have escaped serious injury and I found myself praying for a fatal neck-break rather than a smashed leg. Then, as she lay on her back against the tree, we saw that the load was intact: which somehow accentuated the un-reality of the whole episode. "We must *help* her!" sobbed Rachel. I had been standing rigid with shock; now I dropped recklessly into the scrub tangle where for long, horrible and bloody moments I was fighting my way through onto open ground. As I emerged, Rachel shrieked semi-hysterically – "Mummy! Mummy! She's all right! She's standing up! She's eating the maize!" I stared, then felt weak with incredulous gratitude as I saw our most beloved mula on her feet – guzzling as enthusiastically as she always does when the opportunity arises.

This was the sort of field we've often marvelled at, wondering how anyone could plough, sow and harvest on such a gradient. We slithered and stumbled to and fro, for once heedless of the havoc we were wreaking on precious foot-high maize. Then at last we were standing beside our miraculously-preserved Juana: today it's hard not to believe in guardian angels. She ear-twitched im-patiently when I interrupted her delicious snack to congratulate her on her escape. The only visible damage to the load was the final rupture of our pannier-bags which are no longer Siamese twins. Rachel remarked cheerfully, "If there was a mule-loading contest in the Olympics you'd win a Gold Medal!" Occasionally one's offspring says the right thing at the right time.

We were wondering how to get Juana out of this trap – there seemed to be no possible mule-exit – when someone shouted from above. A young campesino woman, going to fetch water, was standing on the fateful bank and we later discovered that she had witnessed the whole drama. She pointed to a thick eucalyptus wood in a far corner of the field, at track level – then waved and disappeared

During the next hour and a half I felt like one of those wretches in the Inferno who are condemned to push boulders up mountains throughout eternity. Because of the gradient we unloaded Juana, who after all *had* had a shock – though she was affecting to think nothing of it – and stacked our gear and tack under that miracle tree. Then Rachel slowly zigzagged upwards; apart from the near-vertical slope, she was leading a mule most reluctant to leave this banquet of young maize. I followed, carrying the first of five instalments of gear; on such a hill, with loose soil underfoot, it was impossible to carry a big load. At the edge of the wood Rachel took each item from me and humped it up the final difficult stage to the path, showing her usual resourcefulness. Yet to my shame I yelled angrily at her when she dropped the last pannier-bag. By then I was reeling with exhaustion, blinded by sweat and suffering from reaction: and Rachel was the obvious target. Oddly, there's never any temptation to vent spleen on an animal. Is this because a dumb beast can't afterwards take part in a verbal, rational reconciliation and accept apologies?

As we were reloading the campesino lass reappeared, accompanied by three other barefooted young women, and presented an armful of new-cut Alf to Juana. She would accept no payment. I tried to find out who owned the damaged field; our mishap had destroyed so much of the young crop that now my conscience was writhing. But that maize belongs not to a local individual but to some remote Co-op away down the valley.

Our friend insisted that we must rest and eat at her home; I daresay we both looked what Rachel graphically describes as 'Whacko'. We were led around the edge of another enormous maize-field, mercifully level, to a two-storey adobe house, red-tiled and substantial – though what we glimpsed of the interior was filthy and chaotic. For the visitors, wobbly home-made cane chairs were placed outside the kitchen-hut in the small yard, overlooking an untidy but gay flower-garden. Through the doorless entry to the kitchen we could see and hear the fire being blown by our kneeling hostess. Her dirt-encrusted young, aged two and four, were playing rather half-heartedly on a floor strewn with maize-husks and egg-shells. Their two-month-old baby brother died recently of dysentery. As we ate mounds of boiled maize, topped by two fried duck eggs each, our hostess apologised repeatedly for having no rice – the prestigious grain - but we assured her, truthfully, that we prefer maize. Meanwhile several hens and ducks, and a large brown dog and a small black kitten were in hopeful attendance on us. By the time we'd finished eating the sun's rays were so fierce that one kind girl, seeing us dripping sweat, moved our chairs into the shade while our hostess was brewing mugs of delicious herbal tea that gave us an extraordinary 'lift' – God knows what was in it. None of these girls spoke more than a few words of Spanish, yet we were restored as much by their caring attitude as by the sustenance they provided. We have become so used to being ignored by campesinos that our gratitude for this cherishing was extra-keen.

After such a start, the rest of today had to seem easy. It was downhill all the way, into the furnace of the Abancay valley. The last stage of the descent overhung the Rio Abancay – shallow, swift and emerald green. Just downstream from a fine old stone bridge (defaced, like so many structures in Peru, by political graffiti) the river is confined to a short canyon between sky-filling mountains of sheer rock. Here the shadowed water undergoes a sudden metamorphosis, flowing deep, quiet, smooth and jade-green.

We climbed steeply – again accompanied by clouds of fruitflies – through unkempt cane plantations and fertile but idle farmland: something never seen where traditional farming patterns have been left undisturbed. A neglected cactus hedge allowed us access to this dismal ex-hacienda where sickly crops are surrounded by overgrown pathlets, creeper-strangled orchards and blocked irrigation channels – either dried up or wastefully flooding. Swarms of black midges, no less dementing than the fruit-flies, were mercifully dispersed when a strong warm wind sprang up at sunset. This is one of our most penitential sites. The tent is surrounded by a long bristly weed that stings mildly and many large sharp stones are deeply embedded in the lumpy earth. Nor is the abundance of firewood any compensation; our coffee-tin was burst during this morning's misadventure, making a hideous mess in one pannier-bag. For a moment I was baffled on finding everything stuck together with black glue . . . Four of our books must be thrown away: a devastating blow. Also Rachel's torch was smashed and our maps badly stained. Yet when we look at Juana, happily devouring that horrid weed, we still feel today was our lucky 13th.

Camp on very high grassy Ledge. 14 December

Last night I woke repeatedly to scratch inflamed bites. The heat was oppressive, though we left the tent wide open, and at 5.30 the valley lay still and humid beneath an overcast sky. While striking camp we were attacked continuously and simultaneously by clouds of black midges, tiny grey flies and our old amigos the brown fruit-flies. They swarmed so densely on our faces that we could scarcely see what we were doing; and they even got me on areas not normally exposed when I was generously fertilising the hacienda. We were a burning mass of new bites as we continued through that sad estate, remarking on how lovely it must have been when well tended. Soon we came upon the melancholy ruins of the mansion and paused to admire its handsomely carved verandah pillars and the delicate floral frieze all around the balcony. Nearby a gigantic water-mill still revolves on a tumultuous tributary of the Rio Abancay. The simple chapel has been newly whitewashed and repaired; a few candles flickering in front of the Virgin's altar represented the only sign of life about the place.

From the courtyard we followed a broad, tree-lined track – part of the Camino Real. Rachel was leading and I was walking level with Juana's rump. Suddenly I yelled – "Rachel! STOP!" She had been staring up at a flock of parrots, swooping noisy and green across the now-blue sky, and had almost trodden on a tarantula. The full significance of this encounter will be appreciated only by those who know that I am mortally afraid (it's a true phobia) of the tiniest spider. Even to write the word makes me shudder slightly and to come face to face with a tarantula early in the morning on an empty belly after a bad night was almost too much; one relishes local colour but there are limits . . . The creature was unbelievable, walking slowly across the track from left to right; the size of a rat – but a rat with eight legs – so huge and hairy and malevolent-looking that when I realised the implications of our tent having been open all night, in this monster's territory, I nearly fainted. On reaching the right-hand verge it had second thoughts, turned and went back to base more quickly, then crouched in the dead leaves with glaring eyes, looking like all the nightmares I have ever had come true . . . But then, as we hurried past, I suddenly felt non-phobic; precisely *because* this thing was so enormous it seemed more a beast than an insect. (Or, as Rachel would have me call it, an arachnid.) This does not of course mean that I would ever happily share a tent with it.

The people of this region are, by Andean standards, extraordinarily friendly and hospitable. Is it a coincidence that we are now in the ancient heartland of the Quechua tribe? As we breakfasted in Abancay, where an excited throng of children gathered outside the eating-house, one little girl came in and earnestly advised us to rub lemon-juice on every inch of exposed skin, as an insect-deterrent. Most of the population registered shock, horror and sympathy on seeing our bites. Several people told us that the valley's insects explain why one never sees local children going bare-limbed, despite Abancay's notorious heat. (The town stands at 8,500 feet but its encircling mountains make it an inferno.) Yet the insects don't explain why so many people of all ages wear thick woollen garments, often both a sweater *and* a cardigan! In the town centre a mestizo woman, standing at her shop door, sent her little daughter running after us waving two bottles of Fanta. When we stopped to buy coffee, sugar and ship's biscuits, the tiny wizened Indian shopkeeper gave us several glasses of a refreshing homemade fruit cordial. Then, on the outskirts of the town, an old woman beckoned us into her shebeen and gave us each two bowls of powerful chicha – indignantly refusing payment. This potation was too much for Rachel so I had three bowls and continued in a merry mood, uninhibitedly scratching my bitten bottom en route, to Rachel's mortification. In some ways she's inexplicably conventional.

Today's climb was a non-stop lung and muscle endurance test, without any of those gently sloping ledges which usually provide respites between the more severe gradients. But it was also optional; six times our redura crossed the carretera, so we were spared the psychological pressure of *having to* keep going. When we stopped to rest on a soft turfy bank a tiny campesino woman, herding sheep with her ragged grandson, studied us for some moments from a little distance. Then she approached shyly, to present us with part of her picnic lunch: a portion of cold potato stew on a cabbage leaf.

Towards sunset we came upon this wide ledge, close to a summit, which offers lush grazing, a miniature well of bubbling fresh water *and* scrub firewood – a rare bonus at this altitude. As for the view, it ranks among our Top Three. The eastern snow-peaks are on a level with us across a narrow gorge too deep for its floor to be visible. Far below, to the north, the river gorge lies at the base of that grey rocky range we crossed yesterday. Beyond are many other lines of peaks and one perfect powder-blue triangle stood out against a blood-orange sunset. For half-an-hour the western sky was such a glory of changing colours and cloud-shapes that we couldn't concentrate on fire-making.

At dusk we were joined by a ragged twelve-year-old shepherd boy. He warned us that tomorrow's redura is very difficult, then produced from amidst his rags eight boiled potatoes; having watched us climbing for hours this afternoon, he thought we must be very hungry. One remembers such kindness long after the elaborate hospitality of elegant friends has been forgotten. Ten minutes later José's father and small sister arrived to pay their respects: they live in a hovel around the nearest corner. Father endearingly insisted on leaving one of his three large Heinz dogs tethered nearby to guard us against thieves – as though we were his precious animals!

I'm writing outside the tent, lying on smooth turf beneath a full moon. Often I pause to gaze at the nearby snow-peaks, radiantly silver above the ebony abyss of the ravine. It saddens me to think that this is our last Andean full moon – but that's ungrateful. We are fortunate indeed to have lived for so long with so much beauty.

Camp on Floor of Village Post Office. 15 December

We awoke to hear heavy rain on the tent. Then, out of the sodden, grey, cold dawn, José reappeared with a chipped enamel bowl holding four hot maize dumplings with savoury fillings. We unwrapped these goodies from the maize leaves in which they had been steamed and relished the luxury of a hot breakfast while José sat cross-legged in the shelter of the front flap, his hard-soled bare feet tucked under him, and questioned us about Ireland. When the rain eased off he pointed out the first stage of our redura, an unmistakable section of the Camino Real, its paving still discernible, running across a bleak expanse of puna into the clouds. The restricted visibility worried me; unless one can see far ahead, gaps in puna reduras can be hopelessly confusing. This morning however we were confused not by a gap but by a landslide at the base of a steep 500-foot embankment. I did a solo recce and at the third attempt found a way to the top, which was also the summit of a mountain. I whistled and waited. Then a sudden wind rose and as the others joined me the clouds ahead were blown away. Together Rachel and I stood surveying a wide jumble of peaks and valleys – all blue-grey and golden-brown – beyond which lies the Apurimac gorge, our last major challenge (as it was the conquistadores') on the Royal Road to Cuzco.

Beyond an immense grassy bowl-valley, treacherous with boggy patches, we were on a faint goat-trail that wound level around four scrub-covered mountains. At its best this path was eighteen inches wide and the drop into a densely wooded ravine varied from one to two thousand feet. To add to the tension, we had a load problem. This morning an incipient girth sore prompted me to place the load slightly forward: and if it isn't precisely placed it's insecure. When it began to slip during the descent our sagacious Juana stood statue-still; she has more common-sense than a lot of humans I know. One would have said it was a physical impossibility to load a mule on such a path but the Andes have taught us that anything is possible if you're desperate enough. The only casualty was Rachel's Diana-bag, which is having quite an adventurous trip. It went rolling down the bare slope – faster and faster, jumping higher and higher – and came to rest 1,500 feet below. Rachel altruistically volunteered to retrieve it and a very breathless daughter rejoined me some considerable time later. Meanwhile I'd led the unloaded Juana to a slightly less perilous spot, and taken the load and tack onwards by instalments. I then reloaded in the normal way, having made a protective pad, dusted with antiseptic powder, to go between the girth and the tiny sore.

That descent (Stage One on the way to the Apurimac) took us into quite a thickly populated area; our next and final climb will be out of the Apurimac gorge onto the Cuzco highlands. Soon after 2 we paused to examine the famous rock of Sahuite, a huge boulder standing isolated on a grassy cliff and carved with animals, houses, agricultural implements and other unidentifiable objects. This has been described as an Inca relief map of a pre-Conquest village, but nobody is certain about its origin or significance.

Beyond Sahuite we slithered steeply into a broad, long, culti-

vated valley. At 4.45 we rejoined the carretera and a sweaty hour
later entered this little village of Lucumos, having paused on the
outskirts to buy an enormous bundle of Alf. The usual throng
gathered around as we sat outside one of two shops gulping chicha
and eating bananas. I was feeling uneasy; soon it would be dark,
and I dislike camping near a village. Then Hernan appeared,
bustling self-importantly down the rough, dusty village street: a
slim mestizo, aged thirty-ish, with bright, quick eyes and an
organising manner. He invited us to stay in the Post Office and
repeatedly emphasised in a loud voice that he would charge us
nothing for our lodgings. Before we moved he retrieved the 290
soles I had just spent on tinned sardines and buns and insisted on
paying himself. (In the other shop a plump youth behind the
counter had already refused payment for our drinks and laboriously written a note to his mother in Cuzco asking her to help us.)
We have arrived at the ungrateful conclusion that Hernan enjoys
showing off his affluence. He is of some consequence here, as Post
Master, Alcalde and the area's only entrepreneur.

When Hernan's wizened father had removed a selection of
pre-historic agricultural implements from the windowless Post
Office there was just enough room for our flea-bags on the mud
floor. I'm writing this at a tiny corner table on which Lucumos's
wind-up telephone constantly crackles but never rings. In a six-
holed letter rack four letters await collection. My candlelight is
attracting swarms of weird insects – red, brown, green, grey –
which are incessantly crawling up and down the wall in front of me
and across the table. Mercifully none is a spider.

Camp in hot neglected Hacienda Field. 16 December

Hernan insisted on our breakfasting before we left – a delicious
meal of crisp brown maize cakes, baked by his Mamma, and
several mugs of hot strong black coffee. When we set off at 6.30 the
sky was overcast, after a night of heavy rain, and providentially it
remained so all day, thus sparing us that extremity of heat endured in the Pampas gorge.

Soon after 8 we came to the village of Curahuasi and paused to
look at the few remains of a famous Inca tambo. Pedro de Cieza de
Léon recorded that here the great Ninth Inca, Pachacuti, 'gave to
a captain of the Chancas, by name Tupac Huasco, a princess of
Cuzco as wife, and he held her in high regard'. This was in the

middle of the 14th century and Pachacuti had just left Cuzco to conquer the Central Andes, a feat which would have been impossible but for the existence of the 'Huaca-Chaca' – the 'Holy Bridge' over the Apurimac.

At Curahuasi one enters the world of the Apurimac, a region with its own mystique, centred on The Bridge – for over five centuries one of the engineering wonders of the world. It was built c. 1350, during the reign of the Inca Roca, and became the longest continuously used bridge in the Americas. It enabled millions to cross 'The Great Speaker' – including the conquering Incas, who without it could not have moved an army north, and the conquering Spaniards, who without it could not have held Cuzco. Like all the many Inca suspension bridges, this Bridge of San Luis Rey hung from hand-twisted maguey-fibre cables; it was 148 feet long and in the dry season its centre point hung 118 feet above the water. (During the rains the Apurimac rises 40 feet or more.) The cables were regularly renewed every two years by the Indians of Curahuasi, to whom Pachacuti entrusted this task after his defeat of the Chancas, decreeing that all Curahuasi's work-service tax (mit'a) must be devoted to the bridge's upkeep. The locals' skill and diligence were so remarkable that throughout the Colonial period the Spaniards never interfered with the traditional organisation of this labour of Hercules and it was continued after Independence. Only when modern technology made possible the use of iron chains for suspension cables, and wheeled traffic at last penetrated the Andes, was the Huaca-Chaca allowed to decay. It finally collapsed in 1890.

Beyond Curahuasi a kind youth told us that the carretera follows the Royal Road for most of the way and Pedro de Cieza de León's comments don't contradict this: 'The road is well laid out along the slopes and mountains, and those who built it must have had a hard time breaking the rocks and levelling the ground, especially where it descends to the river, and the road is so rough and steep that some of the horses loaded with gold and silver have fallen into the river, where it was impossible to rescue them . . . It is a fearful thing to see the risks the men who go out to the Indies undergo'. Our friend showed us a redura that is no longer obvious; few people now cross the Apurimac on foot. This path rejoined the carretera on the first 'shelf' and we were on the motor-road for the rest of that six-hour descent. It is a narrow, dusty and very stony road. We enviously recalled de León's description of Pachacuti leading his 40,000 soldiers north from Cuzco some 500 years ago: 'He set out from Cuzco in a litter rich with gold and precious stones, surrounded by a guard with halberds, axes and other arms. With him went the lords, and this Inca displayed more valour and authority than all his ancestors. His Coya and other wives travelled in hammock-litters, and it is said they carried many loads of jewels and provisions. Ahead of him went road-cleaners, who left not a blade of grass nor a stone, large or small, on the Royal Road to the lodgings of Curahuasi'. The provisioning of such an army, on the march through such barren terrain, must have taxed even the remarkable organisational abilities of the Incas.

As we began the descent we could see far below what seemed like low hills within the gorge; six hours later, gazing up at them from river-level, they seemed what they are – towering mountains. The cruel immensity of this gorge is beyond anything else we've seen and beyond anything anyone could imagine. It is too harsh and sombre to be called 'beautiful' or 'magnificent': a place of infinite desolation, yet so soaked in history that one walks all the way with ghosts. And the greatest of these is the ghost of a bridge.

When we first heard the 'Great Speaker' we were still some 2,500 feet above the invisible river and, though I'd been expecting that mighty voice, I was momentarily puzzled. Such an eerily echoing roar, amplified by the utter silence of the Andes, was unlike any other water sound I've ever heard. What must the conquistadores have made of this almost sinister reverberation – unceasing for aeons, indifferent to victory or defeat – when first they ventured down these precipices?

We stopped once during the descent, at a shack selling beer and coke. Nearby we passed the only dwellings seen all day: four straw-roofed bamboo hovels, separated by miserable patches of wilting maize and cane. By the roadside a few bony cattle and goats were lethargically masticating withered shreds of scrub. What sort of life can be led by the locals, who have virtually nothing to herd or cultivate? Are these the descendents of workers moved from the coastal desert of Nazca by thrifty Incas, to culti-vate tropical fruits on this gorge's few fertile ledges? Highlanders could not work near the Apurimac; they literally lay down and died if expected to exert themselves in such heat. Even today the temperature must have been near 100° F, despite the overcast sky.

We first saw the Great Speaker at noon, some 1,500 feet below us, apparently immobile in its tortuous chasm; that was exactly four hours before our crossing of the modern bridge. At river level the road wriggles for miles along the base of friable sandstone cliffs too high for the eye to measure. Beyond the tumultuous red-brown torrent rise matching vertical cliffs, all split and fissured by elemental extremes and frequent earthquakes. Higher still rise the snow-peaks of Salcantay and Huamantay – invisible today. A sparse growth of spear cactus and spiny acacia merely emphasises the savage starkness. Walking so close to the roaring, swirling power of the Apurimac, we were oddly moved to think that it rises only about 100 miles to the south-west, in the fierce mountains of Chumbivilca, and (as the Amazon) flows into the Atlantic 3,800 miles away on the far side of a continent. "Wouldn't it be fun to follow it all the way?" said Rachel. I disagreed, while wiping from my bitten face the now-familiar paste of sweat, blood and dust. I'd prefer to walk 1,000 miles on the puna than ten miles at this debilitating altitude.

We were standing on the still-impressive remains of the Huaca-Chaca's stone tower when the notorious Apurimac afternoon gale swept suddenly through the gorge – a wind that made even the Huaca-Chaca's enormous weight sway like a hammock and terrified the bravest of the conquistadores. Examining the gorge walls at this point, and remembering how the bridge was built, one understands why Victor von Hagen wrote: 'The Incas, living on a neolithic cultural horizon tied to stone tools, still conceived a communication system that stands extremely high in comparison with the Romans who had three thousand years of experience to draw on . . . An Inca road is in many respects superior to a Roman road. The Apurimac Bridge, for example, was part of a highway which came from heights the like of which no Roman had ever seen. The passes the Romans conquered were as nothing compared to those in the Andes; Mont Blanc, the highest peak in Europe, is 15,800 feet high; yet here in Peru we walk over Inca roads *built* at this height'. The most detailed description of the Huaca-Chaca's structure was given by Garcilaso de la Vega, the Cuzco-born part-Inca historian who wrote: 'The Apurimac Bridge has its pillar support made up of natural rock on the Cuzco side; on the other side is the stone tower, made of masonry. Under the platform that holds this tower, five or six large wooden beams are inserted as thick as oxen – they stretch from one side to another, placed one higher than another like steps. Around each of these beams, each of the suspension cables is twisted once so that the bridge will remain taut and not slacken with its own weight, which is very great'.

Because of the violent wind-gusts, and the loudness of the Great Speaker's voice, it took some time to persuade Juana to cross the modern bridge, a little way upstream from the Bridge of San Luis Rey. Abruptly she swung away from it and stood stiff-legged, her rump to the river, displaying every known symptom of equine apprehension. The conquistadores were perhaps fortunate that the Incas had burned the Huaca-Chaca, forcing the invaders to ford the Apurimac. As they crossed a month before us, at the driest time of year, the water only came up to their horses' withers; yet this seems the most astounding of all their achievements, given the strength of the current and the slipperiness of the stone bed. Antonio de Herrera Tordesillas, King Philip III's official historian of the Conquest, wrote: 'It was remarkable that they crossed the rivers with their horses even though the Indians had dismantled the bridges, and although the rivers are so powerful. It was a feat that has never been seen since, particularly not with the Apurimac'. Our argument with Juana seemed to go on for ever and I had to exercise supreme self-control to prevent my impatience turning to anger – which would *not* have helped. Then at last she accepted the inevitable and, having once set hoof on the bridge, crossed it briskly but calmly. Half way across I suddenly laughed aloud at the absurdity of human impatience. From beneath my feet came the rhythmic raging of the Apurimac's primeval music, which filled this gorge before men came and still will play when men have gone. Keeping one's patience is really a question of remembering one's place in the universe. But that's easier said than done when one is heat-exhausted, fly-tormented and very hungry . . .

On the Cuzco side we continued upstream for four miles, then turned into the narrow valley of the Rio Colorado. Here the road has been damaged by this season's rains, which explains why we met only three motor vehicles today. The noise of the Colorado, scarcely thirty yards away, reduced us to sign language; because of the gradient this torrent seems more like an interminable waterfall than a river. We are camping just beyond the Colorado canyon in another fly-infested and woefully neglected hacienda field. When it rained heavily after dark I stripped naked and stood enjoying the cool downpour on my sweat-prickly skin. As this is doubtless

tarantula territory I'm writing under the most unfavourable conditions, lying nude on my flea-bag in a cramped, tightly-sealed,
oven-hot tent. But even under favourable conditions it would be
impossible adequately to describe today's trek. There comes a
time when we literary conquistadores must lay down our pens and
admit defeat. I can only suggest – think of the *Eroica* as representing our journey from Cajamarca. And then think of the Apurimac
gorge as the Finale.

12

To Cuzco:
Cops, Robbers and Farewells

Camp on grassy Ridge overlooking Village. 17 December

We have just completed our last full trekking day; by noon tomorrow we should be in Cuzco. So this has been a rather unreal day, marked by varying emotions – sadness at the ending of an incomparable journey, mingled with gratitude for our survival and a certain sense of achievement. But the dominant emotion – shared, yet not directly expressed by either of us – is deep grief at the imminent parting from Juana.

After a gradual three and a half hour climb we breakfasted in the village of Limatambo, where Pizarro slept after his first crossing of the Apurimac. The urban-looking restaurant – enormous, empty, jerry-built and sleazy – had more house-flies to the square foot than you'd believe possible. Garish murals, depicting brave Incas defying cruel Spaniards, covered three walls. Juana was grazing the verge outside and we sat watchfully by a smashed window. For months we've been leaving the load unguarded, but in Limatambo one senses the more sordid tentacles of modern civilisation reaching out from Cuzco.

Not far beyond the village we stopped at the Hacienda Tarahuasi to enjoy what John Hemming has described as 'the best preserved Inca temple platform, with 28 tall niches, and the longest stretch of fine polygonal masonry that I know'. The nearby Archaeological Research Centre is closed for lack of funds. And Limatambo's Tourist Hotel, in a well-kept colourful garden, is closed for lack of customers. So is another newish building, with many broken windows, disconcertingly sign-posted as 'The Limatambo Country Club'. Some over-ambitious developer has recently failed to turn this region into a tourist centre.

At noon we found a formidable redura and, after a morning of sticky heat, the downpour that soon began was welcome. It continued throughout the afternoon as we climbed, with few level respites, onto an immense grassy ridge, boulder-strewn and riven by deep gullies. Here the going got rough: the rain had made our path almost impassable. Rachel fell several times and soon we were both covered in sticky mud. We were also sodden and chilled; one can't wear long ponchos while climbing slippery slopes. Twice we went astray at complicated junctions; on each occasion Quechua-speaking shepherd boys used sign-language to put us right. I thought often of the conquistadores, who had a far more traumatic time as they struggled towards the crest of this same Cerro Vilcaconga.

At noon on 8 November 1533 an advance party of 40 horsemen under Hernando de Soto began this last steep ascent before Cuzco, and like us they hated the intense midday heat. One of them, Ruiz de Arce, wrote: 'We were marching along with no thought of a line of battle. We had been inflicting very long days' marches on the horses. Because of this we were leading them up the pass by their halters, marching in this way in groups of four'. They were about half way up when Soto, well ahead of his men, saw thousands of Indians swarming over the crest above. As the Inca troops charged, hurling boulders before them, they covered the entire mountain-side. When Soto shouted back to his men to form a battle line it was too late; they had had to scatter to avoid the Indian missiles. Many mounted and tried to spur their horses to the level top of this ridge; but no horse could gallop, few could trot and some wouldn't even walk. The animals' obvious exhaustion encouraged the Indians and soon five Spanish heads had been split open by clubs, maces and battle-axes; some of the richest conquistadores were among the dead. Soto then tried to entice the Indians down to the comparatively level ground around Limatambo, where horsemen would have an advantage. Some Indians took this bait and about twenty were killed. The rest retreated to the top of the ridge and both invaders and defenders prepared for an uneasy night. But the conquistadores' uncanny good fortune was soon restored. At 1 a.m., as they huddled sleepless, cold and fearful on an exposed hillock, doing what they could for eleven wounded men and fourteen wounded horses, a distant European trumpet sounded through the night. Another force of forty Spanish cavalrymen had heard of the battle and were doing a daring nocturnal forced march.

No one could better John Hemming's description of the sequel.

'The Indians greeted the new day confident of victory, only to find that the battered force of the previous afternoon had mysteriously doubled. The jubilant Spaniards formed line of battle and advanced up the hill-side. The Indians retreated and any who remained on the slope were killed. The arrival of a thousand men from Cuzco did not save the situation, and the natives' only salvation was the descent of a ground mist ... The battle of Vilcaconga was described by its survivors as "a fierce fight". Quisquis's men at last made use of steep terrain to come to grips with the enemy. They proved that Spaniards and their horses were vulnerable and mortal. They destroyed part of Soto's tiny vanguard. Had they gone on to destroy his entire squadron, they might have become sufficiently emboldened and experienced to have crushed Almagro's and Pizarro's smaller isolated contingents. Native troops annihilated far larger Spanish forces in similar difficult country in later years. But this is speculation. The fact was that Quisquis acted too late. He failed to exploit the many earlier river crossings, steep ascents and tight valleys where his men could have trapped Pizarro's impudent force of invaders ... The Inca Empire did not, as is sometimes supposed, go under without a struggle. Whenever the native armies were led by a determined commander they fought with fatalistic bravery ... But they were now confronting the finest soldiers in the world. Spanish tercios were considered the best in Europe throughout the 16th century and the men who were attracted to the American conquest were the most adventurous. Whatever one may think of their motives, it is impossible not to admire their bravery. In skirmish after skirmish their first reaction was to charge straight into the thick of the enemy. Such aggressiveness was intended as a psychological shock-tactic, and its effect was heightened by the invaders' reputation for success, invincibility, almost divinity.'

As we approached the long crest of the Cerro Vilcaconga (this crossing doesn't seem like a pass) the cloud lifted and the sky quickly cleared. We stood in pale gold evening sunshine looking down over gentle hills and a fertile plain towards the ridge above Cuzco. Directly beneath us miles of grassland sloped to a shallow, cultivated bowl-valley holding a scattered village. We said nothing. Juana scratched her forehead on my shoulder, as she habitually does when we stop to gaze. I put my arm around her neck. Jubilation would I suppose have been in order, now that we could actually *see* the last stage of a 1,300 mile walk over some of the toughest terrain on this planet. But neither of us was feeling even mildly jubilant.

An hour later, by which time it was raining again, we camped not far above the village, by the edge of the track; nowhere else was level enough. We've been inspected by several groups of locals, none of whom I much liked. I find it hard to believe that this is the last of so many happy nights in our tiny tent-home.

Izcuchaca. 18 & 19 December

Yesterday's crisis prevented diary-writing though I was in action for 23 out of those 24 hours. We are still seventeen miles from Cuzco. Moral: Don't Count Your Cuzcos Before You Reach Them . . .

When I went out to change the picket at 12.30 a.m. yesterday morning, brilliant moonlight revealed that all our tack had been stolen. As usual we'd left it beside the tent, covered with a water-proof cape weighed down with stones. After the first moment of rage and frustration (how could Juana now carry the load?) I tried to 'think positive'; this might have happened *any* night, instead of on the last night, and wrecked our whole trip. Then, remembering countless warnings about the corrupting effects of Cuzco's tourist trade, I resolved to guard Juana for the rest of the night and settled down to re-read Pedro de Cieza de León. Twice more I changed the picket, the second time moving Juana to just behind the open tent, where I could hear her cropping until a sudden downpour obliterated the sound. At 5 I went out to change the picket yet again – but Juana was gone. I felt queasy with shock. The picket was still *in situ* but the rope had been cut close to her head-collar. Immediately I recalled one of our numerous evening visitors remarking on the loudness of heavy rain on the taut tent; and he had also closely examined the tack. In addition to shock and grief, I was seething with that unworthy fury which follows on the realisation that one has been outsmarted.

Ignoring the downpour we packed up fast, intending to hitch-hike to Izcuchaca to enlist police aid without delay. Juana couldn't be far away, yet our trying to search a potentially hostile village would be futile. But how to find the carretera? And how to transport our gear? Then, as the first grey light seeped through the clouds, our guardian angel atoned for his recent lapse by sending a cheerful Indian boy, wearing a torn poncho and motor-tyre sandals, up the path from the village. He was driving three ponies and stopped to ask, "Where's your mule?" I explained, adding that within hours we'd be back with several policemen from Izcuchaca. This was a good opportunity to broadcast our intentions; here horse-rustling is a major crime and punished accordingly. Even to be suspected of it could land a man in jail for several years, awaiting trial, so most villagers will co-operate with the police on this matter lest they themselves should be arrested on suspicion. Often the police are not too fussy about their methods; their main objective is to retrieve the stolen animal by fair means or foul.

The pony-herd helped us to carry our gear to the carretera: a three-mile walk through chilly drifting mist. I gave him 100 soles; later we discovered that he had stolen the waterproof cape, our small saucepan and Rachel's beloved fideog.

The sky cleared as we stood by the roadside, soaked and shivering. Ahead, snow-peaks glimmered against the cold paleness of the morning sky. So far, *doing things* had cushioned me from the full impact of our disaster. Now, while waiting twenty minutes for a lift, I felt completely devastated to think of Juana gone – without a good-bye or a thank you – to a probably unsuitable home. Such an affectionate creature needs love in return. Also, it was acutely frustrating to have our trek curtailed within half-a-day's march of Cuzco.

A road engineer, at present supervising repairs near the Apurimac bridge, drove us to this friendly, busy little town (pop. approx. 5,000) where the amiable policia were semi-paralysed, as usual, by their own bureaucracy. They didn't share our view that every moment's delay must be to the thief's advantage. The proper steps had to be taken, in the right order. Firstly, the Izcuchaca Superintendent had to wire a detailed report of the theft to his CO at Abancay. Secondly, the CO, having considered the report, had to wire back his authorisation for action to be taken. Thirdly, only a Seite policeman could go to the relevant village of Ocasacancpa, which is in the sub-district of Seite. (We'd passed Seite, a hamlet just off the carretera, a few minutes after being picked up.) Fourthly, before walking the three miles to Ocasacancpa the Seite policeman would have to travel twelve miles in the other direction, whenever he could squeeze onto one of the area's infrequent truck-buses, to receive in person a search warrant from the Izcuchaca Superintendent. 'A dull hopelessness' is the appropriate cliché for my reaction to all this; by the time the search for Juana began, she could be half-way to Lake Titicaca where there is a keen demand for good mules. *La Policia* are hampered in rural Peru not only by their low average IQ but by the lack of telephones and motor transport. The Superintendent here has his own private Volkswagen but he won't ever use it for official purposes.

A bench was placed in the sun outside the police station. And there we sat for hours being questioned by cheerful fruit-sellers, bread-boys and chicha-girls, in between their sales to captive customers when motor vehicles stopped at this police 'Control'. While Rachel read – she can get lost in a book whatever crisis happens to be in progress – I counted ten policemen lounging or strolling about, apparently with nothing to do but chat to the locals. Yet not one of them could be sent with us to Ocasacancpa.

Amerigo arrived at noon. Tall for a Peruvian, and affable, he had a three-day beard and a sweat-beaded brow because he'd walked the last three miles from Seite. As no message had yet come from Abancay, we couldn't board the suitable truck-bus that stopped at the Control at 12.15. When the message did come, at 1.25, we had to wait another hour for the next over-crowded vehicle, in which it was difficult to breathe: standing in the back, one's rib-cage lacked space for the minimal expansion required. The road is so rough, and we stopped so often, that the thirteen-mile journey took fifty minutes.

At Seite I urged Amerigo to hurry because less than three hours of daylight remained, but he pointed to a nearby shebeen and insisted that cerveza was essential fuelling for the walk ahead of us. Uncharacteristically, I argued against beer drinking. But Amerigo displays the impermeable obstinacy of the very thick and it was 4.05 when we set off for Ocasacancpa on a narrow path that led up from maize-fields to undulating grassland, then steeply down into the bowl-valley containing the hamlet.

Amerigo made no attempt to question the locals, so I stopped often to ask for news of a brown mula branded JL. Then, for the first time since Juana's disappearance, it began to seem that we might see her again; all the campesinos' reactions indicated that she was around, and visible, though no one was prepared to say precisely where. On the cultivated floor of the valley, where the path ran from hovel to hovel between flowering hedges, we saw Carlos, our pony-herd amigo, racing towards us down a slope accompanied by another youth. Both looked triumphant – and expectant. Carlos explained that he and his brother had spent all day informing the locality about our plan to return with the police, and about our enormous international importance (appearances notwithstanding), which we carried documents from Cajamarca to prove, and about the power of gringoes to have campesinos imprisoned for life. As a direct result, our mula had been found wandering in a maize field just an hour ago. Carlos and Pedro had caught her, with great difficulty, and put her to graze on the ridge above their casa where she was now tethered. I studied Carlos's face as he spoke, and remembered his slick petty thieving, and wondered . . . Campesinos rarely venture out alone in the dark. Had his pre-dawn appearance been *not* a 'guardian angel' co-incidence but part of a complicated plot? There was however a fifty/fifty chance that he was speaking the truth; and when he pointed out a familiar figure silhouetted on the skyline my joyous relief prompted me to give him the benefit of the doubt and another 100 soles.

Amerigo refused to make any effort to find our tack; he seemed to feel that he had more than done his duty by being a passive witness to our recovery of a stolen mule. Nor were Carlos and Pedro eager to help – and it was getting late. We decided to forget the tack; within half-a-day's march of Cuzco it could be regarded as expendable.

By 7 p.m. we were back at Seite. Foolishly, I'd believed the Superintendent when he'd promised that Juana, if found, could travel from Seite to Izcuchaca by cattle truck: therefore we were tentless. This promise, like most Peruvian 'official statements', was a mere flight of fancy. So we then had to walk thirteen miles to Izcuchaca through a raven-black night, without a torch, on a muddy, rocky track pitted with holes, while icy rain fell steadily.

At the start of that five-hour walk we were already exhausted after a harrowing day. I had bought a dozen bread-buns in the Seite shebeen, for sustenance on the wing, but Rachel was too tired to eat them. Rarely in my life have thirteen miles seemed so long. During the first two hours, eight or nine buses and trucks passed us, with no thought of dimming, and for the first time our well-mannered Juana, who had never before met a headlamp, shied in panic and twice tried to bolt. While struggling with her in the path of impatient Peruvian drivers, on that stretch of narrow carretera, we were probably in greater danger than at any other time since leaving Cajamarca. We came to dread the distant roar and glow of a vehicle and I found myself walking all the time with clenched fists, my nails dug in my palms. By day we could have looked for a 'lay-by': in total darkness we daren't move off the road until the headlights had revealed what lay on either side – by which time it was too late because Juana was panicking. Had I foreseen this complication I would have *begged* for shelter in Seite despite that hamlet's subtly hostile vibes. We felt quite weak with relief when the traffic ceased abruptly because the Izcuchaca and Apurimac Controls had closed the road for the night.

Between Seite and here we met not one other pedestrian, though this is quite a densely populated area. At 10.10 we first saw Izcuchaca's few dim lights, seeming brilliant in the utter blackness. By then both Juana and Rachel were stumbling frequently through exhaustion. Momentarily those lights, apparently close, cheered us. But as the road undulated and twisted they came to seem like Will o' the Wisps, never any nearer, and it was exactly midnight when we arrived outside the Control. We picketed Juana on good grass in the police station back-yard. Then for ten minutes we had to stand outside our ramshackle colonial hotel, desperately banging on its nail-studded double door until a small boy with a torch admitted us. When we fell into bed, leaving our sodden clothes in piles on the floor, I had been on active duty for 23 hours and 50 minutes – and Rachel for 19 hours.

This morning Rachel slept until 10.45 but I had to be outside the Mercado by 6.30 to secure an adequate supply of Alf. We spent most of the day at the police station, enmeshed in red tape. The Superintendent, much impressed by our Cajamarca documents, insisted that the most strenuous efforts must be made to recover our tack. He urged us to return to Ocasacancpa with Amerigo. I said I would willingly return, but not with Amerigo. It seems however that this case cannot now be transferred because it's down in the records as Amerigo's . . .

After supper, when we went to give Juana her night supply of Alf, we found that the picket had been stolen (from the police yard) and Juana tethered instead to a plank. The policemen on duty shrugged and said, "These things will happen" – or words to that effect. Evidently *The South American Handbook* is not being alarmist when it says of the Cuzco region: 'WARNING: Thieves are becoming bolder and more numerous'.

Cuzco. 20 December

Everything – as the man said – is relative. Our sorrow at the thought of parting from Juana has been lightened by her loss and recovery; at least we can now choose with whom to leave her. We got off to a late (7.45) start. Without tack, loading took twice as long as usual. At last I devised a system less collapse-prone than most of my practical improvisations; we had to re-load only three times in seventeen miles. But this precarious arrangement made it advisable to follow the carretera instead of the Camino Real.

At first the road ran level around the base of lowish curved mountains. To the east, enormous herds of cattle were grazing on the wide fertile plain of Anta; and beyond that sterner peaks rose clear against a cobalt sky. Yet this landscape was not 'our' Andes – nor, of course, had we expected it to be. The Cuzco to Machu-Picchu railway was visible; electricity pylons strode arrogant and ugly across the plain; a brash advertisement for Singer Sewing Machines disfigured the handsome remains of an aqueduct and a fertiliser factory marked the beginning of the long climb to the pass above Cuzco. Yet, surprisingly, these modern intrusions induced no feeling of anti-climax; here the 'Spirit of Place' is too strong for surface scars to matter.

The city of Cuzco was itself worshipped in Inca times. Garcilaso de la Vega records that if two Indians of equal status met on one of the four roads radiating from Cuzco, the traveller coming from the city was greeted as the superior. (Much as Muslims who have visited Mecca are forever after revered.) Indians seeing Cuzco for the first time knelt to do homage before approaching that sacred spot, where each Inca's palace was preserved after his death as a sacred shrine containing his mummified body on permanent display, tended by servants of his own clan who regularly offered the mummy food and drink. The Spaniards were quick to realise the importance of competing with the splendour and solemnity of Inca ceremonies and traditions. They soon set up the gorgeous Feast of the Body of Christ (Corpus Christi) to rival the gorgeous Feast of the Sun (Inti Raymi). Statues of Christian saints replaced carvings of heathen gods, but often the Cuzco Indians dressed their gods in the voluminous, jewel-encrusted robes of the saints and carried them thus in Christian religious processions. They still do, on occasions. Which perhaps is why advertisement hoardings and electricity pylons don't matter too much around Cuzco.

Ascending the Arco Punco ridge, we remembered the last battle of the Cuzco campaign when the Inca army fought fiercely to defend this ridge. 'We found all the warriors waiting for us at the entrance to the city. In the greatest numbers, they came out against us with a great shout and much determination.' Juan Ruiz de Arce complained: 'They killed three of our horses including my own, which had cost me 1,600 castellanos; and they wounded many Christians'. Some of the advance party of forty cavalrymen were driven down the slope but 'the Indians had never before seen Christians retreat, and they thought that they were doing it as a trick to lure them onto the plain'. Thus the Indians, by giving Pizarro's main army time to come up, lost their last chance to defeat the invaders. That night the two armies camped on adjacent hills, the Spaniards with their horses bridled and saddled, the Indians with their camp-fire burning brightly. But when the sun rose the Indian hill was deserted; the apparent invincibility of the conquistadores had finally demoralised the Inca troops. And so: 'The Governor drew up the infantry and cavalry at the first light of dawn the following morning, and marched off to enter Cuzco. They were in careful battle order, and on the alert, for they were certain the enemy would launch an attack on them along the road. But no one appeared. In this way the Governor and his men entered the great city of Cuzco, with no further resistance or fighting, at the hour of High Mass, on Saturday, 15 November 1533'.

Cuzco remains invisible to travellers from the north-west until they are directly above its red roofs. As we approached the summit of Carmenca hill, at noon, the sun sent a brilliant white-gold shaft through a blue-black cloud-mass beyond the Cuzco valley. A moment later we were on the hill, overlooking the straggling little city – suddenly so close that we could pick out many landmarks already familiar from photographs. "There are no modern buildings!" exclaimed Rachel joyfully. "And no tin roofs! It's a *lovely* city!" The Spaniards thought so too. Full of proud excitement, they wrote to King Charles, 'This city is the greatest and finest ever seen in this country or anywhere in the Indies. We can assure Your Majesty that it is so beautiful and has such fine buildings that it would be remarkable even in Spain'.

A policeman at a nearby Control post asked me, "From where have you walked? From Izcuchaca?" I hesitated briefly before admitting, "From Cajamarca". ("Ssh!" said Rachel. "He'll think you're boasting!") The young man stared at me in silent disbelief. And then for a dotty moment I too wondered if what I had said could be true. The conquistadores knew this feeling. They wrote to their King: 'The Spaniards who have taken part in this venture are amazed by what they have done. When they begin to reflect on it, they cannot imagine how they can still be alive or how they survived such hardships and long periods of hunger'.

Here sentiment prompted us to leave the carretera and enter Cuzco by the *ruta de la conquista*, a rough track preserved as it was when Pizarro led his men along it into the conquered capital – to lay the foundations for almost 300 years of colonial rule. At 1.15, as we approached the Plaza de Armas – in Inca days the great Square of Aucaypata, larger than St Mark's Square in Venice and the very heart of the Empire – Rachel did a quick sum and announced that the conquistadores had beaten us by a week. They left Cajamarca on 11 August and arrived in Cuzco on 15 November. We left Cajamarca on 9 September and have arrived in Cuzco on 20 December. The Spaniards' progress was of course slightly slowed by their having to fight four major battles en route. But we had no Indian guides and one member of our expedition was aged nine/ten. I looked past Juana to Rachel in the lead, her short legs covering the last stage of (for her) a 900-mile walk. And then – why deny it? – I felt very proud of her. Especially because there was never once, through hunger, thirst, heat, cold or exhaustion, a whimper of complaint. Rachel would not wish me to say so, but as mini-conquistadores go she's done pretty well.

Suddenly we were in the busy, sunlit Plaza de Armas, surrounded by renaissance and baroque magnificence – four great churches, imposing colonial arcades, mansions built for conquerors. We stood silent, feeling strangely indecisive. So this was *it* – Cuzco. What had been our goal for three months and ten days no longer existed *as* a goal. We were there. Cuzco was all around us. And now we had to face the dreaded moment of disbanding the team . . . Rachel too looked non-exultant. "We should celebrate," I remarked vaguely. "Why?" asked Rachel, moving closer to Juana. I turned towards the posh Hotel Conquistador, just off the Plaza, and called over my shoulder, "This is ridiculous – we've got to pull ourselves together!" So we did, and booked into a double-room with bathroom, soft wall-to-wall carpeting, a telephone, wireless, central heating *and* an electric fire – all of which cost 800 soles. To me this seemed outrageous until I forced myself to 'think sterling' and realised it was only £2.25. Rachel uneasily surveyed all this lavishness. "We'll find somewhere more suitable to-morrow," I reassured her. "Just for one night we must have a room with a bath, before we go to stay with the Waltons."

While the porter was taking our load upstairs (obviously he'd never before seen gringo baggage of that calibre) the receptionist was finding a corral – in a doctor's lock-up garage for which we have to pay *1,000 soles* per night. It almost broke our hearts to leave Juana standing disconsolate on an oily concrete floor with a meagre bundle of Alf which it had taken us two hours to collect from various cuy-owners.

On the way back to our hotel I bought a new shirt and new shoes. Then, before my bath, I symbolically consigned my boots, jeans and bush-shirt to the WPB. As from this evening, a modicum of respectability will be required. Our trekkers' privileges are no more.

The same. 21 December

In Izcuchaca we were told that there is no demand for riding-mules in this motorised region but that the Cuzco Tourist Office organises pony-trekking during the dry season. At home no one would condemn a beloved animal to such a career; here one-day treks, with a long rainy season vacation, offer an easier life than regularly carrying loads to market and pulling primitive ploughs up precipices. So this morning we presented ourselves to Sancho, the young man who apparently runs the Tourist Office, and asked him if he would like to buy an affectionate, good-looking, intelligent, docile and hardy young riding mula.

Sancho at once lost his 'professional' welcoming smile and looked pathetically confused. "You want to *hire* a mule to ride – yes?" "No," I said, "we want to *sell* a mule."

At that point two young women who dispense tourist brochures in an adjacent office came to the door and explained: "These ladies have walked from Cajamarca with a mule." Sancho laughed uneasily, not sure how to take this joke. "It's *true*," insisted one young woman. "We saw them arriving yesterday and they are staying at the Hotel Conquistador and the porter has seen their documents from Cajamarca."

Sancho's bewilderment deepened. He frowned at us. "*Why* did you walk from Cajamarca? It is a long way and the roads are bad.

It is possible to fly from Cajamarca to Lima, and then from Lima to Cuzco. It is not necessary to walk."

I avoided Rachel's eye lest she might giggle derisively, thus mortally wounding Sancho and wrecking our chances of doing a deal. "We'll fetch the mule," I said briskly. "She isn't far away. When you've seen her you can think about it – there's no hurry."

Juana had just finished her breakfast Alf – a lavish supply, purchased early at the Mercado – and she greeted us ecstatically, eagerly trotting out of her alien prison. Our way back to the Plaza took us past what remains of the Temple of the Sun and up the renowned Callejon Loreto between some of those unique Inca walls of which John Hemming has written: 'The Incas' skill as masons is their most impressive artistic legacy . . . They succeeded in cutting and polishing their stones with dazzling virtuosity. Adjoining blocks fit together without visible mortar. Even when the blocks interlock in complicated polygonal patterns, their joints are so precise that the crevices look like thin scratches on the surface of the wall.' But we were in no mood to enjoy these magnificent monuments. Now that Juana had to be sold, all our attention was focused on getting that horrible ordeal over and done with as quickly as possible.

Our absence had allowed Sancho to make the necessary mental adjustments and he was again smiling. "You are like Pizarro!" he greeted us. "You have shown how easy is travel in Peru for foreign ladies! Now I telephone *The Lima Times* and they write about you!"

It was immediately evident that Sancho doesn't know a mule from a donkey. His father, he said, is the expert. So he locked up his office (there are few tourists in Cuzco at this season) and we all set off for his home on the outskirts of the city.

Despite its architectural splendours and illustrious history, one can't really think of Cuzco as a *city* in our sense of the word. It seems more like a prosperous market-town, with extensive agricultural suburbs where small tiled adobe houses line rough muddy laneways and farm animals and poultry wander happily, untroubled by motor-traffic. It took us an hour to reach Sancho's home, a large two-storeyed farm-house in its own cobbled courtyard, concealed from the road by a high mud wall with a wooden double door. Sancho's mother greeted us, an unlikeable mestizo woman whose sharp eyes peered suspiciously from a fat cunning face. She looked contemptuously at Juana and snapped, "Muy flaco!" (very lean) which alas! is true. But Sancho's father

approved and we settled on 27,000 soles; I'd asked 30,000, he'd
offered 25,000. The bureaucracy of mule-trading will however be
another day's work. Tomorrow Sancho and I must go to a notary
(surprise! surprise!) and transfer Juana's papers in his presence.
So we left our mula happily settling down to a pile of maize husks,
having arranged to return tomorrow afternoon to exchange the
notary's documents for cash.

We have now moved from the Hotel Conquistador, whose
poshness proved illusory. Our initial baths exhausted the hot
water supply; when Rachel leaned lightly on the handbasin it fell
to the floor; the central heating didn't work; the electric fire
behaved like a Catherine wheel if switched on and, when the
door-handle fell off, locking us in, we discovered that the telphone
was a mere decoration. We are much happier in the Residencial
Plaza, also just off the Plaza de Armas, where for 380 soles we have
a double room (sans bedding) with a big table beneath a dim
electric light bulb. There is no window, but the door opens onto
a balcony running around three sides of an open patio where
geraniums blaze and sheets are hung to dry. Rachel's only complaint is that the communal loo suffers pungently from drought.

The same. 22 December

We spent most of today with Sancho, commuting between the
District Police Headquarters (as in Cajamarca, the police had to
be deeply involved) and the office of the Public Notary, where for
hours everybody ignored us. Then at last our 'case' was taken up
by an ancient and phenomenally slow-witted gentleman with
wispy silvery hair, bushy black eye-brows, a grey cravat and a
shiny black suit. When all four certificates (made out on special
embossed paper bought by us at the post office) had each been
stamped three times by different clerks we set off for Sancho's
home. On the way we booked on tomorrow's truck-bus to the
Waltons' tea-plantation – which happily is beyond reach of more
conventional forms of transport – where we were invited for
Christmas when we met Carolyn and John at San Rafael.

Chez Sancho we got a shock. Already Juana had been moved
(by *goods train!*) to an uncle's pasture down the Urubamba Valley,
'because now in the rains there are no riding tourists and she needs
to get fat'. After the first horrid blank moment we were glad. *Not
saying* good-bye is always much easier.

Bibliography

Peru Before Pizarro George Bankes (Phaidon, 1977)

Cuzco: Magic City Alfonsino Barrionuevo (Editorial Universo S.A., 1968;

Backpacking and Trekking in Peru and Bolivia Hilary & George Bradt (Bradt Enterprises, 1980)

Peru G.H.S. Bushnell (Thames & Hudson, 1957;

Four Faces of Peru W. Byford-Jones (Robert Hale, 1967)

The Incas Pedro de Cieza de Leon (University of Oklahoma Press, 1976)

Vision of Peru Violet Clifton (Duckworth, 1947)

The Peoples and Cultures of Ancient Peru Luis G. Lumbreras – translated by Betty J. Meggers (Smithsonian Institution Press, 1974).

Man and Land in Peru Thomas R. Ford (University of Florida Press, 1955)

Aristotle and the American Indians Lewis Hanke (Hollis & Carter, 1959)

The Conquest of the Incas John Hemming (Macmillan, 1970)

The Last of the Incas Edward Hyams & George Ordish (Longmans, 1963)

Andean Adventure Lilo Linke (Hutchinson)

Peru Robert Marett (Ernest Benn, 1969)

Peruvian Pageant Blair Niles (John Murray, 1937)

Indians of the Andes Harold Osborne (Routledge & Kegan Paul, 1952)

The Peru Traveller Seldon Rodman (Ward Lock, 1967)

Family in Peru John Sykes (Anthony Blond, 1962)

Highway of the Sun Victor von Hagen (Travel Book Club)

The Vision of the Vanquished: The Spanish Conquest of Peru through Indian Eyes Nathan Wachtel – translated by Ben and Sian Reynolds (Harvester Press, 1977)

Incas and Other Men George Woodcock (Faber & Faber, 1959)

Letter to a King Don Felipe Huaman Poma de Ayala, translated by Christopher Dilke (Allen & Unwin, 1978)

History of the Conquest of Peru William H. Prescott (Bickers & Son, 1878)

South American Handbook published annually by Trade & Travel Publications, Bath

Index

Abancay, 235, 244, 246
Acobamba, 157, 160
Acolla Marco, 167, 168
Agia, Miguel, 237
Agrarian Reform, 6, 27, 89–90, 145, 236
altitude, 36, 37, 54, 85; sickness, 60–1, 62
Ambo, 147
Andahuayalas, 209, 226, 227–34, 235
Andes, 14, 54–5, 112, 123, 125–6, 167, 200, 208; approach to, 1; between Cajabamba and Huamachuco, 34–8; compared with Himalayas, 48, 61; grandeur of, 22, 45–6, 48, 211; harvests in, 29; snow-peaks, 46–7, 85, 105, 252; see also individual mountains, rivers and towns
Arce, Ruiz de, 256
Atahualpa, 2–4, 10, 92, 174, 237
Ayachucho, 201, 204, 206–7; Battle of, 206; University of, 206
Ayachuco Archaeological-Botanical Project, 111
Ayala, Felipe Guarnan Poma de, 233

banks, 11, 207, 208, 209, 228–9
Barcapalca, 123
bats, 142–3, 144
Belaunde, Terry Fernando, 76, 134
birds, 26, 31, 46, 67, 79, 84, 112, 239, 245
blacksmiths, 120, 193, 225–6
bogs, 86, 124, 211
Bradt, Hilary and George: *Backpacking and trekking in Peru and Bolivia*, 46, 79n.

bridges, 2, 24, 73, 102, 103, 112, 127, 134, 135, 172–3, 204, 213, 221, 244; Bridge of San Luis Rey, 250, 253; 'Huaca-Chaca', 250, 252–3
British Agricultural Mission, 6, 13
buses, 137–8, 183, 192–3, 212–13

Cajabamba, 27–8, 80
Cajamarca, 1, 2, 4–5, 13, 21, 71, 138, 165, 210
Calderbank, George and Amelia, 5, 6, 9, 11
Camino Real, 29, 30, 31, 34, 36, 37, 161, 227, 245, 247, 248, 250, 263
campesinos, 1, 6, 11, 19, 30–1, 39, 49–53, 63, 113–15, 121, 140, 145, 158, 210, 246; aloofness of, 45, 116, 141; drinking hours, 168; fiesta and, 98, 99, 108; funerals, 183, 232; hostility of, 58–9; incuriosity of, 26, 48; mistrust of gringoes, 231; religion of, 230; steal equipment, 217–19; steal Juana, 258–61
camp sites, 18, 21, 25–6, 32, 44, 49–52, 74, 78–9, 113, 122–3, 140, 147, 153–4, 158, 163–4, 185–6, 205, 211, 212, 222, 223, 247
Cerro de Pasco, 147, 150
Cerro de Vincos, 105, 121
Cerro Vilcaconga, 256, 257
Chancas, 226
Chavez, Captain Francisco de, 75
Chavín, 64, 69, 105, 112, 113, 115–21, 207
Chiclayo, 1
Chicmo, 224–5
children, 71, 88, 90, 93, 110, 129–30, 131, 207

uncommunicativeness of, 129, 130
insects, 21, 43, 71, 82, 94, 142, 205,
  206, 221, 240, 244, 245, 246, 249
Izuchaca, 259–60, 262

Jacas Chico, 141–2
Jangya-Cocha, 123
Jauja, 169–84
Jayuri, 240
Junín, 152, 153; pampa, 150, 151, 154;
  Lake, 150, 152

Lacabamba, 74, 75–7
lakes, 67–8, 86, 124, 125, 150, 152
landslides, 48, 70, 135
La Unión, 105, 121, 131, 134–5
Léon, Luis de, 65, 66
Leon, Pedro de Cieza de, 35, 41, 74,
  85, 108, 173, 186, 249, 250
Liberation Church of South America,
  40, 98
Lima, 29, 89, 145, 203
Limatambo, 254
llamas, 148, 149–50, 151, 154
Lucomos, 249

Maldonado, Diego, 226–7, 233
Marãnon Gorge, 135, 140
markets, 19, 21, 160; in Ambo, 147; in
  Cajamarca, 4; in Huamachuco, 39;
  in Huánuco, 145; in Huari, 109; in
  Jauja, 169, 171–2, 177–80; in
  Pampas, 197; in San Marcos, 20
Matara, 16–18
Mayor, 202–4
Mercadillo, Captain Alonso, 162
Massia, Alfonso, 238
mestizos, 4, 10, 39, 49–53, 63–4, 71, 87,
  126, 157–8, 204; of Locabamba
  area, 74; lack of communication,
  104; lack of response, 90; defeat
  Spanish army, 206; taunting by, 187
Mexico, 28, 51
migration, 29, 203
mines, 47, 56, 63, 64, 148; mining
  communities, 66, 68–9, 70, 149, 150,
  151

Ocros, 212, 215

Osborne, Harold: Indians of the Andes,
  97–8, 110

Pachamamma, 121
Pachas, 135
Pampas, 67, 69, 71–3, 80, 191, 204
Peru, 231, 237; absentee landlords, 27;
  Communist Party in, 155, 171;
  criticism of, 114, 155, 159–60,
  162–3; government spending, 26;
  jail in, 231; Junta, 6, 155, 186; lack
  of nationalistic feeling, 76, 177; rice
  crop, 4, 101
Piscobamba, 93, 101–2
Pizarro, Francisco, 3–4, 41, 75, 162,
  165, 173–4, 227, 241, 254, 264
Pizarro, Hernado, 172, 241
police, 9–10, 17, 66, 105, 116, 136–7,
  180, 186, 191, 193, 197–9, 203, 215,
  216, 225, 259–61, 262, 264–5, 268
Pomabamba, 90, 91–3, 94, 97–101
Pomachaca, 158–60
Poma, Huaman: Letter to a King, 26,
  110, 111, 173
poverty, 15, 76, 141
Prefecture, 8–9
pueblos, 15, 19, 21, 36–7, 73, 152, 160,
  202
Pumpuyac, 123

Quechua, 100, 123, 128, 210, 215, 232,
  237
Quichupunta Pass, 140–1
Quilcayhuanca, 123

Rachel's diary, 19, 43, 56–7, 60, 79–82,
  139–40
reduras (short cuts), 16, 19, 27, 62–3,
  91, 102, 142, 150, 167, 187, 202, 213,
  216, 222, 223, 235, 236, 241, 246,
  247, 250, 255
Rio (river), Abancay, 244, 245;
  Apurimac, 248, 250, 251–3, 254;
  Colorado, 253; Conchucos, 73, 82;
  Higueras, 143; Huallaga, 143;
  Huarpa, 204, 205; Mantaro, 202,
  203, 204; Marañon, 135; Montaro,
  167; Negra, 29, 32; Palca, 155;
  Pampas, 215, 220, 222;